Negotiating Cultural Rights

Negotiating Cultural Rights

Issues at Stake, Challenges and Recommendations

Edited by

Lucky Belder

Senior Researcher, Renforce Research Programme, Europa Institute, Faculty of Law, Economics and Governance, Utrecht University, the Netherlands

Helle Porsdam

Professor of Law and Humanities and UNESCO Chair in Cultural Rights, University of Copenhagen, Denmark

EE Edward Elgar PUBLISHING

Cheltenham, UK • Northampton, MA, USA

Cover image courtesy of the designer Alex Castiglioni working for Aqueduct London (Nuova Accademia di Belle Arti, Milan)

Published by
Edward Elgar Publishing Limited
The Lypiatts
15 Lansdown Road
Cheltenham
Glos GL50 2JA
UK

Edward Elgar Publishing, Inc.
William Pratt House
9 Dewey Court
Northampton
Massachusetts 01060
USA

A catalogue record for this book
is available from the British Library

Library of Congress Control Number: 2017941905

This book is available electronically in the **Elgar**online
Law subject collection
DOI 10.4337/9781786435422

MIX
Paper from responsible sources
FSC® C013056

ISBN 978 1 78643 541 5 (cased)
ISBN 978 1 78643 542 2 (eBook)

Typeset by Columns Design XML Ltd, Reading
Printed and bound in Great Britain by TJ International Ltd, Padstow

Contents

Contributors

Shahira Amin is an independent journalist based in Cairo. A longtime contributor to CNN's Inside Africa, Amin is also a documentary film-maker producing films for UN agencies. She currently contributes to Freemuse and Al Monitor. Amin has won several international awards including Julio Anguita Parrado Award 2012 for courageous journalism, Global Thinkers Forum Award 2013 for Excellence in promoting gender equity and BMW Foundation's Responsible Leaders Award 2016.

Lucky Belder is Senior Researcher in the Renforce Research Programme at the Europa Institute of the Utrecht University Faculty of Law, Economics and Governance. Dr. Belder's research on governance of the arts and sciences, cultural heritage and cultural diversity, and fundamental issues in intellectual property regimes contributes to her advisory work for Dutch governmental agencies and international cultural institutions.

Yvonne Donders is Professor of International Human Rights and Cultural Diversity and Head of the Department of International and European Law at the University of Amsterdam. Her research focuses on analysing from a legal as well as a multidisciplinary perspective issues related to reconciling universal human rights and cultural diversity, including the promotion and protection of cultural rights. She is further a member of the Dutch National Commission for UNESCO, the Human Rights Committee of the Advisory Council on International Affairs, the Editorial Board of the Netherlands Quarterly of Human Rights, and the Advisory Council of the National Institute for Human Rights.

Hanne Hagtvedt Vik is Associate Professor of International History of the University of Oslo. Her research has centred on the history of human rights and development aid. Recently her research has turned to the emergence of international indigenous peoples rights and the dynamic relations between local, national, regional and international realms in the case of the rights of the Sami people. Her work has been published in the Journal of Global History, the International History Review and the Journal on Group and Minority Rights.

Lotte Hughes is an historian and Senior Research Fellow at The Open University, UK, who specializes in contemporary Kenya. Dr. Hughes leads the interdisciplinary ESRC-funded research project 'Cultural Rights and Kenya's New Constitution' (2014–17), which also speaks to global developments in the study of culture and cultural rights. Key publications include *Moving the Maasai: A Colonial Misadventure* (2006, reissued in paperback 2016).

Jannice Käll gained her Ph.D in Legal Theory at the Dept. of Law at Gothenburg University, Sweden. Besides her LL.M. in Law, Dr. Käll holds an M.Sc. in Intellectual Capital Management. She has many years of experience in research and practice concerning innovation in high-technology firms and start-ups, the design of national innovation systems, intellectual property and contract law, as well as critical legal theory.

Fiona Macmillan is Professor of Law at Birkbeck, University of London, and Visiting Professor of Law at the University of Roma Tre and the University of Gothenburg. She is currently the Director of the International Society for the History and Theory of Intellectual Property (www.ishtip.org).

Matthias Mann leads the Department of Proteomics and Signal Transduction at the Max Planck Institute of Biochemistry in Munich, which develops and applies methods of mass spectrometry (MS)-based proteomics in a variety of biological areas. He is also affiliated with the NNF Center for Protein Research at University of Copenhagen and has authored and co-authored more than 600 publications with over 100,000 citations according to ISI (h-factor more than 154), making him one of the most highly cited researchers worldwide.

Helle Porsdam is Professor of Law and Humanities and UNESCO Chair in Cultural Rights at the Center for Legal Cultures, University of Copenhagen. She received funding for a HERA (Humanities in the European Research Area, ESF) project on copyright, creativity and cultural heritage institutions (2010–13) and is currently heading a Velux-funded project on digitization and cultural heritage institutions. Among her publications are *Legally Speaking: Contemporary American Culture and the Law* and *From Civil to Human Rights: Dialogues on Law and Humanities in the United States and Europe*.

Dalindyebo Shabalala is Visiting Assistant Professor at Case Western Reserve Law School and a Fellow of the Institute on Globalization and International Regulation at Maastricht University. His research addresses on the interaction of international intellectual property law with human rights and climate change law. His current research focuses on the rights of indigenous peoples to their traditional knowledge.

Farida Shaheed a sociologist by training and activist by choice, is the Executive Director of Pakistan's oldest feminist organisation, Shirkat Gah – Women's Resource Centre, and former (and first) UN Special Rapporteur in the field of Cultural Rights. Widely published work focuses on the interface of identity, politics, power and rights; numerous national and international awards include the Prime Minister's Award and Women's Human Rights Award.

Stina Teilmann-Lock is Associate Professor of Design Studies at the University of Southern Denmark. Dr. Teilmann-Lock is the author of *The Object of Copyright: A Conceptual History of Originals and Copies in Literature, Art and Design* (2016) and has published widely on art, design and intellectual property law.

Acknowledgements

The editors wish to thank all the contributors to this volume as well as the two UN Special Rapporteurs in the field of cultural rights, Farida Shaheed and Karima E. Benounne and the people from the Special Procedures Division of the UN Office of the High Commissioner for Human Rights in Geneva, Dragana Korljan, Mylène Bidault, and Johanne Bouchard.

The editors furthermore wish to thank the Danish Velux Foundation who funded Helle Porsdam's project, 'The Past's Present: Digital Transformations and Cultural Heritage Institutions' (pf.ku.dk). Members of this collaborative project met in Copenhagen in November 2015 at the Royal Library and the National Museum, two of the external partners for Porsdam's project, to plan this volume. It was the former, and now sadly deceased, Director of the Royal Library, Erland Kolding Nielsen, who helped us organize a dinner on November 13, 2015 at the Royal Library' wonderful restaurant 'Søren K', named after Søren Kierkegaard. And it was during this dinner that Danish composer and conductor Bo Holten had members of his vocal ensemble 'Musica Ficta' perform various songs by the famous Danish composer Carl Nielsen in order then to ask all conference participants to come and join him at the piano. Once we were standing around his piano, Holten managed to make us all join in a circle canon or round, focusing on the old song known in French as 'Frère Jacques, Frère Jacques.' No one present that evening will ever forget how we all sang this song in our own respective languages – loud and clear, with a feeling of unity and cultural kinship through song!

What made this event even more memorable was the fact, as we learned later that evening, that at the very moment we were joined in song, gunmen and suicide bombers hit a concert hall, a major stadium, restaurants and bars in Paris and left more than one hundred people dead and hundreds more wounded. Nothing could have brought home to us more forcefully the importance of finding common ground around and guarding against the abuse of cultural rights!

Introduction: outlining the field of cultural rights and its importance

Lucky Belder and Helle Porsdam

THE MANDATE AND THIS VOLUME

The Human Rights Council established the mandate of the United Nations Special Rapporteur in the Field of Cultural Rights in 2009 with Resolution 10/23. It was Cuba that, as a member of the Council, introduced this Resolution and conducted the procedural and diplomatic process leading up to its adoption by the Council, and it is Cuba that is in charge of the yearly resolutions of the Council as well as of the renewal of the mandate every three years.[1]

Pakistani sociologist and feminist human rights activist Farida Shaheed was appointed as the first Independent Expert and continued as Special Rapporteur in the period between 2009 and 2015. During her tenure she published ten thematic reports on the following topics: preliminary views on the conceptual framework for the mandate (2010), the right to access and enjoy cultural heritage (2011), the right to enjoy the benefits of scientific progress and its application (2012), cultural rights of women on an equal basis with men (2012), the right to the freedom of artistic expression and creativity (2013), the writing and teaching of history (2013), memorialization processes (2014), the impact of advertising and marketing practices on the enjoyment of cultural rights (2014), and the impact of copyright and patent policies on the enjoyment of the right to science and culture (two separate reports published in 2015).[2]

Shaheed's list of thematic reports may, as Mylène Bidault (the Office of the High Commissioner for Human Rights staff member overseeing the drafting of Shaheed's reports) puts it, 'appear eclectic'. But the

[1] See Bidault (2016).

[2] All reports are available on the website of the Office of the High Commissioner for Human Rights at http://www.ohchr.org/EN/Issues/Cultural Rights/Pages/AnnualReports.aspx.

themes are not only 'all linked and articulated together in various ways and degrees'; they also by and large follow the structure of Article 15 of the International Covenant on Economic, Social and Cultural Rights (ICESCR) which, together with Article 27 of the Universal Declaration on Human Rights, forms a major legal basis for cultural rights.[3] These provisions protect the right of every person to: (i) participate in cultural life; (ii) to enjoy the arts and the benefits of scientific progress and its applications; and (iii) to benefit from the protection of the moral and material interests resulting from any scientific, literary or artistic production of which he or she is the author.

Together, Shaheed's ten thematic reports provide a new standard on cultural rights. This volume highlights these reports and discusses how cultural rights are now part of a global discourse for supporting inclusive social and political development, and for fostering intercultural dialogue for the mutual understanding of cultures. We see the volume as a contribution to current debates concerning cultural rights and have invited the contributors to reflect upon the main conclusions concerning the meaning and the position of cultural rights in Shaheed's reports, as well as on what the implications of these conclusions may be for international relations, the international legal order, and for cross-cultural understanding.

At a scholarly level, new and important works on culture, cultural heritage, and human rights are helping to increase the interest in this particular corner of human rights research. The last few years have seen the publication of, among others, Helaine Silverman and D. Fairchild Ruggles, *Cultural Heritage and Human Rights* (Berlin: Springer, 2007); Yvonne Donders and Vladimir Volodin (eds), *Human Rights in Education, Science and Culture* (UNESCO and Ashgate, 2007); Francesco Francioni and Martin Scheinin, *Cultural Human Rights* (Leiden, NLD: Martinus Nijhoff, 2008); James A.R. Nafziger, Robert Kirkwood Paterson, and Alison Dundes Renteln (eds.), *Cultural Law: International, Comparative, and Indigenous* (Cambridge: Cambridge University Press, 2010); Olivier de Schutter (ed.), *Economic, Social and Cultural Rights as Human Rights* (Cheltenham, UK, and Northampton MA: Edward Elgar, 2013); Federico Lenzerini, *The Culturalization of Human Rights Law*; Ana F. Vrdoljak, *The Cultural Dimension of Human Rights* (both Oxford University Press, 2014); Aurora Plomer, *Patents, Human Rights and Access to Science* (Cheltenham, UK, and Northampton MA: Edward

---

3 Bidault (2016), 22.

Elgar, 2015); and Christophe Geiger (ed.). *Intellectual Property and Access to Science and Culture: Convergence or Conflict?* (CEIPI-ICTSD, 2016).

TWO KEY ISSUES IN THE FIRST REPORT

In her first report, Shaheed points to key provisions from the International Covenant on Civil and Political Rights (ICCPR) as well as to Article 13 ICESCR (the right to education) and various provisions and instruments relating to indigenous people and minorities as being relevant for her mandate. The first report identifies and addresses two key issues on which there has been much disagreement over the years: the relationship between cultural diversity and cultural relativism, and the relationship between group rights and individual rights.

(a) The Relationship Between Cultural Diversity and Cultural Relativism

Many originally thought and argued that cultural rights would automatically lead to the promotion of cultural relativism, and that all human rights would suffer as a result. As William Logan put it much later, 'cultural rights are clearly related to cultural diversity and cultural diversity is an obvious challenge to the very idea of universal human rights'.[4] In her first report, Shaheed chose to settle this issue by affirming that cultural rights, like all human rights, are universal. In 2009, General Comment 21 on the right to the enjoyment of cultural life had stated that the protection of cultural rights is incomplete without the ethical imperative of the protection of cultural diversity.[5] Respect, protection and promotion of cultural diversity being essential for ensuring the full respect of cultural rights means neither, however, that cultural diversity can be invoked to infringe upon or limit the scope of human rights guaranteed by

---

4 William Logan (2012) in reference to the Academy of European Law 2005 'cultural rights are clearly related to cultural diversity and cultural diversity is an obvious challenge to the very idea of universal human rights', p. 239.

5 Recognition of the importance of 'cultural diversity' is global. This is reflected in e.g., the Charter of the European Union; the Culture Conventions of the Council of Europe, the 2006 Declaration on ASEAN Unity in Cultural Diversity; and The 2006 Charter of the African Renaissance of the African Union.

international legal instruments, nor that all cultural practices are automatically condoned by these instruments, Shaheed argues:

> The principle of universality of human rights, one of the core principles of international human rights law, on the one hand, and cultural rights and cultural diversity on the other, are sometimes considered as opposed. This view stems partly from a misplaced tendency to equate cultural diversity with cultural relativism, which has the effect of raising fears and misunderstanding regarding the recognition and implementation of cultural rights … Therefore, not all cultural practices can be considered as protected in international human rights law.[6]

Complex as the relationship between the unconditional protection of cultural diversity and the protection of cultural rights may seem, they are mutually supportive.[7] Respect for human rights entails the creation of an enabling environment for cultural diversity. Such an environment will in turn promote cultural rights, but it will also allow people to be sensitive to the dangers involved when the interests of some are trespassing on the interests of others. This should ideally make it impossible for people anywhere to refer to tradition, culture and/or religion as legitimizing infringements of human rights, especially women's rights.[8]

In her reflections on the significance and challenges of the cultural rights mandate (Chapter 1 in this volume), Shaheed again addresses the relationship between cultural rights and cultural diversity. Always dynamic and forever changing, culture inevitably relates to power and to disagreement and negotiation concerning meanings and worldviews, she writes.[9] All societies have a dominant culture whose members seek to enforce their own cultural views, and these views are under constant challenge by members of minority groups who wish to have their respective views and needs to belong recognized: 'Power differentials impact the ability of individuals and groups to effectively contribute to the identification, development and interpretation of what should be considered as a common "culture" both in terms of shared cultural heritage from the past and in terms of contemporary cultural life.'[10]

It is important, furthermore, Shaheed argues, to separate both culture *per se* and the preservation of culture or cultural heritage from cultural

---

6 A/HRC/14/36, esp. paras 32–34. See also Bidault (2016).

7 Ibid., para. 24.

8 Gender is one of the issues that the mandate asks the Special Rapporteur to focus on.

9 Farida Shaheed, Ch. 1, this volume.

10 Ibid.

rights. Safeguarding cultural heritage is the responsibility of UNESCO. The cultural rights mandate concerns human creativity and the possibility for everyone to participate in and contribute to cultural life in an active way: 'The mandate is about ensuring that the necessary conditions exist for everyone to access, participate in and contribute to cultural life on a basis of equality and without discrimination; to question existing traditions and create new ones.'[11] It is when the two – culture and cultural rights – are conflated that the end result may be cultural relativism.

(b) The Relationship Between Individual Rights Versus Group Rights

Shaheed likewise confronts head-on a second issue that has often been raised in relation to cultural rights: the relationship between the individual and the collective dimensions of these rights. Group rights have been recognized in countless human rights instruments, she notes. They do exist in practice in international human rights law today, especially in the UN Declaration on the Rights of Indigenous Peoples, just as various general comments by the Committee on Economic, Social and Cultural Rights have emphasized that cultural rights may be enjoyed alone, or in association with others or as a community. But this does not lead to:

> the denial of individual cultural rights: individuals always enjoy their rights, inter alia, to participate or not to participate in one or several communities; to freely develop their multiple identities; to access their cultural heritage as well as that of others; and to contribute to the creation of culture, including through the contestation of dominant norms and values within the communities they choose to belong to as well as those of other communities.[12]

To approach access to cultural heritage as one of the key elements of the realization of cultural rights by focusing on the rights of the individual stakeholder in cultural heritage, as Shaheed does in her first report, solves the dilemma of individual versus group rights. The uniqueness of every human being, the bearer of multiple and complex identities, means that the right for everyone to take part in cultural life is considered as the right to take part in communities of shared culture and engage freely in cultural affiliations.[13] Cultural practice is always collective, and 'while an individual's identity showcases uniqueness, the collective identities

---

[11] Ibid.

[12] A/HRC/14/36, para. 10.

[13] Ibid., para. 23.

emphasise similarity,' as Shaheed beautifully puts it in her reflections on her mandate.[14] The relationship between individual and collective rights is one that does need to be further explored, though, she correctly states in several of her reports. It will no doubt be taken up by her successor as Special Rapporteur, Karima Bennoune.

TWO THEMES/ISSUES THAT UNDERLIE AND BIND TOGETHER ALL TEN REPORTS

All Shaheed's reports display her trust in the rich possibilities for the field of cultural rights. This is particularly the case with regard to two issues, which may be said to bind her reports together, and which she repeatedly cross-references: cultural rights as empowering rights and the link between culture and science.

(a) Cultural Rights as Empowering Rights and Discourse

Cultural rights are potentially empowering once we realize, Shaheed writes, that they 'include freedoms and entitlements … [for] all persons, without discrimination based on their particular identity(ies), and in a way that enhances the enjoyment of all human rights'.[15] The message that cultural rights are for all persons – and not just for certain groups or minorities – is an important one to send at a time where majorities in various elections in Europe (Brexit) and the United States (the presidential election of 2016) seem to have been motivated, in part, by a feeling that (human) rights are not for them, but only for minority groups, and that their problems are of no concern to the international (human rights) community. The conception of cultural and other human rights as universal and not relative (though sometimes still context-dependent), as rights to be relied on in practice and not just in theory, is once again a timely and important one to develop and refine.

Delivering the opening address to the World Conference on Human Rights in Vienna in 1993, then Secretary-General of the United Nations, Boutros Boutros-Ghali, offered an interesting reflection on the complexity of human rights. At one and the same time both absolute and historically defined human rights, he said, have 'a dual nature':

---

[14] Shaheed, Ch. 1.
[15] A/HRC/14/36, para. 20.

> Human rights should be viewed not only as the absolute yardstick which they are, but also as a synthesis resulting from a long historical process. As an absolute yardstick, human rights constitute the common language of humanity. Adopting this language allows all peoples to understand others and to be the authors of their own history. Human rights, by definition, are the ultimate norm of all politics.
>
> As an historical synthesis, human rights are in their essence, in constant movement. By that I mean that human rights have a dual nature. They should express absolute, timeless injunctions, yet simultaneously reflect a moment in the development of history. Human rights are both absolute and historically defined.[16]

Human rights – and here most people would agree – are by no means perfect. But precisely because they are both absolute/timeless and historically dependent, they constitute one of the few, if not indeed the only, (semi)-universal ethical discourse we have today. At a time of increasing globalization, where respect for cultural diversity takes center stage as a global concern, and where migration and advances in technology have increased the level of cultural exchange and intermingling, but have also fostered cultural clashes and incompatibilities that were previously masked by distance, we need a common forum or arena in which we can explain, negotiate, and come to new understandings. Culture permeates all human activities, including legal systems, in all communities. It is therefore important for us to work with law not only as a technical practice for ensuring social control, but also as a cultural vocabulary that recognizes people's aspirations for rights and justice, thereby enabling a common discussion among diverse communities who have no other common vocabularies.

Cultural rights have everything to do with cultural identity. The cultural heritage of a community is a way of expressing its identity, for example. This gives it a particular importance, both inside the community and with respect to its relations with the outside. Cultural heritage not only addresses the question of how a community is comprised and according to what values, it also functions as a way of telling those outside the community about the community and why it might deserve to be valued.[17]

In this relation, it bears repeating that human rights are the work of many actors and the product of global interactions. It was Cuba, as we saw, that was the prime mover behind Resolution 10/2. And new research has

---

[16] B Boutros-Ghali, A/CONF.157/22: Address by the Secretary General of the United Nations at the Opening of the World Conference on Human Rights (1993), 3.

[17] See Macmillan, 2017.

shown that there is a vital connection between the decolonization process and human rights, that the duality of race and religion has been a driving force in the breakthrough for international human rights law, and that Jamaica and Liberia have been influential normative powers in twentieth century politics concerning human rights – all of which challenges us to rethink how Western the notion of human rights really is.[18]

Ahmed An-Na'Im, one of the first scholars to take the issue of cultural rights seriously, once maintained that 'the lack or insufficiency of cultural legitimacy of human rights standards is one of the main underlying causes of violations of those standards'.[19] Cross-cultural legitimacy is important; people around the world are more likely to observe normative propositions if they believe them to be in accordance with and sanctioned by their own cultural traditions. This is no doubt the reason why, on the occasion of the 60th anniversary of the Universal Declaration of Human Rights (UHDR), the UN declared Culture to be one of six cross-cutting themes of the UN Agenda, the others being Dignity and Justice, Development, Environment, Gender, and Participation.

The 2008 choice of Culture as a cross-cutting theme was explained as follows:

> … The concept of Human Rights is bound closely to the belief that culture is precious and central to our identity. The way we are born, live and die is affected by the culture to which we belong, so to take away our cultural heritage is to deny us our identity. At the same time, we can all benefit from our experience of other cultures and we have something to offer them in return.[20]

In the last few decades, cultural rights have become increasingly relevant in the context of globalization (post-colonialism, post 9/11, shifts in global power structures, cultural diversity) and the protection of intellectual property rights. Furthermore, cultural rights are seen as key to the realization of the Millennium Development Goals.[21]

---

18 See Jensen, 2016. See also Lenzerini, 2014.

19 An-Na'im, 1992, 19.

20 See http://www.ohchr.org/EN/UDHR/Pages/CrossCuttingThemes.aspx.

21 See Background Paper, 7 March 2014 for a meeting held at United Nations Headquarters in New York on Monday, 5 May 2014, in cooperation with UNESCO. The Background Paper and the accompanying letter are available at http://www.un.org/en/ga/president/68/pdf/letters/03072014TD%20Culture%20and%20Sustainable%20Development.pdf (last accessed on July 25, 2014).

See also the UNCTAD creative economy reports published every two years on global creative industries UNCTAD/PRESS/PR/2013/16, released 15 May 2013.

This is particularly interesting as cultural rights have traditionally been underappreciated. As Shaheed correctly points out, there is support for these rights in the International Bill of Human Rights as well as in the more recent UN Declaration on the Rights of Indigenous Peoples (2007). Also, UNESCO has produced both soft law within several distinct areas of cultural rights and policy – the right to education, linguistic rights, traditional culture and folklore, and cultural diversity – and binding treaties relevant to the area of cultural rights and to the protection of cultural heritage, both material and immaterial.

(b) The Link Between Culture and Science

The second theme that underlies all Shaheed's reports is the link between culture and science. Both relate to the pursuit of knowledge and understanding as well as to human creativity. Just as the right to participate in cultural life enables people to continuously be creative and contribute to society's cultural meanings and manifestations, so the right to science gives people the freedom to engage in critical thinking and to investigate and contribute new knowledge in the field of science.

In her thematic report on the right to enjoy the benefits of scientific progress and its application (see Chapter 4), Shaheed relates the link between culture and science to the need to protect academic research and academic standards. It is interesting in this context to recall how the word 'scientist' was born. It happened, science philosopher Laura J. Snyder tells us, at the third meeting of the British Association for the Advancement of Science in 1833. The famous poet Samuel Taylor Coleridge was present at this meeting, and he succeeded in alienating everyone by attacking the host, William Whewell, for referring in his opening remarks to the scholars in the audience as 'natural philosophers'. They were no such thing, Coleridge argued; they were practical men who got their hands dirty by experimenting with electricity or digging for fossils. After quieting down the audience who took this as an insult, Whewell actually agreed that Coleridge had a point and coined the phrase 'scientist' to describe the emerging professionalized practice of modern science.[22] Whewell came to the phrase 'scientist' by analogy with 'artist': much as the artist is typically more interested in doing art than in philosophizing about what it is or ought to be, so the modern scientist conducts experiments (and digs) in accordance with a clear set of rules set by

---

22 Snyder, 2011, pp. 1–2.

academic standards on research, including checks and controls, and may not be expected to speculate about the more philosophical aspects of science.[23]

As we shall see, in her 2012 report on the right to enjoy the benefits of scientific progress and its application (discussed in Chapter 4) as well as in her two 2015 reports on IP both of which relate IP policy to the right to science and culture (discussed in Chapters 10 and 11), Shaheed describes access to both science and culture as major, transformative tools for realizing and making dreams come true. Likewise, in an interview that we conducted with her in November 2015 in Copenhagen, Shaheed stressed how learning to appreciate the connection between science and culture has been one of the most useful lessons she has learned as UN Special Rapporteur.[24] The connection between the two is based, Shaheed also writes in Chapter 1 of this volume, on human creativity being involved in both cultural and scientific activity. This is especially interesting in light of the general assumption that the domains of science and technology are very different from the domains of the arts and humanities – an assumption that is often expressed with reference to the famous 'two cultures' debate between the two Cambridge, UK colleagues, C.P. Snow and F.R. Leavis about higher education and core curricula.[25]

C.P. Snow gave his famous lecture, 'The Two Cultures and the Scientific Revolution,' at the University of Cambridge in 1959.[26] What has since come to be known as 'the two cultures' debate concerned the gap – and the proper balance – between the technological and natural sciences on the one hand, and the humanities on the other. In his lecture, Snow (a writer of fiction who also had a PhD in chemistry) had argued that the British educational system had over-rewarded the humanities (especially Latin and Greek) at the expense of scientific and engineering education with the result that people in politics, administration, and industry were ill-equipped to manage the modern scientific world.

The reaction of Professor of English and famous literary scholar F.R. Leavis to Snow's lecture was delivered in his 1962 Richmond Lecture, 'Two Cultures? The Significance of C.P. Snow.' Snow mainly dealt in

---

23 Ibid., 3. – We wish to thank Peter Hjertholm for drawing our attention to this interesting, historical event.

24 'UCPH Talking About – Negotiating Cultural Rights', Helle Porsdam interviewing Farida Shaheed, November 13, 2015 – available at http://video.ku.dk/secret/12446221/64f4083b0fdbbbde433687327261b013.

25 For a longer and more thorough discussion of this, see Porsdam, 2013.

26 Snow, 1998.

clichés and preached a way of salvation, Leavis argued, that entailed welfare for all in terms of material, quantitative standards of living and advantages of technology only. What quantitative methods are not very good at handling can in fact well be the things that matter most: the big questions about life and death which may at its best produce great art and literature. Things were changing so rapidly, and critical reflection was needed to help make sense of it all – and to prevent the worst scientific blunders which, in the atomic day and age, could have catastrophic results. Moreover, important ethical issues could well be at stake, Leavis maintained – issues that perhaps scientists themselves would not be aware of.[27]

The 'two cultures' debate has since surfaced in different contexts. Thinking about the relationship between science and culture when she was first appointed Special Rapporteur, Shaheed had what she calls in her reflections (Chapter 1) an 'epiphany' – namely:

> that at the core of cultural rights is human creativity, regardless of whether this is in terms of science, technology or artistic expression. The right to science is encompassed in the broader right of all human beings to not only create (an essential part of cultural life), but also to enjoy the fruits of the creativity of others while preserving the right of authors, read as including all manner of creators, to the moral and material benefits of that creativity.[28]

It does, in other words, make sense to regard and discuss the three parts of Article 15,1 ICESCR as being not so much at odds with each other, but instead as belonging together.

In her report on the right to enjoy the benefits of scientific progress and its application, at which we shall take a closer look in Chapter 4, rather than simply lining up side by side quantitative knowledge with more qualitative, cultural approaches to knowledge, Shaheed consequently advocates for something closer to a merging of science and culture. Likewise, in her two last reports on intellectual property, the issue of the moral and material benefits of creativity is linked very prominently to the right to science. There really no longer seems to be two, but only one culture or 'cultural capability' left.[29] The possible implications are interesting – as Lea Shaver, who served as a consultant

---

27 Leavis, 1962, 25–6.
28 Shaheed, Ch. 1, this Volume.
29 A/HRC/20/26, para 20.

to Shaheed on her report on the right to enjoy the benefits of scientific progress and its application,[30] puts it:

> … there is no clear dividing line between 'culture' and 'science.' Consider, for example, the issue of ensuring widespread access to scientific publications and scholarship. Would this belong in the 'culture' report, because it deals with text and publication? Or is it an issue of science, because the subject matter of the publication pertains to engineering and medicine? If the latter, must we treat scholarship about physics differently from scholarship about poetry? Indeed, scientific inquiry, theory, and literature, as well as technological innovation and products, are themselves properly recognized as cultural manifestations.[31]

THE CHAPTERS

Reflecting the 'two cultures' debate and Shaheed's argument that there is no clear dividing line between culture and science, the present volume is an interdisciplinary endeavour. When it comes to the setting of cultural (as well as other human) rights – the way in which they are formulated in international treaties and domestic and international law, and applied in practice in national constitutional and legal systems – law is obviously a key discipline. But it is not the only one; a purely legal approach fails to take into account the ethical, historical, political, economic, anthropological – and in the case of Article 15.1(b) ICESCR on the right to benefit from scientific progress and its applications also the natural/technical sciences – dimensions of these rights. These are just as important and it is only by integrating data, tools, perspectives and theories across faculties and disciplines in law, the humanities, and the social and natural/technical sciences that we can begin to get a sense of the full cultural rights picture.

A first, introductory chapter is written by **Farida Shaheed**. It forms a companion piece to Chapter 2, written by **Lotte Hughes**, on Shaheed's first report – a report that was especially important as it outlined the mandate of the UN Special Rapporteur in the field of cultural rights and discussed basic definitions and topics of relevance to the field. Several of Shaheed's most important arguments and reflections on her mandate and her time as Special Rapporteur have already been touched upon. We are privileged to be able to print Shaheed's reflections. It is not all that

---

[30] Shaver, 2016, 30: 'producing drafts, participating in all meetings organized to solicit expert feedback on the drafts, and collaborating on their finalization'.

[31] Ibid., 31.

common for a Special Rapporteur to offer such reflections, and Shaheed's will help map for future generations the beginnings of and the early developments within the new and exciting field of cultural rights. Lotte Hughes' comments, in Chapter 2, on Farida Shaheed's first Report are based on her research in Kenya on the interplay between customs and cultural practices of local communities and government policies. Her experiences present a unique opportunity to discuss some of the issues that are distinguished in the first and most general Report. Of particular interest is her analyses of the use of the 'ubiquitous' term community. Hughes warns that this overused and under-defined term should be applied with care, as she finds that this term has served an array of social, political and legal ends, and often seems to result more in the exclusion of non-participants than in a better understanding of the participants in a specific group. Alternatives like collective or social group would better describe a particular group in a particular context. Hughes' account of her research on the contacts between local communities and the Kenyan Government demonstrates clearly how the application of terms like community, or identity in real situations may not reflect what was intended to be achieved by the protection of cultural rights on a more abstract level.

Another issue discussed by Hughes is that of 'self-ascription' – a concept that refers to the identification of groups not only by objective, but also by subjective factors. Hughes points out the delicate line between real and 'invented' traditions. She questions the UN practice that seems to avoid objective criteria to decide which claims should be considered to have a legitimate historical base, and who should be recognized as a representative for these claims.

In Chapter 3, **Lucky Belder** discusses the second 2011 Report on 'Access to Cultural Heritage'. Affirming the importance of cultural diversity, the report's conclusions and recommendations are all based on the implicit assumption that cultural diversity is conditional to ensuring an enabling environment for the access to cultural heritage, Belder demonstrates. She begins the chapter by marking the occasion that for the first time, a UN document explicitly links a human rights-based approach to the right to express one's identity and the right of access to cultural heritage.

Next, she focuses on which actors could be considered responsible for this right of access to cultural heritage. Recent developments in international human rights law signal an increasing role for non-state actors, and Belder concludes that the implementation of cultural rights has come to include a principle of responsibility that relates not only to states, but also to other public institutions as well as to corporate enterprises and civil society. In the final part of her chapter, Belder establishes that the 2015 UNESCO Declaration on the protection and promotion of museums and collections incorporates this principle, by calling upon museums as institutions, but also on museum professionals and civil society at large to observe and implement the principles of instruments for the protection of cultural heritage.

Chapter 4, written by **Helle Porsdam** and **Matthias Mann**, concerns Shaheed's 2012 report on the right to enjoy the benefits of scientific progress and its applications. Shaheed starts her third thematic report by stressing the strong link between the right to science and other human rights, especially the right to participate in cultural life. She then outlines the normative content of the right to science, and this normative content and the recommendations made in 'The right to science' report form the point of departure for the four sections of Porsdam's and Mann's chapter.

In the first section, they focus on the link Shaheed makes between the right to science and the right to culture. The second section discusses 'the access perspective': the need to ensure that science and technology will be of benefit to everyone, not least the most vulnerable groups around the world. Then Porsdam and Mann turn, in section 3, to 'the protection perspective': the need to foster an environment that protects the individual researcher and enables him/her to produce and then subsequently disseminate, alone or together with his/her group, scientific knowledge. Finally, section 4 analyzes and comments upon Shaheed's 'areas for further consideration': the right to science and intellectual property; the equitable sharing of benefits and transfer of knowledge; and third-party actors and their obligations (the private-public divide). Porsdam and Mann end by suggesting a fourth area that, in their opinion, merits further consideration – namely, the possible clash between (fundamentalist) religion and science. Along the way, they also offer other suggestions for topics or areas that they think need attention and/or clarification.

Yvonne Donders is the author of Chapter 5. Culture is often seen as an obstacle to the enjoyment of human rights by women. The 2012 report by the Special Rapporteur called 'Enjoyment of cultural rights by women on an equal basis with men' focuses on a more positive role of culture for women. Culture is not only an impediment to, but also an important instrument for the realization of their human rights. The report fits in the more general approach taken by the Special Rapporteur to emphasize the importance of cultural rights for the enjoyment of other human rights, Donders demonstrates. This report is a very comprehensive document on cultural rights and women. Its title suggests that the report is mainly about the equal enjoyment of cultural rights by women and men, but, as Donders points out, the report deals with much more than that. Notably, it elaborates on the role of women in the development, preservation and decision-making of issues that relate to culture.

In other words, Donders shows, the report is not only about the (cultural) rights of women, but about cultural rights and gender. Gender roles and especially gender stereotypes play an important role in the (lack of) advancement of women's cultural rights and in the defense of cultural practices harmful to women. The report provides an important contribution to the discussion on these topics by not painting a mere negative picture of the relationship between cultural rights and women, but by emphasizing the importance of cultural rights to empower women and to transform cultures. As such, the report could, Donders concludes, serve as a helpful tool for states and other stakeholders to better understand and implement cultural rights for all, including women and girls.

Both Chapter 6 and Chapter 7 discuss Shaheed's 2013 report on 'The right to freedom of artistic expression and creativity.' **Shahira Amin** bases her chapter (Chapter 6) on her own country, Egypt. Rights groups have, she states, hailed Egypt's 2014 Constitution as 'one that protects and guarantees freedom of artistic expression,' saying it was more progressive than previous constitutions. Yet, a huge gap still exists between constitutional protection for expression and the reality on the ground faced by Egypt's artists.

The 2011 Revolution had raised hopes for increased freedom of expression – for decades constrained by strict censorship – but, sadly, a culture of repression still prevails. Outlining a number of recent Egyptian cases, Amin shows how art that addresses politics, religion and sex continues to be censored in the name of protecting public order, morality and state interests. The new Constitution, which passed with overwhelming support in early 2014, states that 'public morals, ethics, traditions, customs, values, culture and heritage determine society's evolution and guarantee the rights and liberties of all individuals'. The reality is different, however. The effects of censorship on the arts and the unjustified restrictions on artistic expression are stifling artists in post-revolution Egypt.

Stina Teilmann-Lock approaches Shaheed's report on artistic freedom from a somewhat different angle. Her focus (in Chapter 7) is on intellectual property law and freedom of expression, and she points to a sometimes overlooked motivation identified by Shaheed, namely the 'protection of corporate interests'. There is a desire to silence criticism of corporate activities by artists, and to protect a specific logo or brand from mockery or parodic use. Indeed, in a world where branding has become a major generator of cultural significance there is likely to be a conflict of interest between corporations that aim to control the meanings associated with their brands and artists who aim to critique the cultural significance of such brands, Teilmann-Lock demonstrates, following Shaheed. In disputes of this type corporations have been seen to invoke their intellectual property rights as a means to curb artistic expression of which they disapprove on economic grounds.

One such clash between a corporation and an artist is mentioned by Shaheed (in a footnote): that of *Nadia Plesner* v. *Louis Vuitton*. This case was the result of a controversy involving the Danish-born visual artist Nadia Plesner and the holders of the right to use the luxury brand 'Louis Vuitton'. As Teilmann-Lock shows, the case is an example of how legislation – whose intended purpose was obviously not to impose censorship – can turn out to be one of the 'multi-faceted ways in which the right to the freedom indispensable for artistic expression and creativity may be curtailed'. Intellectual property law is designed to protect the rights of creators and innovators so as to stimulate investments in commerce and arts that will be beneficial to society. However, Teilmann-Lock concludes, the way in which intellectual property rights are enforced may, in effect, transform them into an instrument of censorship to be invoked by corporations or other private actors.

Shaheed's two consecutive reports 'Writing and teaching of history' (2013) and 'Memorialization processes' (2014) are the topic of Chapter 8, authored by **Hanne Hagtvedt Vik**. During her travels as the UN Special rapporteur in the field of cultural rights, Shaheed frequently encountered intense disagreements over events in the past and found that across the world people(s) are prevented from accessing historical narratives not only of their own cultural heritage, but also of that of others. Her history and memory reports deal with post-conflict and divided societies and build on the observation that international human rights treaties proclaim the right of all humans to their cultural heritage, and that this includes knowing the past. But to which cultural heritage and history do we have the right, Vik asks? And what would characterize human rights-based approaches to the past? Shaheed offers normative statements and guidance primarily for states, but also for other actors involved in historical research, teaching and memorialization processes.

Shaheed's principal proposition is the advancement of 'multi-voiced narratives' of the past. This and other propositions emanate from a commitment to making sure that history teaching and memorialization do not lead to the (escalation of) conflicts, that victims are recognized, and that the teaching of history and memorialization build on the principles behind the rights to freedom of opinion and expression, as well as the rights to information and academic freedom. Shaheed is concerned that historical narratives may be manipulated for the sake of forging national (and other) identity. These concerns and purposes embody inherent tensions, however, some of which are perhaps irreconcilable. Having summarized the two reports and reflected on some of the reports' main propositions and assumptions, Vik ends by suggesting a future path for the present Special Rapporteur with regard to the fields of history and memory.

Chapter 9 concerns Shaheed's 2014 report on 'The impact of commercial advertising and marketing practices on the enjoyment of cultural rights.' **Dalindyebo Shabalala's** commentary of this report brings up the issue of the focus of the report on the frame of competition law, and the effects of advertising as commercial practice resulting in the imposition and manipulation of choice and options. In response, Shabalala leans towards a 'cultural ecology' approach, presenting a broad interpretation of advertising, not so much referring to the commercial nature of the speaker, but more to advertising as a method of persuasion that may be harmful to the free access to information. Persuasive methods may be applied by commercial enterprises inducing consumers to buy certain products, but, increasingly, similar methods are used by political or religious groups. Shabalala supports the conclusion of the Rapporteur that a mix of regulatory measures and self-regulation is called for, and that an independent regulator should engage in monitoring and standard setting in access to and the use of media rather than in enforcing rules post-violation.

The last two chapters offer commentaries on Shaheed's two 2015 reports on intellectual property as it relates to the right to science and culture. In Chapter 10, **Fiona Macmillan** looks at the report on copyright policy. In drawing critical attention to a wide range of issues impacting on the operation of copyright law and, especially, the international copyright regime, Shaheed's report has courageously gone where few other institutions of public international governance have dared to go. This territory is not uncharted, however, as Macmillan points out. A considerable number of academic and activist commentators have already set up camp there. The challenge now is to build upon this report by bringing to light further matters of substantial importance in understanding the relationship between copyright and the realization of cultural rights. In this chapter Macmillan offers comments on a range of issues raised or touched on in the copyright report, but which she considers deserve further consideration. There is a yardstick according to which these issues have been selected, and this yardstick is a set of principles and observations that she suggests are fundamental to finding our way to a system that recognizes and promotes creativity and cultural rights.

Measuring itself according to this yardstick, Macmillan's chapter examines six critical issues raised by the copyright report: private property over cultural output; the problem of corporate ownership of copyright; the uses of human rights discourse; the particular position of Indigenous Peoples; the challenges posed by digital technologies; and the problem of the apparently ever-decreasing (or, maybe, ever-increasing) cultural commons.

The theoretical framework to which **Jannice Käll** relates her comments in Chapter 11 is that of the so-called 'new materialists' who suggest that we currently live under 'advanced capitalism'. Following 'the new materialists' she argues that the conflicts between patents and human rights make very specific sense in relation to a new materialist understanding of capitalism, and that the conceptual battle between patents and human rights also needs to be fought against the force(s) of advanced capitalism. In order to highlight the severity of the patent regime today as it aligns with capitalism, it is important to pay special attention to issues that rupture the dominating idea of the human as a person who produces and has control over culture and science through property.

Käll addresses the general emphasis in Shaheed's final report on the importance of supporting the creation of free and non-political forms of science. As outlined in the Report, it is today specifically worrisome that patent control is used as a means to govern science even when it is publicly funded. Thus, the politicization of science through marketization and the role of neoliberalism in turning the university into something akin to a company may be understood as a specific threat to the realization of science.

REFERENCES

A/HRC/14/36 (2010)

A/HRC/20/26 (2012)

An-Na'im, Abdullahi A. (1992), *Human Rights in Cross-Cultural Perspectives: A Quest for Consensus* (Philadelphia: University of Pennsylvania Press).

Bidault, Mylène (2016), 'Intellectual Property Policies and the Right to Science and Culture: The Work of the Special Rapporteur in Context,' in Christophe Geiger (ed.), *Intellectual Property and Access to Science and Culture: Convergence or Conflict?* Global Perspectives for the Intellectual Property System, CEIPI-ICTSD, Issue Number 3, 2016, 21—9.

Geiger, Christophe (2016) (ed.), *Intellectual Property and Access to Science and Culture: Convergence or Conflict?* Global Perspectives for the Intellectual Property System, CEIPI-ICTSD, Issue Number 3.

Jensen, Steven L.B. (2016) *The Making of the International Human Rights*, (Cambridge University Press).

Leavis, F.R. (1962), *Two Cultures? The Significance of C.P. Snow.* The Richmond Lecture (London: Chatto & Windus).

Lenzerini, Federico (2014), *The Culturalization of Human Rights Law* (Oxford: Oxford University Press).

Logan, William, 'World Heritage and Human Rights: Preserving our Common Dignity through Rights Based Approaches' (2012) 18(3) *International Journal of Heritage Studies* 231–44.

Macmillan, Fiona (2017), 'Cultural Heritage and the Unseen Community'. Forthcoming in S. Whatley, C. Waelde, A. Brown and S. Harmon (eds), *Dance, Disability and the Law: Invisible Difference* (Intellect Books).

Porsdam, Helle (2013), 'Digital Humanities: On Finding the Proper Balance between Qualitative and Quantitative Ways of Doing Research in the Humanities,' *Digital Humanities Quarterly* 7.2/2013 – available at http://www.digitalhumanities.org/dhq/vol/7/3/000167/000167.html.

Shaver, Lea (2016), 'Intellectual Property and the Right to Science and Culture: The Reports of the Special Rapporteur in the Field of Cultural Rights,' in Christophe Geiger (ed.), *Intellectual Property and Access to Science and Culture: Convergence or Conflict?* Global Perspectives for the Intellectual Property System, CEIPI-ICTSD, Issue Number 3, 2016, 30–41.

Snow, C.P. (1998), 'The Two Cultures. The Rede Lecture, 1959,' in *C.P. Snow The Two Cultures* (Cambridge: Cambridge University Press).

Snyder, Laura J. (2011), *The Philosophical Breakfast Club: Four Remarkable Friends Who Transformed Science and Changed the World* (New York: Broadway Paperbacks).

1. The United Nations cultural rights mandate: reflections on the significance and challenges

Farida Shaheed

Being the first mandate holder in any area of human rights carries the distinct privilege of freely exploring the scope and normative content of that right as well as the opportunity to lay out a framework to respect, protect, and promote those rights by defining their scope and content. This privilege comes with responsibility and challenges, however. This duality of privilege and challenge as the first mandate holder was an aspect that I was acutely aware of throughout my tenure first as Independent Expert and then Special Rapporteur in the field of cultural rights.

All first mandate-holders undoubtedly face challenges. With respect to cultural rights, however, the usual challenges were compounded by several less usual factors. To start with, unlike other areas of human rights where there is a fairly clear notion of what the human rights violations might be, if not always the solutions, in the case of cultural rights there was little clarity about exactly what this mandate would be about. The ambiguity and lack of precision is reflected in the title of the mandate itself: 'in the field of cultural rights', rather than simply 'cultural rights'. Compare this with, for example, the title of the mandate of the 'Special Rapporteur on the promotion of truth, justice, reparation and guarantees of non-recurrence', which may be a mouthful and over-ambitious in terms of 'guarantees of non-recurrence', but certainly provides a clear sense of what is being looked at, or even that of the 'Special rapporteur on violence against women – its causes and consequences' which again suggests the scope of the mandate. While ambiguity can also be viewed as an advantage in that it leaves the scope wide-open, it presented a serious challenge. (Early on, we stopped using the formal term except in official documents in favour of the simpler 'cultural rights').

The evident skepticism about whether cultural rights were indeed a human right as a distinct area is reflected in the mandate starting off as an Independent Expert position, rather than as a Special Rapporteur. This is especially significant given that cultural rights are clearly enunciated as an integral component of human rights in article 27 of the Universal Declaration of Human Rights and further explicitly elaborated under article 15 of the International Covenant on Economic, Social and Cultural Rights (ICESCR). Several articles of the International Covenant on Civil and Political Rights also relate to cultural rights, as I would later spell out in my reports. The skepticism on the part of many states was evident to me as soon as I assumed the mandate and persisted regardless of the resolution bringing into existence the mandate in 2009, and despite a day of general discussion on the right to take part in cultural life a year earlier in 2008.

Part of the problem stemmed from the paucity of previous work on cultural rights, reflected in the frequent comment prior to my mandate, that cultural rights were a generally underdeveloped area in comparison to other human rights.[1] Fortunately, some academics were engaged in exploring cultural rights from the international human rights perspective. There were virtually no civil society groups working on cultural rights at all, groups either worked on human rights or on culture. There were a few exceptions dedicated to cultural rights, such as the Fribourg Group that produced the Fribourg Declaration on Cultural Rights in 2007,[2] but this was not a registered entity at that time.[3] Alternatively groups worked on a particular aspect, as for example, the American Association for the Advancement of Science that narrowly focused on the right to scientific progress and its application, ignoring all other aspects of Article 15 of the ICESCR. The dearth of previous work that could help explore the scope and content of the right rendered the task of explicating the scope and

---

1 Patrice Meyer-Bisch, *Les droits culturels, une catégorie sous-développée des droits de l'homme, Actes du VIIIe Colloque interdisciplinaire sur les droits de l'homme à l'Université de Fribourg* (Editions Universitaires Fribourg, Suisse, 1993). See also Elsa Stamatopoulou, 'The right to take part in cultural life', submission to the Committee on Economic, Social and Cultural Rights, day of general discussion on the right to take part in cultural life (E/C.12/40/9), pp. 7–8.

2 Fribourg Declaration on Cultural Rights (2007), available from www.unifr.ch/iiedh/assets/files/declarations/eng-declaration.pdf.

3 The Fribourg Group has since enlarged and initiated the setting up in November 2016 of a new entity called the Observatory on cultural rights and diversity which aims at continuing research, training and advocacy on cultural rights.

normative content of cultural rights, the purpose of the mandate, all the more challenging.

The paucity of previous work and skepticism are interrelated, of course: the less the work done on a particular aspect of human rights, the less clear its significance is likely to be. For the cultural rights mandate, the uncertainty surrounding what exactly cultural rights were combined with the paucity of related work resulted in an overarching challenge. This was convincing people and, given that the United Nations is comprised of states, state representatives in particular, that cultural rights were human rights meriting attention by making visible cultural rights and their significance in terms of human rights for all. The initial skepticism and uncertainty at the beginning of my tenure was confirmed when it was coming to a close by one ambassador to the United Nations who candidly told me that when I assumed my position 'no one really knew what the mandate was about or what to expect'.

A first breakthrough came in March 2012, when the mandate was converted from an Independent Expert to Special Rapporteur through Human Rights Council Resolution 19/6 and without any comment being made by any state. The lack of comment was seen as significant because at the time the mandate was being established a number of states, while not asking for a vote, had not hesitated to express their skepticism. It is perhaps noteworthy too, that this resolution was tabled before the end of my first three-year tenure and formulated in a way to ensure that I would continue to hold the mandate. The change in attitude was also evident when the mandate started reporting to the Third Committee of the General Assembly in New York, as well as the Human Rights Council in Geneva in 2012. (Although this brought the pressure of writing two thematic reports a year, instead of one.) Having started with a fairly primordial challenge of having to convince people of the value and importance of cultural rights, it is with considerable satisfaction that I can say that at the end of my tenure, the work of the mandate ensured that cultural rights had been accepted as an important area of human rights by states, regardless of whether they agreed with all my reports or not.

KEY PARAMETRES FOR DEEPENING UNDERSTANDING OF CULTURAL RIGHTS

Given the dearth of materials, developing the cultural rights mandate would have been still more difficult had it not been for the general comment No. 21 (2009) of the Committee on Economic, Social and

Cultural Rights (CESCR) on the right to participate in cultural life.[4] The comment was in the final stages of preparation when the cultural rights mandate came into existence and, fortuitously, the perspective of the Committee coincided with my own. The comment resonated deeply with my own thinking in several key aspects. In particular, the understanding that culture is to be considered 'a living process, historical, dynamic and evolving' (para. 11), 'not as a series of isolated manifestations or hermetic compartments, but as an interactive process whereby individuals and communities, while preserving their specificities and purposes, give expression to the culture of humanity' (para. 12), reflected my own thinking. So, too, did the assertion that 'the cultural life of the community' today had to be understood in the plural as 'communities' (pp. 7–9). This seemed to be one of those obvious facts that nevertheless need to be explicated in written text. The general comment served as an important springboard in the initial development of cultural rights under the mandate.

My own understanding was, and remains, that the significance of cultural rights only becomes apparent by moving away from the concept of culture as specific manifestations of self-expression and simultaneously recognizing that culture permeates all human activities and institutions equally, whether artistic expressions or legal systems.[5] Culture, I often say, is like a prism through which we perceive, understand and engage with the human, manufactured and natural world around us, and through which we, in turn, are perceived and understood by others. Culture therefore provides people with a sense of self, underpins collective and individual identities alike and is manifested in individual and collective self-expression, understanding and practices. But neither culture nor identity is ever static. What is not explicated in comment No. 21 is that (a) identities, individual as well as collective, are also in a constant state of creation and (b) culture is always a site of contestation over meanings and worldviews in which new understanding, discoveries and

[4] UN Committee on Economic, Social and Cultural Rights (CESCR), *General Comment no. 21, Right of everyone to take part in cultural life (art. 15, para. 1a of the Covenant on Economic, Social and Cultural Rights)*, 21 December 2009, E/C.12/GC/21, available at: http://www.refworld.org/docid/4ed35bae2.html.

[5] See for example, Farida Shaheed, 'The Interface of Culture Custom and Law – Implication's for Women and Activism' in *Women's Law in Legal Education and Practice in Pakistan North-South Cooperation* (eds), Rubya Mehdi and Farida Shaheed (New Social Science Monograph: Copenhagen, 1997).

insights confront the old, the established, and the normative. Hence, the normative defined by concepts of culture, is also in a constant state of flux: being created, contested and recreated within the social praxis of diverse groups interacting in all human endeavours in the economic, social and political arenas as well as in what are traditionally understood to be cultural spheres of life.

I also concurred with the Committee's view that cultural rights encompass an aspect of collective rights as well as of individual rights, and that cultural rights may be exercised not only alone, or in association with others but also as a community.[6] This has a particular significance for indigenous and local communities, but also for all others as culture itself is a collective process. The collective aspect of cultural rights was also taken up by the Committee in its general comment No. 17 in reviewing the moral and material rights over authorship over any scientific, literary or artistic production of which he or she is the author with reference to the ICESCR, reflecting the fact that some authorship is collective, rather than individual – something I also elaborated on in several of my thematic reports, notably the reports on cultural heritage, the right to enjoy the benefits of scientific progress and its applications, and copyright.

Apart from the resonances with my perspective on cultural rights, general comment No. 21 provided a pivotal and practical insight. This was the clarification that the right to participate in cultural life is to be considered as having three distinct aspects: (a) the right to access; (b) the right to participate in; and (c) the right to contribute to cultural life.[7] Using the basic human rights premise that human rights must apply to all and the yardstick of considering each aspect from the viewpoint of the most disempowered and marginalised, this apparently simple unpacking has proved extremely useful for it implies a series of basic questions to be asked. Questions include, for example, who has access and who does not, and to what is this access? What blocks or enables participation and of which people/groups of people? What does contribution mean, and what is needed to ensure that everyone is able to contribute to cultural life on a basis of equality and without discrimination? These questions proved equally valid for researching the right to enjoy the benefits of

---

6 See also Jaime Marchan Romero, 'Derechos culturales: la practica del Comité de derechos economicos, sociales et culturales', working paper submitted to the seminar on implementing cultural rights: nature, issues at stake and challenges, p. 5, available at http://www.ohchr.org/EN/Issues/CulturalRights/Pages/Documentation.aspx.

7 General comment No. 21, *supra* note 4, para. 15.

scientific progress and its applications, as for artistic freedoms, history teaching and memorialisation processes, advertising, etc. and have greatly facilitated the elaboration of normative content of cultural rights.

CULTURE, CULTURAL DIVERSITY AND CULTURAL RELATIVISM

A separate challenge in terms of developing the cultural rights mandate concerned the unmistakable initial concern of numerous states that cultural rights would translate into cultural relativism, thereby undermining the universality of human rights; as evident in the nature of the questions my first two reports evoked. Presumably this concern was related to the terms of reference of the mandate 'to study the relationship between cultural rights and cultural diversity'.

This I saw as less challenging. While I am convinced that rights can only be fully enjoyed when they become integrated into a people's culture, I have long maintained that no society ever has a singular culture and that cultures relate to power. Regardless of other constituent factors, every society in the world has a dominant culture, promoting the viewpoints and perspectives of those with the power to enforce their norms and impose sanctions for transgressions, as well as subaltern cultures of those with less power or those contesting the current configurations of power.[8] Collective identities are inextricably linked to the underlying structures and dynamics of power related to accessing and exercising control over economic, political and cultural resources in every society. Consequently, from the very first report I have stressed that not only is culture dynamic, it is inherently linked to issues of power. Power differentials impact the ability of individuals and groups to effectively contribute to the identification, development and interpretation of what should be considered as a common 'culture' both in terms of shared cultural heritage from the past and in terms of contemporary cultural life. Equality and diversity *within* each community (however defined) is just as crucial as equality and diversity across communities for belonging – to a family, community or society – does not automatically confer equality *within* that community. Consider, for example, the

[8] Farida Shaheed, 'Violence Against Women Legitimised by Arguments of 'Culture' – Thoughts from a Pakistani Perspective.' in *Due Diligence: The Responsibility of the State for the Human Rights of Women* (ed.) Carin Benninger-Budel (Netherlands: Martinus Nijhoff Publishers, 2008).

situation of women or persons with disabilities, or those with less economic power in any community.

This makes it imperative to deconstruct 'the community'. Instead of presuming a homogenous community in which everyone lives happily together as equals, it is vital to analyse both who is assumed to be the authoritative voice of 'the' community and by whom, in particular the state, this is assumed. Demystifying the construct of 'the community', which is so closely associated with culture, reveals who defines and decides what the values of a particular community are, helping to identify the positive obligations of the state. With respect to states, it is important to remember that there are more ethnic groups than nation states and that 'nations, and ethnic groups and cultural communities are ideologically plural even if they share common cultural mores'.[9] From the perspective of human rights norms and standards, it is equally important to bear in mind the tendency of nation states to protect dominant nations or groups.[10] The tendency to protect dominant groups becomes especially problematic, for example, when the voice of 'the' community is taken to exclusively mean a few patriarchs who have power, as elaborated in my report on the enjoyment of cultural rights by women on an equal basis with men.[11] The presumption that certain patriarchs (or unelected others) are entitled to speak for all, is all the more problematic given that this tendency persists even in states which otherwise uphold the democratic norm of people voting in their representatives. It is incumbent on states to ensure, as a positive obligation, that everyone has an equal opportunity to access, participate in (which has to include decision-making) and contribute to cultural life.

In terms of diversity, I also stress that individuals are not binaries, the either/or configurations of statistics. In reality, each individual is the bearer of a multiple and complex identity which makes her or him a unique human being while simultaneously enabling her/him to be part of communities of shared culture (see A/HRC/14/36, para. 23). This complex identity is the result of multiple processes of socialisation but equally results from engagements and interactions with the world around us and new stimuli that can evoke a rethinking of received wisdoms and

---

[9] Ephraim Nimni, 'Collective dimensions of the right to take part in cultural life', submission to the Committee on Economic, Social and Cultural Rights, day of general discussion on the right to take part in cultural life, (E/C.12/40/17), p. 8.

[10] Ibid., pp. 10–11.

[11] Report 2012 – 'The enjoyment of cultural rights by women on an equal basis with men', A/67/287.

ways of viewing ourselves, others and our surroundings. While an individual's identity showcases uniqueness, the collective identities emphasise similarity. Collective identities never encompass all the characteristics of any individual: the use of the pronoun 'we' privileges only certain parts of individual identities, selecting specific markers of a complex personal identity that highlight a link with a particular group of people. In many ways 'we' is a social construct as it only comes into play vis-à-vis another. Nevertheless, this social construct plays a central role in the concepts and processes of inclusion/ exclusion that define who we are and who we are not; who the other(s) is/are; what we can and cannot do and what we expect the other to do or not do.

Still, people are *simultaneously* part of several communities of shared cultural values. The specific implications are that cultural rights must translate into ensuring that every voice is given an opportunity to be heard equally, in particular those who are marginalised, disempowered and with least opportunities of voicing their concern. Rights must underpin each person's ability to simultaneously be part of as many or as few communities as they choose as well as joining, leaving and (re)joining these at will; to critique the existing parameters and mores of all the cultural communities in which they want to participate and be able to freely create new communities of shared cultural values, and to do all this without fear of punitive action.

It is of paramount importance to distinguish cultural rights from culture per se even though cultural rights are closely and inherently linked to culture, for it is the failure to distinguish between the two that opens the door to cultural relativism. The conflation of culture with cultural rights has meant that throughout my mandate I found myself repeating that the mandate was not about preserving culture as it is or even safeguarding cultural heritage, however valuable this may be. This is the remit of UNESCO. Cultural rights are also certainly not about traditions, except for 'The greatest tradition [which] is the tradition of reinventing tradition', as the social psychologist Ashish Nandy says.[12] The mandate is about ensuring that the necessary conditions exist for everyone to access, participate in and contribute to cultural life on a basis of equality and without discrimination; to question existing traditions and create new ones. This means ensuring equal opportunities to be heard and to experience cultural life as a participant and to be a contributor to it.

---

[12] See Ashish Nandy *The Intimate Enemy – Loss and Recovery of Self under Colonialism* (2nd edn, Oxford India Paperbacks: New Delhi, 2009).

Every culture, contemporary as well as past, has aspects to it which are not in keeping with human rights standards and all cultures violate human rights at some point or aspect. Therefore, as stated by Adbulaye Sow, 'it is myopic [and] misinformed to say that cultures are essentially pro or anti-human rights. They are in fact neither of the two and a fertile arena for contestation'.[13] All societies must strive to reorient culture to be in keeping with human rights. Nowhere is this more apparent than in the case of gender given that culture has consistently been used to keep women, girls and persons of other genders disempowered, and to deny their rights.

THE CHALLENGE OF GENDER AND CULTURE

Culture is often used in the context of the Convention on the Elimination of all forms of Discrimination Against women (CEDAW) to explain the lack of progress. This, despite article 5 under which states are to:

> take all appropriate measures to modify the social and cultural patterns of conduct of men and women, with a view to achieving the elimination of prejudices and customary and all other practices which are based on the idea of the inferiority or the superiority of either of the sexes or on stereotyped roles for men and women.[14]

Indeed, knowing how women are pushed into participating in all kinds of harmful practices in the name of culture, my very first statement as a mandate holder stressed that the right to participate in cultural life includes the right *not* to participate in any cultural event, ritual or process that undermines human dignity.

As the mandate resolution explicitly calls for a perspective on gender (as well as persons with disabilities), it was interesting that early on in my mandate, at one of my first side events on women and cultural rights, some states commented that while the mandate should have a perspective on gender, it should not focus on gender per se. My response was that even if the resolution had not called for this perspective, I would have included gender because gender is central to all cultures everywhere for it is only one of three incontrovertible facts of life, the other two being

---

[13] Abdulaye Sow. Le droit de participer à la vie culturelle. (E/C.12/40/17) pp. 8–9.

[14] Convention on the Elimination of All Forms of Discrimination against Women (CEDAW), available at http://www.un.org/womenwatch/daw/cedaw/text/econvention.htm.

birth and death. Gender is not only a social construct; it is a cultural construct present in every society and community, large or small, with its accompanying gender rules: the permissible and impermissible, the laudable and the condemnable, as well as punitive actions for transgressions.[15] It is therefore impossible to speak of cultural rights and ignore gender.

The key role of culture in imposing and keeping in place patriarchal structures and systems to the detriment of women and girls has been written about at length. There is no doubt that women are prevented from accessing as well as participating in cultural life through restrictions imposed in the name of cultural practices. Culture is used to justify numerous other violations of rights: being subjected to various forms of violence; denied political, economic and educational rights for example. In terms of cultural life, the ability of girls and women to contribute to cultural life is impeded by cultural restrictions as well as not having the wherewithal (resources and opportunities) to explore and develop their creativity, and it is often impossible for women to challenge gender norms or leave their communities without fear of punitive actions. Culture does not exist outside human communities; it is determined by people and the rules and structure and systems put into place.

From the perspective of developing the mandate, the challenge this presented was that most women's rights activists conceived of culture as primarily an obstacle to women's rights. Hence, in 2009, no activists were looking at cultural rights from a gender perspective. As a feminist and long-time women's right activist one of my concerns on assuming the mandate was to explore whether and how the lens of cultural rights could help to tackle the complex interface of culture and women's rights. Having researched the CEDAW committee reports and comments, and having concluded that it would be difficult to always prejudge what exactly could be categorised as harmful practice in a given context, I started advocating a paradigm shift: from viewing culture as an obstacle to women's rights to demanding equal cultural rights of women and girls at par with men and boys within the first year of the mandate. I shared this perspective with civil society groups focused on women's rights and also met informally with the CEDAW Committee on a couple of

[15] See for example, Farida Shaheed, 'Citizenship and the Nuanced Belonging of Women', in *Scratching the Surface: Democracy, Traditions, Gender* (ed.) Jennifer Bennett (Lahore, Heinrich Böll Foundation, 2007). See also Nira Yuval-Davis, *The Politics of Belonging: Intersectional Contestation* (London, Sage, 2011).

occasions, in the hopes that the Committee would be able to adopt this new perspective. When it became evident that the Committee's pre-existing work commitments mean this could not happen in the near future, I was persuaded to write a report on the topic to help identify specific questions that can help to hold states accountable to their international obligations. This has the net advantage of holding states accountable to their international obligations while avoiding the likely contentious discussions around which culture may be 'better' or 'worse'.

DEFINING THE PARAMETRES OF CULTURAL RIGHTS AND KEY LESSONS

Several factors contributed to defining the scope and content of cultural rights. If one driver was examining the various parts of article 15 of the ICESCR to explore how to translate these into more concrete measures, equally important catalysts for content and scope emerged in the course of country visits and interactions as well as communications regarding a violation of rights. Examining and elaborating on one right, led to explorations and reports on other aspects. For example, the pivotal role of history that led to two consecutive reports on history teaching and memorialization processes, was catalysed by meeting people on every country visit striving to retrieve, document and make known their history both as a means of strengthening their own identity and so as to make others acknowledge this history and therefore, them as a people. In parallel, I also met people contesting the contents and/or the way in which history was currently being taught, or simply feeling left out in the educational process that defines who 'we' are in a particular country. The report on artistic freedoms, for its part, was galvanized by the increasing number of communications I started receiving as a mandate holder reporting violations of the rights of people engaged in artistic expression.

A significant challenge in defining the scope of the mandate was the constant reference to science as well as culture, scientific progress as well as artistic creativity in both the Universal Declaration and even more explicitly in article 15 of the ICESCR. The CESCR had examined and elaborated on very specific aspects such as the moral and material interests and copyright issues, but had not explored what the right to science as such meant. Hence, when soon after assuming my mandate, someone suggested to me that I should write a report on this aspect, I was reluctant. This was not only because this was definitely outside my own comfort zone, but also because the literature I perused revealed a tendency to focus either on 'culture' or 'science'. Indeed, it was suggested that, depending on the writer's perspective, either culture or science had been added merely because it was in UNESCO's mandate. When I consulted the Committee for possible guidance, the response was not encouraging. Writing such a report was seen as difficult as there was no case law on which to build. Nevertheless, although hesitant, I decided to write a report anyway as I believe one of the responsibilities of a mandate holder is to explore difficult issues.

There were two important catalysts for my understanding of the right to science; first, an article by Lea Shaver gave me invaluable insights, and led me to adopt her term 'the right to science and culture'.[16] The second catalyst was a fundamental question posed by Mara Busto of the Office of the High Commissioner for Human Rights (OHCHR) during the expert group meeting on the subject, for which I am extremely grateful. Her question was: What does the right to enjoy the benefits of scientific progress and its application mean beyond the right to health and other aspects of scientific inquiry? Thinking about this vital question in conjunction with reading about aspirations being a cultural competency gave me a breakthrough in understanding. The epiphany was that at the core of cultural rights is human creativity, regardless of whether this is in terms of science, technology or artistic expression. The right to science is encompassed in the broader right of all human beings to not only create (an essential part of cultural life), but also to enjoy the fruits of the creativity of others while preserving the right of authors, read as including all manner of creators, to the moral and material benefits of that creativity. As expected, this report was highly praised by a number of states and not at all well-received by others; and the use of the shortened 'right to science' was questioned. It is therefore interesting to note that the term right to science and culture (or culture and science) is now becoming quite common.

Different arcs of investigation helped to continuously further explore and define the scope of the mandate. The artistic freedoms report, for example, brought to light the importance of public spaces as arenas for cultural life and threw up questions regarding who decides on the utilisation of such spaces. This directly led to the subsequent report on advertising, but it also contributed to the report on memorialisation, museums and monuments. The artistic freedom as well as the right to science reports galvanized the work on copyright and the difficult interface of cultural rights and intellectual property laws. Working on

[16] Lea Shaver, 'The right to science and culture', *Wisconsin Law Review*, 2010.

intellectual property laws was especially challenging and involved a very steep learning curve for me. In like manner, the cultural heritage report led to the later reports on history and memorialization. The development of the reports and accompanying research helped overcome what initially seemed to be an almost insurmountable challenge of defining the scope of cultural rights. Given that culture does permeate all aspects of human life the question was where to draw the line between cultural rights and other human rights.

In terms of normative content, country visits especially brought home several important lessons for furthering cultural rights. Efforts for promoting access to cultural life do exist but there is clearly a need to avoid ghettoization – meaning that it is not sufficient to ensure people's access to their own cultural life. Promoting cultural rights requires a multi-way process. This means that it is not sufficient to merely ensure that a particular group of people have access to their own cultural heritage, such as history or cultural spaces. It is equally important that the majority community learns about the history of minorities and is encouraged to participate in the cultural events and self-expression of marginalised communities – care being taken to ensure that the people whose cultural life is involved are not further marginalised by this. Similarly, the right to contribute to cultural life is a crucial and overlooked aspect, especially for marginalised groups. This was a lesson brought home for me by several people, but especially persons with disabilities who insisted that they want to be able to contribute to cultural life through their own creativity and not merely access the creativity of others.

There were several issues I was unable to explore during my tenure which deserve attention, such as cultural rights in educational institutions, the impact of globalization and development imperatives on cultural rights. The cultural rights of indigenous people and persons with disabilities both deserve full reports. There are two other aspects meriting attention I would like to highlight here. The first is the impact of tourism on people's cultural rights. This is especially important given the current focus on culture as a driver of development. There is a real danger that the push for tourism as a source of income will force people into performing their culture for the sake of others, rather than living it. What this means for human rights is not clear yet. I am not implying that all tourism is bad, just that this is an issue that came to light as already constituting a problem in the research on cultural heritage. The second issue relates to cultural rights in state institutions such as orphanages and foster homes, but equally importantly also prisons and hospitals for medical and psychological treatments. This issue was brought to my attention first by a woman who wrote me a letter regarding welfare services and their disregard for her cultural rights, but it also came to light in the course of country visits regarding prisoners not being able to speak in their own language with other prisoners, as this was considered a security risk. These are areas I hope future mandate holders as well as scholars and civil society groups will take up.

THE SIGNIFICANCE OF CULTURAL RIGHTS

In terms of significance, the fact that cultural rights relate to peoples' identity, self-expression and creativity as individuals, groups of individuals and as communities, places them at the centre of human rights. Furthermore, as highlighted in my report on cultural rights for women on a basis of equality with men, cultural rights are empowering rights that can open access to all other rights for many marginalised groups of people. In the case of women and girls, I am convinced that many other social, economic and political rights simply will not be accessible – or fully enjoyed – until women and girls enjoy cultural rights on a basis of equality with men and boys.

Attesting to the interdependence and interrelatedness of human rights, cultural rights in fact bridge rights enshrined in the International Covenant on Civil and Political Rights as well as under the ICESCR, as clearly reflected in particular in the reports on women, artistic freedoms, history teaching and memorialization processes. When I assumed the mandate, not only did few people understand what cultural rights were, many felt these were 'soft rights' that perhaps would not showcase violations in the same way as other rights. However, precisely because human rights are interdependent, regardless of which particular aspect of human rights is used as a window to examine a particular situation, it will inevitably reveal the same basis of discrimination and exclusions of certain people, even though the specific manifestation of the rights' violations will differ. However, I believe that cultural rights are transformative: they are empowering rights, providing important opportunities for the realization of other human rights. The lack of equal cultural rights, combined with economic and social inequalities, makes it difficult, if not impossible, for people to enjoy personal autonomy, to exercise their civil and political rights, and in particular to participate in the political life of their community or country.

In many ways it is the combined impact of several reports that give weight to the scope and normative content as proposed by the mandate. For example, some questioned the report on the right to cultural heritage because they did not think this particular right constituted a real human right. They gained a better understanding when the right to cultural heritage was seen in the context of the later report relating to the right to enjoy the benefits of scientific progress and its applications. For others the importance of cultural heritage and who decides what this is became more evident after the report on women. This report highlighted the crucial role of everyone's right to determine what constitutes cultural heritage, that is, things received form the past that are considered so important that they are to be passed on to future generations. There was an even greater and wider appreciation of the value of cultural heritage when seen in the light of the reports on history teaching and memorialization processes. Indeed, this is an area which has been taken forward by the current mandate holder. In this sense, the accumulative work on the mandate I believe has been greater than its individual parts.

Today, there is an acceptance of cultural rights that seemed almost impossible when I started the mandate. Equally importantly, the reports have led to concrete actions and have been used in support of cultural rights by states and non-state actors alike. The mandate's work has, for example, contributed to the development of cultural policies in several Scandinavian countries. The UN Women regularly refers to the report on women, just as several states have acted upon the recommendations submitted and several non-state actors, such as school principals, have instituted changes in accordance with recommendations. The reports have led to language being adopted in the UN, to more reporting on cultural rights under ICESCR, renewed attention to the right to science and culture, including the intersection with intellectual property laws and to a showcasing of the importance of artistic freedom in an unparalleled way. They have contributed to discussions in the European Parliament. Civil society actors have also used the country reports to take forward their agendas. This leaves me both relieved and with a sense of accomplishment. Nevertheless, cultural rights are all too often still considered to be secondary. Too many people still think of cultural rights as a luxury, which can be compromised when priorities must be set. Nothing could be further from the truth, for cultural rights are essential to people's sense of self as well as future aspirations; they are markers of a vibrant and democratic society and a key ingredient in overcoming conflicts. I hope my work has helped clarify this. As a way of highlighting the crucial role of cultural rights I did suggest to the Committee on Economic, Social and Cultural Rights that, for a while at least, it should reverse the order of reviewing states parties reports: instead of starting with questions about economic rights, it should start with asking questions about cultural rights, then social rights and end with economic rights.

Finally, I have to say that my six years as mandate holder from November 2009 to October 2015 when my second term ended, was an exciting journey of discovery that confirmed the statement made in the first thematic report that, 'In many aspects, cultural rights are pivotal to the recognition and respect of human dignity, as they protect the development and expression of various world visions – individual and collective – and encompass important freedoms relating to matters of identity'. This is a journey I have made together with Mylène Bidault who worked with me on the mandate at the OHCHR and is as passionate about cultural rights as I am and has worked on the subject in great detail. The journey was made possible thanks to innumerable people whose generosity of spirit humbles me; not just the experts who helped undertake the research, but equally others who went out of their way to share their expertise, time, and insights to move the analysis and thinking on cultural rights forward, both in terms of specific meetings and during my country visits. I have learnt enormously from so many, in the process gaining some wonderful friends. I know that it would simply not have been possible to explicate cultural rights without their invaluable inputs and can only hope that the mandate will continue to enjoy such support, eased by the increasing number of people and groups working on cultural rights and by the fact that the question and skepticism that met the idea of cultural rights is now a thing of the past.

2. Implementing cultural rights (nature, issues at stake and challenges) – Report 2010 (A/HRC/14/36)

Lotte Hughes

INTRODUCTION AND BACKGROUND

This chapter will, in its response to the 'first report', draw on my research experience in Kenya since 1997, studying a variety of subjects that have included the history of Maasai land alienation and forced migration, indigenous peoples' rights and resistance, civil society-led engagement with cultural heritage, state heritage management, museums, and issues around memory and memorialization, including contemporary memorialization of the Mau Mau rebellion that took place in the 1950s in colonial Kenya. It is also relevant to explain that I currently lead a collaborative interdisciplinary research project which is examining how Kenyans are exercising new cultural rights, enshrined in the 2010 constitution.[1] My chapter will therefore draw on empirical knowledge of Kenya in particular, and Africa more broadly. I am an historian of Africa and empire with a Kenya specialism.

When presenting in Copenhagen in November 2015 the paper on which this chapter is based, I warned that my paper would be provocative. I also apologized in advance if the Rapporteur had gone on, in later reports, to deal with the issues I raised. I had not read the later reports and was asked to confine my remarks to the one assigned to me; I assume that my fellow speakers did likewise. This first report inspired me

[1] I would like to thank research colleagues Harriet Deacon, Zoe Cormack, Steve Ouma Akoth and Nicola Stylianou for their comments on an earlier draft paper, on which this chapter is based. For more information on the ESRC-funded project we work on, Cultural Rights and Kenya's New Constitution (2014–17), whose team also includes Mark Lamont, Gordon Omenya and formerly Heather Scott, see http://katibaculturalrights.com/.

to think about broader issues arising, which Ms Shaheed could not have been expected to address at that early stage. In raising these issues as topics for discussion, no blame was or is apportioned to Ms Shaheed for failing to touch on them in her initial report. It simply got me thinking around the subject, and inspired the following reflections.

SUMMARY OF THE FIRST REPORT

The report's own Summary states that the independent expert set out to develop 'preliminary views on the conceptual and legal framework of her mandate'.[2] She focused on the challenges regarding the scope and content of cultural rights, and reviewed the relevant existing provisions in UN human rights instruments. She then presented her preliminary thoughts on the interaction between the principle of universality of human rights, the recognition and implementation of cultural rights and the need to respect cultural diversity. Aware of the fact that many other UN 'mechanisms' have mandates which relate to cultural rights, Ms Shaheed also committed herself to 'coordinating with other mechanisms'. Finally, she selected some priority issues that she proposed to address during her time in office. These related to two main topics: (a) cultural rights, globalization of exchanges and information, and development processes; and (b) participation, access and contribution to cultural life, without any discrimination.

To extract some key points, Ms Shaheed noted that cultural rights have often been described as underdeveloped in comparison to other human rights. Because they have received less attention, they are sometimes seen as rights of 'lesser priority'. Nonetheless, they are an integral part of human rights, which are universal, indivisible, interrelated and interdependent. She asserted that cultural rights are in many respects 'pivotal to the recognition and respect of human dignity, as they protect the development and expression of various world visions – individual and collective – and encompass important freedoms relating to matters of identity'.[3] She pointed out that there is no official definition of cultural rights. Wisely, she said she would not attempt to define culture, on the grounds that it is unnecessary and may be inappropriate. But she went on to cite various 'expert' views; for example, she indirectly quoted Rodolpho Stavenhagen (former UN Special Rapporteur on the human

[2] Shaheed, 2010, Summary, p. 1. http://www2.ohchr.org/english/bodies/hrcouncil/docs/14session/A.HRC.14.36_en.pdf

[3] Ibid., p. 3.

rights and fundamental freedoms of indigenous peoples) as saying 'culture can be understood as a product, as a process and as a way of life', which goes beyond ethnicity, language and religion.[4] Importantly, she noted that human rights instruments are living instruments, and that it is vital to keep 'sufficient room for new developments and interpretations to arise', as 'new situations, demands, or foci of oppression' emerge.[5]

Ms Shaheed was required to find out how best to distinguish which human rights can be considered cultural, then to define the content of these rights. The legal instruments she most relies upon and cites include General Comment No. 21 adopted in 2009 by the Committee on Economic, Social and Cultural Rights, and other comments by that committee; the Universal Declaration on Cultural Diversity; the UNESCO Convention on the Protection and Promotion of the Diversity of Cultural Expressions; the Fribourg Declaration on Cultural Rights; the Universal Declaration of Human Rights; and the International Covenant on Economic, Social and Cultural Rights.

I will first address some apparent assumptions, before going on to discuss and problematize certain issues arising from the report. These include issues around terminology (I am especially querying over-use of the ubiquitous term 'community'); the meaning of cultural diversity and cultural development; self-ascription, especially with regard to indigeneity; constructions of identity, and the politics of identity and belonging. The apparent assumptions identified and discussed may not be so much Ms Shaheed's, as those embedded in the international rights instruments she surveys, as well as those embedded in the UN system as a whole.

MY RESPONSE TO THE REPORT

Since this was the first of a series of reports, written before Ms Shaheed's work had got fully underway, it understandably reads like a wish list and is fairly prescriptive. She set herself an exercise – to review the existing protocols and identify areas for further exploration. The subject of cultural rights is (understandably for a piece of work commissioned by the UN) approached and unpacked within the context of internationalized human rights, which is not necessarily how 'local' cultural stakeholders,

---

4 Ibid., p. 5.

5 Ibid., p. 4, quoting Patrick Thornberry, 'Cultural rights and the universality of human rights', submission to the Committee on Economic, Social and Cultural Rights, day of general discussion on the right to take part in cultural life (E/C.12/40/15), p. 6.

especially within civil society, may regard these rights (more on this below). We need to understand the two intertwined sets of rights, as Ms Shaheed does, as continually evolving, and to historicize their relationship. This is not the place and neither is there space to provide deep historicity, but in my response I will insert history and historicity into the equation where possible. Furthermore, I hope to demonstrate that culture and cultural rights are themselves cultural products – not necessarily products of legal instruments and international rights discourses but also (for example) socio-cultural-political encounters at every level. And, furthermore, that culture is best understood not as a stable and primordial given but as a human construct.

Cultural Diversity

I would like to start by questioning and exploring whether cultural rights necessarily imply and involve cultural diversity, and vice versa. Ms Shaheed writes: 'Provided that cultural rights are fully understood as being part of the wider human rights system and therefore grounded in existing norms and principles of international human rights law, they allow for an enriched understanding of the principle of universality of human rights by taking into consideration cultural diversity.'[6] Moreover, the Universal Declaration on Cultural Diversity states 'full respect for human rights, and in particular for cultural rights' both creates an enabling environment for, and is, a guarantee of cultural diversity (arts 4 and 5).[7] It may be useful at this point to note law professor Christoph Beat Graber's analysis of how cultural diversity came to be a key concept in international law. He links it to the 'intensification of economic globalization during the last decades of the twentieth century', and discusses it in relation to international trade (Graber, 2006, 553–4).[8]

I read the first of these statements (by Ms Shaheed) as meaning that the global multiplicity of cultural rights, taken as a whole, can enrich and expand our understanding of universalized human rights. But at national and local level, the ways in which culture and cultural rights are assigned or self-assigned to specific groups, many of them ethnic, can smack of essentialism and exclusivity. One often sees an unfortunate unwillingness

---

[6] Ibid., p. 3.

[7] Ibid., p. 25.

[8] This insightful article aims to explain how cultural diversity has become an issue of international law and provides critical assessment of the strengths and weakness of the Convention on Cultural Diversity. It also discusses culture and development.

by one cultural grouping (I prefer the terms group or collectivity to community, more on this below) to embrace cultural diversity on a national scale, let alone a global one – indeed, groups may actively resist such a move or concept, as part of their resistance to forced assimilation and multicultural 'mongrelism'. These are understandable impulses, especially where there is a history of forced assimilation during and following colonial times. In an attempt to secure benefits of one kind or another for the group (such as recognition, compensation, a bigger slice of the national cake, political power, economic development or tourism revenue) many ethnic groups, in countries such as Kenya and South Africa for example, seek to privilege and reify 'their' culture over others, which is surely antithetical to the embrace and championship of diversity? (Examples will follow.) These are issues that scholars of multiculturalism have long wrestled with; for example, see Charles Taylor's 1992 work, and other contributors to the important 1994 edition which reproduced Taylor's original essay and spoke to this, thereby pushing his original enquiry further. In her introduction to the 1994 volume, which she also edited, Amy Gutmann discusses some of the tensions between 'the liberal democratic value of diversity' and the very different concerns of citizens who seek to secure their culture and identity via efforts 'to preserve distinct and unique cultures over time' (Gutmann, 1994, 9). She goes on:

> Liberal democracy is suspicious of the demand to enlist politics in the preservation of separate group identities and the survival of subcultures that otherwise would not flourish through the free association of citizens. And yet democratic institutions, more than any others, tend to expose citizens to a diverse set of cultural values. Hence liberal democracy enriches our opportunities, enables us to recognize the value of various cultures, and thereby teaches us to appreciate diversity not simply for its own sake but for its enhancement of the quality of life and learning. The liberal democratic defense of diversity draws upon a universalistic rather than a particularistic perspective (ibid., 10).

Kenya's new (2010) constitution is underpinned by a liberal democratic ethos, and also contains notions of separateness; for example, the devolution of government to 47 counties each with their own separate governments, which the constitution brought about, aims among other things to foster national unity by recognizing 'diversity', but also recognizes 'the right of communities to manage their own affairs' and aims to protect and promote the interests and rights of minorities and marginalized communities (art. 174). However, many of my research contacts, who include Kenyan citizens engaged in non-state heritage activities, and who are concerned about the reclamation of 'their' group's history and heritage from colonial and neo-colonial masters, would profoundly disagree with the ideas expounded above by Gutmann, principally the belief that cultural values are universal rather than particular. However, when exposed to other 'cultures' within Kenya, by which Kenyans invariably mean ethnic groups, individuals and groups may come to appreciate the shared values, 'traditions' and histories that unite far more than they divide.[9]

Are Cultural Rights and Diversity Necessarily Central to Development Processes?

Under 'Areas of concern and priority issues for the mandate',[10] the Special Rapporteur cites UNESCO's pleading for 'a cultural approach to development', and recognition of cultural specificities 'necessary for the viability of any sustainable development project'.[11] Indeed, all development should be culturally sensitive, and include fundamental elements such as protection, access to justice, education, and the intellectual development of individuals, and not simply involve (as development too often implies) the attainment of national economic goals and growth. However, I think we should exercise caution with regard to broad-brush, normative statements such as 'cultural diversity ... is one of the roots of development' (she is quoting the Universal Declaration on Cultural Diversity, art. 3)[12] for no better reason than it allegedly 'widens the range of options open to everyone ... [and is] also ... *a means to* achieve a more satisfactory intellectual, emotional, moral and spiritual existence' (again a direct quote from the Declaration, emphasis added by this author).[13] Why and how? It is not Ms Shaheed's job to explain. But the fact of diversity (cultural and other kinds) is surely not a means to

---

9 This was one of the lessons that emerged from organizing inter-ethnic exchange visits for community peace museums and other Kenyan cultural groups, an activity I carried out with research colleague Karega-Munene in 2009–11 with British Academy funding (Hughes, 2011). Poorer citizens who are unable to travel widely within Kenya often have very little knowledge of other ethnic groups, and are susceptible to believing the stereotypical portrayal of these groups as 'Other' or 'traditional enemies', a notion peddled by elite actors for political gain. But when they get to meet and interact with members of other groups, we observed that they can be agreeably surprised.

10 Shaheed, 2010, pp. 42–52.

11 Ibid., p. 49.

12 Ibid.

13 Ibid.

anything, apart from being one of the characteristics of, and conducive to, a pluralistic society.

The Rapporteur appears to be sensitive to this, but it is worth emphasizing that cultural assets and identities ('people's cultural identities must be recognized and accommodated by the State', a quote from a 2004 UNDP report)[14] are too often regarded by states and (in Kenya's case) devolved county governments primarily as having a commercial value that can and should be exploited for the economic development of specific 'communities', regions and the nation as a whole.[15] 'Recognition' and 'accommodation' sound thoroughly well meaning, but may be perversely interpreted in practice, in ways that citizens may not necessarily welcome or find respectful of their rights. Moreover, the universal trend towards the commodification of culture does not necessarily sit well with how non-state cultural stakeholders regard the value of culture.[16] A leading light in the Kenyan peace museums movement put it this way:

> The basic value of culture that can never be disputed is that culture is a tool through which social fabric is made. For the survival of humankind, human interaction is a divine practice. It is these [cultural] interactions that enable humankind to bring diverse and unique abilities together for the common good of human society … The contribution of culture as far as development is concerned should not be through monetarization of culture but through crafting development practices embedded in particular cultural practice.[17]

---

[14] Ibid.

[15] Proof of this lies for example in the language employed in cultural heritage legislation, at both national and county level in Kenya, and in the ways in which county governments are using 'culture' to market their counties online and in other media. My research colleagues and I will be writing about this at a future date.

[16] This is clear from collaborative research in Kenya. Civil society informants have repeatedly told me and colleagues (past and current) of the felt, emotive and non-monetary value of their cultural heritage; for example, traditional peace cultures are employed in inter- and intra-communal peace and reconciliation initiatives by Kenya's peace museums movement, not in order to advance economic development (Coombes et al., 2014).

[17] Private communication by email to this author, 31 March 2016. Many thanks to Njiru Njeru for sharing these thoughts. He states that these are his personal views but he believes they are shared by other members of the Community Peace Museums Heritage Foundation (CPMHF), the umbrella organization for Kenyan peace museums, which are non-state and non-profit-making initiatives.

I would also like to draw readers' attention to a growing literature, notably Karen Engle's chapter 'Culture as Development' in her insightful 2010 book on indigenous development, and Basu and Modest's 2015 edited volume *Museums, Heritage and International Development,* a critical evaluation of claims concerning culture's importance in world development. The latter text convincingly demonstrates, citing a 2011 UNESCO report among others, that claims concerning culture's significant contribution to development cannot be proved, partly because of a lack of appropriate indicators and measurement tools. A more recent UNESCO report (not discussed in that volume) on culture and development is highly critical of the lack of inter-sectoral cooperation within the organization, which 'considerably weakens' its advocacy efforts towards the integration of culture and sustainable development at every level (UNESCO, 2015, vii).

Engle explores the genesis of ethno-development since the 1970s, 'when indigenous rights advocates began to expose the clash between indigenous rights and modern development models' (Engle, 2010, 191). Ethno-development, or 'development based on the traditional culture of indigenous groups' (ibid., 183), was meant to enable marginalized and indigenous groups to take control of their own development, and resist the imposition of inappropriate development models by external actors. These groups saw Western-led neoliberal development as posing a threat, yet simultaneously offering a future to indigenous peoples so long as 'cultural specificities' such as indigenous knowledge were included, and on condition that they controlled the development themselves. However, Engle illustrates how complicated and divisive these processes can become, when groups are expected (by the World Bank and other players) to develop in ways reflective of 'traditional' culture – which may not be what they want at all, nor reflect how their way of life has changed. One example she gives is gaming on Native American reservations in the United States. What happens when some members of a group decide to choose an alternative development path that does not necessarily chime with 'traditional' social norms – for example by welcoming extractive industries on their lands? Should they not be free to depart from 'traditional' norms and values, even though this risks the slur that they are not 'real indigenes'? Ms Shaheed hints at this conundrum in asking, 'who can be considered as developed, and from whose point of view?'[18]

---

[18] Shaheed, 2010, p. 49.

THE PROBLEM WITH 'COMMUNITY'

I now turn to discussing the Rapporteur's use of the word 'community'. This, or the plural 'communities', appears at least 33 times in her first report. I am guilty of over-using these terms myself (no doubt many scholars are, while the development industry is particularly keen on the notion of 'community' and the need to engage with ubiquitous 'local people'). But I would suggest that the alternatives collective, collectivity or social group are more nuanced, and that we ought to avoid over-use, especially when discussing culture. Here I will draw on discussions in critical heritage studies, particularly the work of Emma Waterton and Laurajane Smith, who write:

> There are a handful of words within the wider social sciences that are continually used, abused and reused, such as 'identity' and 'culture'. These are words that in essence are so fundamental they are difficult to take issue with; it is in their use that they have become so problematic. To this list, we want to add 'community', a term that has taken up a life of its own in recent years, not only within heritage studies but in popular and political life as well (Waterton and Smith, 2010, 4).

What do these authors take issue with? They believe the word or expressions about it 'are embedded with restrictive assumptions concerned with nostalgia, consensus and homogeneity, all of which help to facilitate the extent to which systemic issues tied up with social justice, recognition and subordinate status are ignored or go unidentified' (ibid.). In other words, 'community' is not a 'cuddly' (their word) monolithic, homogeneous grouping, as is often implied. 'For far too long, a simplistic and romantic idea of community has been peddled. ...' (ibid., 5). Let us apply this to the cultural rights debate. Self-description by a group invariably involves essentialization – in other words, the characteristics of a group are boiled down to supposedly essential features, which may in fact not be inclusive of all group members, or reflect changes to the group and its members over time, or be as distinctive as the group (or individuals within it) imagine. Furthermore, under pressure and influence from external forces including political players, development organizations, churches, donors and international rights bodies, social groups that were once fluid and open to in-migration can become concretized and exclusionary. Peter Geschiere has discussed the dangers of this in relation to autochthony and citizenship in Cameroon, where concretization of 'community' and what he calls the 'growing obsession with "autochthony" and belonging' can lead to 'ever more vicious forms of exclusion of "the other", the stranger, the *allogène*' (2005, 12, 10; also developed in his 2009 book). This exclusionary process, at the heart of which struggles over land posit land as a cultural right, is also increasingly happening in Kenya, with sometimes fatal results. Geschiere describes how the Cameroon government's use of the undefined term 'the local community' in new forest laws led to jockeying for position by previously fluid social groups that did not feature 'fixed positions of authority', but which were now keen to establish themselves as the recognized owners of 'community forests'.

In his study of a land claim by Khomani San people in South Africa, Daniel Huizenga has used a different methodology (textual analysis) to examine how 'communities' can be constructed as a result of struggles for rights and resources. Upending the notion that communities produce claims and struggles (no, claims and struggles can also produce communities), his analysis of the documentation of a land claim shows how documents created in support of claimants 'represent a specific way of knowing that contributes to a socio-legal construction of "community"' (Huizenga, 2014, 145). By tracking the use of the term 'community' within a data repository he shows how the term is used for different social, political and legal ends. He concludes that the documentation format, working 'in tandem with popular narratives of loss and reclamation', helps to create a particular socio-legal construction of an indigenous community, one which fails to account for the changing nature of (in this case) a claimant community, the claimants' different goals, and existing inequalities. In the land claim case he is discussing, this has helped to perpetuate women's exclusion (ibid., 156). These ideas can usefully be applied to other settings in which collectivities or other social entities are produced as a result of social processes.

What are the implications of all this for cultural rights? Rights to representation are of course closely intertwined with constructions and notions of community. Who within a 'community' has the authority or power to speak for it, or represent it, in relation to cultural rights or anything else? The Rapporteur hints at disquiet when she talks of discrimination and barriers to participation, but the emphasis in those passages of the report appears to be more on external barriers, not those within social groups themselves. We may have concerns, for example, as to whether the voices of children, youth and women are heard and their rights respected within patriarchal groups where 'traditional' (male elder) authority holds sway, on cultural and a wide range of other matters. The Rapporteur gives a nod to this when she writes, in the context of people's ability to contribute to the identification, development and interpretation of culture and cultural heritage, that 'power differentials must be taken into consideration',[19] and, during a discussion on the relationship between individual and collective rights, that individuals should be able to contest 'dominant norms and values within the communities they choose to belong to …'.[20] No doubt she went on to develop these ideas in subsequent reports.

This reminds me of a day-long discussion I had in 2014 with a Council of Elders in Embu County, which is lobbying the Kenyan government to amend the new constitution so that elders receive more recognition – for example, of their role in dispute resolution and the transmission of culture. In this case, and invariably in Kenya, culture is ethnicized in popular discourse – the elders were referring in our discussion exclusively to the culture of the Embu ethnic group.[21] Though the Council told me it had female members, none were present that day. The chairman turned to me at one point and said derisively: 'A woman has *no* culture, only the culture of her husband or father!'[22] I took a deep breath, then decided to say what I thought: 'With respect, I'm not going to let you get away with that!' Lively discussion ensued about gender issues, and the unfairness (as they saw it) of special concessions for women and youth, in terms of development opportunities and funding. What I took away from this was that the elders (by no means all elderly, some appeared to be as young as 40-something) were actually expressing anxiety about masculinity and the erosion of male power and 'traditional authority' in the modern world, rather than concerns about 'culture' per se. But they had assumed only *they* had the right to speak to or represent the cultural concerns of their social group. How different the conversation might have been if other women, apart from myself (dismissed as ignorant and culture-free by virtue of being a single white Westerner), had been present. That day I heard plenty of collective expressions of 'the meaning given to … existence' and 'world views' – mentioned several times in this First Report as expressions of culture – but not views representative

---

19 Shaheed, 2010, p. 6.

20 Ibid., p. 10.

21 The Embu (or Aembu) are a Bantu group closely related to the neighbouring Gikuyu (also spelled Kikuyu) and Meru peoples. Embu people live predominantly in Embu County, Kenya.

22 Andrew Ireri, chairman of Nyangi Ndiiriri Council of Elders. Focus group discussion with this author at Aembu Community Peace Museum, Nembure, Embu County, 16 November 2014. My thanks to museum curator Njiru Njeru for translation and field assistance.

of the Embu ethnic group as a whole, which this and other councils of elders claim to represent.[23]

When Article 27 of the Universal Declaration of Human Rights refers to the 'cultural life of "the community" [or] "communities"', what does that actually mean?[24] In its use of the singular, moreover, it suggests that individual groups or communities only have a singular cultural life. This paragraph (that is, Shaheed's) goes on to mention how culture can be created 'including through the contestation of dominant norms and values' within and between communities. But the concept of 'community' still comes across as a reified beast – something of a sacred cow and 'nostalgic ideal' form of homogeneous social organization. We should be aware at all times of the 'thick seams of power that structure any given collection of people' (Waterton and Smith, 2010, 8) and not use the term 'community' uncritically.

As these authors note, much the same applies to 'identity', a social construct rather than a given – something most scholars now regard as constantly constructed, reconstructed and deconstructed within wider socio-political processes (for example, see the chapter by Keyes and other contributions to Romanucci-Ross and De Vos, 1995). Identity changes shape according to need, the desire for gain, and political mobilization around 'heritage' (among other things).[25] A contemporary example from South Africa – the mobilization of pre-Zulu identities and promotion of Zulu heritage in the transition period since apartheid ended – is provided by Mbongiseni Buthelezi (2015). He describes how 'many people in KwaZulu-Natal (and elsewhere in South Africa) are probing their identities and confronting what the Zulu kingdom and Zuluness mean to them.' But they are forced, while seeking to understand their pasts, to '(circum)navigate' the 'symbolic centrality' of the Zulu kingdom and its founder, Shaka, since the official narrative of the heritage of the province has come to centre on this (op. cit., 160). In the struggle for control of 'heritage', in this and many other scenarios, identity is anything but a given – it has become a political football.

---

[23] For example, Shaheed, 2010, n. 5 on p. 4. 'World visions' is referred to in ibid., p. 9.

[24] Ibid., p. 10.

[25] Space precludes me from referring to the wider literature on 'community', particularly in a global cultural heritage context. But see for example Crooke (2010) for a discussion of the relationship between community and heritage, and the instrumentalization of 'community', in Northern Ireland.

The Rapporteur touches on how individuals can select different identities in 'particular interactions and engagements'.[26] But I suggest this can and should be pushed further to include consideration of the ways in which culture and identity are produced through encounters – such as those between the local, the national and the global, between different polities, and between groups, sometimes via cultural brokers, also known as 'ethnic entrepreneurs' (Keller, 2014, 46–7). Cultural brokers/ethnic entrepreneurs are not necessarily benign creatures; they can be used by elites to incite violence. Keller gives examples from countries including Rwanda, Nigeria and Kenya. While conceding that the root causes went deeper, he blames ethnic entrepreneurs for fomenting the 2007–08 post-election violence that tore Kenya apart: 'To some extent, this [post-election] crisis was the result of the ethnic entrepreneurs and cultural brokers-cum-politicians who incited ordinary people in an effort to challenge or defend the outcome of the elections' (ibid., 103–4). Through a range of country studies, Keller describes how the pressures exerted by globalization, as well as internal pressures that include land scarcity, the changes wrought by multiparty politics, and economic crisis, can push both 'incumbent regimes' and opposition parties into using cultural brokers/ethnic entrepreneurs to play upon citizens' fears of 'immigrants', encourage the assertion of exclusive rights, elevate autochthony to dangerous levels, and in the worst cases, to instigate violence. He leaves the reader in no doubt about their often insidious role in the concretization and mobilization of 'cultural identity' for political and other ends.

SELF-ASCRIPTION AND OTHER ISSUES

It is striking that the concepts of 'culture', 'cultural rights' and 'indigeneity' tend to be *self-ascribed* categories, unlike the broader universal categories of humanity, human rights and (for the majority of us) non-indigeneity. Or at least, self-ascription is a key concept in the interpretation, implementation and operationalization of cultural rights on the ground. One can of course think of exceptions in terms of the taxonomies of 'tribe' that were arguably introduced by colonial authorities in the colonial era, which (while contested) remain in place to this day in countries including Kenya, South Africa and Zimbabwe. (Rwanda is a unique exception, with all reference to ethnicity and ethnic markers

---

26 Shaheed, 2010, p. 23.

officially outlawed by the Kagame regime.) Indeed, the notion of 'tribe', and self-classification in 'tribal' terms, has become resurgent in several parts of the continent, as Buthelezi (2015) makes clear with regard to 'Zuluness' in South Africa (see my earlier reference to this text). What are the implications of this for our discussion? Self-identification as an indigenous people, for example, is a key pointer to definitions of indigeneity within the global discourse and protocols on indigenous peoples' rights. This was not always the case; anthropologist Dorothy Hodgson has described how African groups previously categorized as minorities were able to use the 'emerging principle … of self-identification' and cultural difference/distinctiveness, introduced in a 1986 report by Special Rapporteur José Martínez Cobo, to 'prove' their indigeneity (Hodgson, 2009, 9).[27] Also for minorities, the UN Office of the High Commissioner for Human Rights (OHCHR) states that definitions must include both objective and subjective factors, that is, self-ascription.[28] This is echoed in other UN documents, such as a paper for the Working Group on Minorities by José Bengoa, who refers to '"objective and subjective" factors, among which the minority's awareness of its own identity constitutes the key element' (Bengoa, 2000, 2).[29] Leaving aside minorities for a moment, the problem that then arises is that any group or collective can theoretically self-identify as indigenous, regardless of whether there is any historical basis for this assertion, and invent a cultural tradition, history and 'origins' story that may have no factual basis – and on the back of such an assertion, claim cultural rights which by extension may also have no basis in historical reality. I will give two examples shortly.

---

[27] Cobo is a former Special Rapporteur of the Sub-Commission on Prevention of Discrimination and Protection of Minorities. Hodgson describes how Manuel Alfonso Martinez, former chair of the UN Permanent Forum on Indigenous Peoples, had previously insisted 'that Africans and Asians were not indigenous and should instead bring their complaints to the [then] newly formed U.N. Working Group on Minorities'. This position did not make him popular with indigenous peoples (Hodgson, 2009, 7).

[28] There is no internationally agreed definition on which groups constitute minorities. It is often stressed that the existence of a minority is a question of fact and that any definition must include both objective factors (such as the existence of a shared ethnicity, language or religion) and subjective factors (including that individuals must identify themselves as members of a minority). See United Nations (OHCHR), References.

[29] My thanks to Jérémie Gilbert for drawing my attention to some of this literature.

More broadly, in the anthropological and other literature, ethnicity is also both objectively and subjectively defined: 'like any form of social identity, ethnicity remains essentially *subjective*, a collective sense of social belonging and ultimate loyalty related to parentage and a belief in common origins' (Romanucci-Ross and De Vos, 1995, 350). I would also emphasize the word belief, since an origins story may not reflect historical reality, but is more likely to be mythical. That then prompts the awkward question: is it a good idea or even defensible for cultural rights defenders to act upon a belief, or give the same weight to 'belief' as they do to fact?

The second problem arising is this: whose job is it to tell the difference between cultural reality and constructions thereof, and to 'call out' invented traditions masquerading as fact? This may sound heretical, but it lies firmly in the Hobsbawm and Ranger camp (1992). I do not wish to deride or dismiss genuinely held beliefs about culture, but want to make the point that if they do not have a basis in historical fact (which is of course contested in itself), and are driven, subverted and tainted by politics, this has major implications for cultural rights defenders, as well as for the groups concerned. Or does the Rapporteur regard the right to self-ascription as part and parcel of the right to 'important freedoms relating to matters of identity'?[30] To answer my question (whose job is it to tell the difference): dare I say it may very likely be independent scholars, since the UN system does not appear to include a sifting mechanism to sort the cultural wheat from the chaff – or does it? The global cultural rights regime appears to automatically give credence to groups which claim to be cultural rights bearers, by virtue of having a distinctive culture and identity, without questioning the legitimacy and construction of such claims. The practice of including indigenous representatives in UN meetings can be seen to have produced an institutional culture in which more credence is given to *who* speaks, than to what they say. As important as rights to participation, consultation and expression are, this practice is, I suggest, both naïve and fraught with danger.

In East Africa and other parts of the world, assertions of this kind to cultural particularity, often linked to indigeneity, are increasingly being made for political reasons, and reasons embedded in the politics of recognition, identity and belonging – none of which are mentioned in this report. This is totally understandable, but I suggest they must be factored into wider and future discussion. (Identity is mentioned several times, but not the

---

[30] Shaheed, 2010, p. 3.

politics of.)[31] These assertions and positionings often involve a strategy called strategic essentialism, which means presenting one's self or more often one's group as possessing certain fixed, simplified and essentialized characteristics useful for strategic purposes, such as securing recognition, land, power, political and/or monetary gain. Briefly, the politics of recognition are centred on demands for external recognition, and are closely linked to the politics of identity. As Charles Taylor has written:

> The thesis is that our identity is partly shaped by recognition or its absence, often by the *mis*recognition of others, and so a person or group of people can suffer real damage, real distortion, if the people or society around them mirror back to them a confining or demeaning or contemptible picture of themselves (Taylor, 1994, 25).

The politics of belonging are often intertwined with these other two activities/processes, and may involve the construction of in-group and out-group identities and collective identification with particular places and territories. The point to take away from all this is that self-identification and self-ascription by groups should not be taken at face value – they are part of 'the complex web of interactions that take place between actors and ideas' (Igoe, 2004, 9) and are linked to strategies of extraversion, a term coined by Bayart (1993) to describe the complex ways in which both groups and individuals have long sought alliances with powerful external players in order to gain power locally.

Drawing on my own research and that of Gabrielle Lynch, I will now give two brief examples of processes of becoming indigenous, which present a distinct challenge to notions of culture and cultural rights that rely upon self-ascription or self-identification.[32] I have observed the phenomenon of 'becoming indigenous' (Igoe, 2004; Hodgson, 2009, 2011) in relation to assertions to land and indigeneity made by a Gikuyu 'community' living in and around a sacred forest near Othaya in Central Kenya (Hughes, 2014). Gikuyu are neither indigenous, nor marginalized nor a minority – arguably, the only indigenous peoples in Kenya (if one uses the 'aboriginality' definition) are or were forest-dwelling hunter-gatherers, everyone else is an incomer. The Gikuyu form Kenya's largest ethnic group, and the one that has benefited most from the riches of post-independence, partly due to the fact that three presidents including

---

31 For example, ibid., pp. 8, 9, 16, 17.

32 My thanks to Gabrielle Lynch for commenting on earlier versions of this chapter.

the current post-holder[33] are or were Gikuyu (current President Uhuru Kenyatta, his father Jomo Kenyatta, Kenya's first post-independence president, and Mwai Kibaki). But some poorer sections of this ethnic group do not see it that way, since the fruits of *uhuru* (freedom from colonial rule) have not trickled down. I discovered one group had been heavily influenced by a UK-based international environmental rights NGO, as well as international indigenous rights discourses circulating in cyberspace, to seek to reinvent themselves as indigenous forest dwellers in order to gain wider recognition and assert their rights to a sacred forest. They attempted to do this, and activists claiming to represent the group continue to do so, partly by means of an invented 'origins story' which asserts that their ancestors had lived in this particular forest since 1650. In fact, as leading Gikuyu historian Godfrey Muriuki (1974) makes clear in his study of Gikuyu origins and migrations, Gikuyu people did not migrate to this area until the end of the nineteenth century – and proceeded to drive out and/or become assimilated with a pre-existing forest-dwelling group of hunter-gatherers called the Athi. If anyone could claim to be indigenous to these forests it is the Athi – but they no longer exist as a distinct group and cannot therefore make counter-claims.

In my second example, Lynch (2012) describes the case of the Endorois people, subject of a landmark decision by the African Commission on Human and Peoples' Rights (ACHPR) in February 2010. Having failed to get anywhere in domestic Kenyan courts, the Endorois took their case for redress to the ACHPR over their mass displacement, by the Kenyan government, between 1973 and 1986 from their 'ancestral' lands at Lake Bogoria to make way for a game reserve. The Endorois also complained that, as a result of the eviction, they had lost access to sacred cultural sites including the lake and a forest. The Kenyan government argued before the ACHPR that the Endorois were not an indigenous people, but a sub-group of the Tugen ethnic group, which is part of the larger Kalenjin community. However, the ACHPR ruled that the Endorois were indigenous, had been unlawfully evicted, and that several articles of the African Charter had been violated by the Kenyan government, including Article 17 which concerns the right to take part in cultural life. But Lynch argues convincingly that the Endorois only came into existence as a people or 'community' relatively recently, as a result of struggles for land and rights. Furthermore, she asserts, the ACHPR's recognition of them as indigenous 'completes a process of ethnic

---

[33] Uhuru Kenyatta was president when this book went to print, but may no longer be after elections in August 2017.

invention that began in the 1990s (Lynch, 2012, 24).[34] When my former colleague, the historian David Anderson, was carrying out doctoral fieldwork in Baringo in the 1980s, no one called themselves Endorois. In colonial times, it was simply the name of a location in southern Baringo (Anderson, 2002, 298).

The African Union subsequently ratified the ACHPR's decision, which confirmed that the Endorois have special rights. But the ACHPR victory was hollow: the Commission has struggled to make the Kenyan government act on its ruling, and the Endorois continue to push for their rights. The government set up a taskforce to look into the matter, but this wound up after a year without any progress having been made, from the point of view of Endorois and their advocates. With the support of Minority Rights Group International (MRG), which supported their ACHPR action, the Endorois Welfare Council which represents the 'community' is challenging the designation of Lake Bogoria as a World Heritage Site, which took place without seeking their consent. It also seeks to ensure the full and effective participation of the Endorois in the management of and decision-making about the 'property', in particular the Lake Bogoria component. This is a distinct shift in approach and language. Most recently, the Endorois are pinning their hopes on grassroots advocacy at county level, especially in relation to a management plan that Baringo County Government is drawing up for Lake Bogoria, that is likely to include benefit sharing with local residents and their involvement in the management of the reserve.[35]

Unfortunately for the Endorois (though they would in any case reject the suggestion that they are Tugen), the Tugen cannot be described as a

---

[34] She has argued elsewhere (Lynch, 2011) that the larger Kalenjin group did not exist as a people before the 1940s. Her 2012 article concludes:

> The [African Commission] outcome is a victory for Endorois leaders and may help other communities tackle state injustice. However, the broad implications for social justice and inter-communal relations are contentious given the decision's reinforcement of an inherently exclusive sense of ethnic territoriality and neglect of gross inequalities in wealth and power. From this perspective, the decision reflects a modern obsession with the 'politics of recognition' to the neglect of a 'politics of redistribution' (Lynch, 2012, p. 24).

[35] My thanks to Lucy Claridge, Legal Director at Minority Rights Group, London, for information and for sharing the document World Heritage 39 COM, WHC-15/39. Com/7B, 2015, from which some of this information is drawn. The taskforce was a disappointment to the Endorois, and failed to produce a report, while government promises to extend its mandate beyond a year were not fulfilled. Telephone conversation with this author, 8 September 2016, and email communication 9 September 2016 and at various times.

marginalized or minority group, the Kalenjin even less so. Former president Daniel arap Moi was a Tugen, and wielded enormous power. Though long retired he still has significant influence in the highly-charged politics of the Rift Valley, which revolve around land and cultural identity. These played a major part in stoking the 2007–08 post-election violence in which more than 1100 Kenyans died and around 600 000 were internally displaced (Mueller, 2014).

As I have written above when discussing the role of cultural brokers/ethnic entrepreneurs, mention of this crisis – which tore Kenya apart and continues to resonate in the run-up to elections in August 2017 – serves to illustrate the fact that assertions of culture, identity and belonging are not necessarily benign but can sometimes feed violence and human rights abuses. Moreover, the common association between people and place (both those made by the groups concerned and in a number of UN rights protocols) should be read critically. Linking people to a particular territory via 'cultural' means (for example, by asserting they have lived there 'since time immemorial', a meaningless and ahistorical term, but one constantly heard in cultural rights, indigenous rights and popular discourses) is both central to the appeal and utility of this idea (it becomes a way of claiming land and asserting rights to associated resources, royalties, employment and so on) but also presents a major danger. This is because it suggests that some other people belong *less* to the same territory – and ought, therefore, to be excluded from it.

TO CONCLUDE

Ms Shaheed is to be congratulated for her first report, which sets out useful preliminary views on the conceptual and legal framework of her mandate. Moreover, it was wise of her not to define 'culture', least of all at the outset of a programme of work which she was about to embark upon, but to seek to find out how others define it.[36] In my discussion of the report, these brief examples (which stand for many) are intended to demonstrate the difficulties and challenges of taking at face value group claims to indigeneity, as well as marginalized minority status, which have major implications for cultural rights defenders as well as the groups concerned. I also hope that my earlier points on terminology will provide

---

36 My research colleagues and I have found that, during our current study, it is more fruitful to examine how culture (or notions of culture) are being *used*, rather than to ask what it is, or limit oneself to a single definition. Many anthropologists have long ago abandoned attempts to define the term.

food for thought for Karima Bennoune, Ms Shaheed's successor, to take forward. In her first report to the UN, she has already cited my point about the implications of taking the term 'community' at face value when talking about culture and human rights (Bennoune, 2016). Who 'owns' culture, who 'speaks for' culture, are questions of fundamental significance not simply in terms of gender and patriarchy, but also in terms of unpacking, deconstructing and dealing with 'stories' of identity. This first and subsequent reports are located within a UN system, approach and discourse that conform to specific and pre-determined norms, which can sometimes be intellectually restrictive. This is a task for another day, but looking at the broader picture we need to explore why the UN finds certain ways of understanding culture and community politically and pragmatically useful; how these are influenced and shaped by states and lobbyists (particularly minority and indigenous); and examine what this produces both on the ground and within the system itself.[37]

REFERENCES

Anderson, David, *Eroding the Commons. The Politics of Ecology in Baringo, Kenya 1890–1963* (James Currey 2002).

Basu, P. and W. Modest, *Museums, Heritage and International Development* (Routledge 2015).

Bayart, Jean-François, *The State in Africa: Politics of the Belly* (Longman 1993).

Bengoa, José, 'Existence and Recognition of Minorities'. (Working Paper, Commission on Human Rights. Sub-Commission on the Promotion and Protection of Human Rights. Working Group on Minorities. E/CN.4/Sub.2/AC.5/2000/WP.2, 3 April 2000) 1–32.

Bennoune, Karima, 'First report to the UN Human Rights Council' (31st session, Agenda Item 3. Promotion and protection of all human rights, civil, political, economic, social and cultural rights, including the right to development, 3 February 2016) 1–21 <www.ohchr.org/Documents/Issues/CulturalRights/A-HRC-31-59_en.doc> accessed 22 August 2016.

Buthelezi, Mbongiseni, 'Heritage vs. Heritage: Reaching for Pre-Zulu Identities in KwaZulu-Natal, South Africa' in Derek R. Peterson, Kodzo Gavua and Ciraj Rassool (eds), *The Politics of Heritage in Africa. Economies, Histories and Infrastructures* (Cambridge University Press 2015).

Coombes, A. E., L. Hughes and K-Munene, *Managing Heritage, Making Peace: History, Identity and Memory in Contemporary Kenya* (I B Tauris 2014).

Crooke, Elizabeth, 'The Politics of Community Heritage: Motivations, Authority and Control' (2010) 16(1–2) *International Journal of Heritage Studies* 16–29.

[37] My thanks to Harriet Deacon for making this point, and for her very useful comments on an earlier draft of this chapter.

Engle, Karen, 'Culture as Development' in Karen Engle, *The Elusive Promise of Indigenous Development* (Duke University Press 2010).

Geschiere, Peter, 'Autochthony and Citizenship. New Modes in the Struggle over Belonging and Exclusion in Africa' (2005) *QUEST. An African Journal of Philosophy* XV11 9–24.

Geschiere, Peter, *The Perils of Belonging: Autochthony, Citizenship and Exclusion in Africa and Europe* (University of Chicago Press 2009).

Graber, Christoph Beat, 'The New Unesco Convention on Cultural Diversity: A Counterbalance to the WTO?' (2006) 9(3) *Journal of International Economic Law* 553–74.

Gutmann, Amy, 'Introduction' in Amy Gutmann (ed.), *Multiculturalism. Examining the Politics of Recognition* (Princeton University Press 1994).

Hobsbawm, E. and T. O. Ranger, *The Invention of Tradition* (Cambridge University Press 1992).

Hodgson, Dorothy L., 'Becoming Indigenous in Africa' (2009) 52(9) *African Studies Review* 1–32.

Hodgson, Dorothy L., *Being Maasai, Becoming Indigenous: Postcolonial Politics in a Neoliberal World* (Indiana University Press 2011).

Hughes, Lotte, 'Sacred Spaces, Political Places: The Struggle for a Sacred Forest' in Annie E. Coombes, Lotte Hughes and Karega-Munene, *Managing Heritage, Making Peace: History, Identity and Memory in Contemporary Kenya* (I B Tauris 2014).

Hughes, Lotte, 'Promoting Peace through Dialogue: Facilitating Cultural Exchange Visits in Kenya' (Ferguson Centre Working Paper No. 1, The Ferguson Centre for African and Asian Studies, The Open University, February 2011).

Huizenga, Daniel, '"Documentation of Community" in the ≠ Khomeni San Land Claim in South Africa' (2014) 37(1) *Political and Legal Anthropology Review* (PoLAR)145–61.

Igoe, James, 'Becoming Indigenous in Africa: The Globalization of Maasai and Barabaig Ethnic Identities' (Working Paper in African Studies No. 248, African Studies Centre, Boston University 2004) 1–27.

Keller, Edmond J., *Identity, Citizenship, and Political Conflict in Africa* (Indiana University Press 2014).

Keyes, Charles F., 'Who Are the Tai? Reflections on the Invention of Identities' in Lola Romanucci-Ross and George A. De Vos (eds), *Ethnic Identity. Creation, Conflict, and Accommodation* (3rd edn, AltaMira Press 1995).

Lynch, Gabrielle, 'Becoming Indigenous in the Pursuit of Justice: The African Commission on Human and Peoples' Rights and the Endorois' (2012) 111 (442) *African Affairs* 24–45.

Lynch, Gabrielle, *I Say to You: Ethnic Politics and the Kalenjin in Kenya* (University of Chicago Press 2011).

Mueller, Susanne D., 'Kenya and the International Criminal Court (ICC): Politics, the Election and the Law' (2014) 8(1) *Journal of Eastern African Studies* 24–42.

Muriuki, Godfrey, *History of the Gikuyu 1500–1900* (Oxford University Press 1974).

Shaheed, Farida, Report of the independent expert in the field of cultural rights, Ms Farida Shaheed, submitted pursuant to resolution 10/23 of the Human Rights Council (2010). <http://www2.ohchr.org/english/bodies/hrcouncil/docs/14session/A.HRC.14.36_en.pdf> accessed 22 August 2016.

Romanucci-Ross, Lola and George A. De Vos (eds), *Ethnic Identity. Creation, Conflict, and Accommodation* (3rd edn, AltaMira Press 1995).

Taylor, Charles, 'The Politics of Recognition' in Amy Gutmann (ed.), *Multiculturalism. Examining the Politics of Recognition* (Princeton University Press 1994).

The Constitution of Kenya 2010 (pocket edition, published by the National Council for Law Reporting with the Authority of the Attorney-General, Uraia Trust, no date).

Waterton, E. and L. J. Smith, 'The Recognition and Misrecognition of Community Heritage' (2010) 16 (1–2) *International Journal of Heritage Studies* 4–15.

World Heritage 39 COM, WHC-15/39.Com/7B, Paris, 15 May 2015. United Nations Education, Scientific and Cultural Organization, Convention Concerning the Protection of the World Cultural and Natural Heritage Committee, 39th session, Bonn, 28 June–8 July 2015.

UNESCO, 'UNESCO's work on culture and sustainable development. Evaluation of a Policy Theme. Final Report' (November 2016) <http://unesdoc.unesco.org/images/0023/002344/234443E.pdf> accessed 7 April 2016.

United Nations, Office of the High Commissioner for Human Rights (OHCHR). Minorities under international law (no date) <http://www.ohchr.org/EN/Issues/Minorities/Pages/internationallaw.aspx> accessed 21 March 2016.

3. The right of access to and enjoyment of cultural heritage – Report 2011 (A/HRC/17/38)

Lucky Belder

1. INTRODUCTION

The Report on Access to Cultural Heritage, hereafter called the Access Report, was published in 2011 and constitutes an important step forward in the cultural rights debate.[1] For the first time, the connection between the right to express one's cultural identity and the right of access to cultural heritage was given centre stage in a United Nations document advocating a human rights based approach to cultural heritage.

It was UNESCO that first addressed access to cultural heritage. This became concrete in a series of international conventions on the protection of objects, manifestations and expressions of cultural heritage: the 1970 Illicit Trade Convention on international trade in cultural objects; the 1972 World Heritage Convention on monumental cultural heritage; the 2001 Protection of Underwater Cultural Heritage; the 2003 Intangible Cultural Heritage Convention; and the 2005 Convention on the protection and promotion of the Diversity of Cultural Expressions. At the same time, these conventions developed an approach to heritage conservation that increasingly recognized the importance of the relevant local communities and their cultural rights. The potential value to the local cultural communities by thinking about cultural heritage in terms of economic and social resources and how they can contribute to sustainable development goals is increasingly acknowledged in the more recent culture conventions. The UNESCO conventions thereby demonstrate a shift in

[1] Report on Access to Cultural Heritage of the Independent expert in the field of cultural rights, Farida Shaheed, March 2011, UN Doc. A/HRC/17/38, <http://www.ohchr.org/EN/Issues/CulturalRights/Pages/AccessCulturalHeritage.aspx> last accessed 1 December 2016.

emphasis from the protection of material cultural objects towards the protection of immaterial and material values connecting these objects to a diversity of individual stakeholders and their communities.

The Access to Cultural Heritage Report by Special Rapporteur Faridah Shaheed refers to the core body of cultural rights singling out Article 15 ICESCR; and Article 27 of the ICCPR; the UN Declaration on the Rights of Persons belonging to National, Ethnic, Religious and Linguistic Minorities; the International Labour Organisation Convention No. 169 concerning Indigenous and Tribal Peoples in Independent Countries;[2] the International Labour Organisation Convention No. 169 concerning Indigenous and Tribal Peoples in Independent Countries;[3] the 2007 UN Declaration on the Rights of Indigenous Peoples (DRIPS);[4] and the Convention on Biological Diversity, containing the reference in Article 8(j) to the 'knowledge, innovations and practices' of indigenous and local communities.

Shaheed also refers to a number of regional instruments: the ASEAN Declaration on Cultural Heritage (2000); the Charter for African Cultural Renaissance (2006); and regional instruments like the European FARO Framework Convention on the Value of Cultural Heritage in Society; the Asian Declaration on Cultural Heritage; and the Charter for the African Renaissance. She thereby links the position of cultural rights to core human rights such as the right of self-determination, the right to education, the right to freedom of expression, and the right to freedom of thought and religion.[5]

This Access Report reflects upon the positive and negative issues that are at play in the framework of the protection of cultural heritage. The first part of this chapter provides a summary of the normative content of the Access Report. The main part of my commentary is dedicated to the question of where responsibility lies for the right of access to cultural heritage. By discussing recent developments in international human rights law that signal an increasing role for non-state actors I will suggest that the implementation of cultural rights involves a principle of responsibility that relates not only to states, but also to other public actors as well as to corporate enterprises and civil society.

In the final part of the chapter, which is dedicated to the 2015 UNESCO Declaration on the protection and promotion of museums and

[2] Ibid., paras 41–43.
[3] Ibid.
[4] Ibid., paras 33–40.
[5] Ibid., paras 44–48.

collections, I will offer an example of the allocation of responsibility to non-state actors.

2. A SUMMARY OF THE REPORT ON ACCESS TO AND ENJOYMENT OF CULTURAL HERITAGE

2.1 Short Overview of the Access Report

The 2011 Access Report takes as its starting point the right to the enjoyment of cultural life as discussed in 2009 in General Comment No. 21 on ICESCR on Article 15 paragraph 1(a). This provision was explained as containing three aspects of the right of everyone to: (a) participate in; (b) have access to; and (c) contribute to cultural life.[6] The Report's focus is on the second of this threesome and aims to further explore the right to the 'adoption of specific measures aimed at achieving respect for the right of everyone, individually or in association with others or within a community or group … to have access to their own cultural and linguistic heritage and to that of others'.[7]

The questionnaire for the preparation of the Access Report presented a working definition of cultural heritage:

> tangible heritage (e.g. sites, structures and remains of archaeological, historical, religious, cultural or aesthetic value), intangible heritage (e.g. traditions, customs and practices, aesthetic and spiritual beliefs; vernacular or other languages; artistic expressions, folklore) and natural heritage (e.g. protected natural reserves; other protected biologically diverse areas; historic parks and gardens and cultural landscapes).[8]

This concept of cultural heritage reflects the definitions in UNESCO's two major Culture Conventions of UNESCO: the 1972 Protection of World Cultural and Natural Heritage Convention and the 2003 Safeguarding of Intangible Cultural Heritage Convention. The definition of cultural heritage in the Council of Europe Faro Convention of 2005 may be regarded as the culmination of a long process of an ever more inclusive definition, referring to:

> a group of resources inherited from the past which people identify, independently from ownership, as a reflection and expression of their constantly

---

6 General Comment No. 21 E/C.12/GC/21. 2009, para. 15.

7 Ibid., para. 50.

8 Access Report, *supra* note 1, para. 4.

> evolving values, beliefs, knowledge and traditions. It includes all aspects of the environment resulting from the interaction between people and places through time.

These words emphasize the dynamics of cultural heritage in the context of its interaction with people in the present time, and through time, providing a link from the past to the future. From that perspective, access to cultural heritage becomes key to the realization of cultural rights in general.

2.2 The Human Rights Issues Related to Cultural Heritage

The Access Report identifies a number of issues at stake in the regulatory framework of cultural heritage. Noting that the international legal framework is empowered and dominated by nation states, the Report finds that the definition and selection of cultural heritage are 'reflective of power differentials'. This may lead to the glorification of cultural symbols of dominant communities, shaping histories, exerting political and social pressure and creating a potential, forced assimilation into mainstream society.[9] The Report therefore considers it necessary to recognize that dominant communities should take into account diverging opinions and interpretations. Likewise, access to and enjoyment of cultural heritage also includes the freedom to participate or *not* to participate in communities of choice.

This issue was highlighted in the preparatory meetings in Geneva and Oslo with representatives from UNESCO and its advisory bodies International Centre for the Study of the Preservation and Restoration of Cultural Property (ICCROM) and International Council on Monuments and Sites (ICOMOS).[10] William Logan, who participated in these meetings, reported that the human rights approach to cultural heritage entails understanding that the conceptualization, management and protection of cultural heritage is part of a set of cultural practices that are defined by the political, social, cultural and economic context. At the same time it was generally accepted that human rights are individual rights, and that both in the identification process and in the public policies related to

---

9 Ibid., paras 10, 11.

10 W. Logan, 'Cultural diversity, cultural heritage and human rights, towards heritage management as human rights-based cultural practice' (2012) 18(3) *International Journal of Heritage Studies* 321, 232.

conservation and access to cultural heritage it is necessary to recognize and respect individual claims to the access to and enjoyment of cultural heritage.[11]

The Report also highlights other current threats caused by the conflicts and competing claims regarding cultural heritage. The destruction of cultural heritage in violent conflicts, both within and between states, constitutes one example. A human rights approach strengthens the arguments for immediate recognition and implementation of the existing international legal instruments on the protection of cultural heritage as well as the investigation and prosecution of individuals that are suspected of being guilty of 'crimes against humanity'.[12] One of the first cases brought before the International Court of Justice is the case against Ahmad Al Faqi Al Mahdi who is suspected of the intentional destruction of cultural heritage in Mali, in violation of the 1907 IV Hague Regulations concerning the Laws and Customs of War on Land; the 1954 Hague Convention for the Protection of Cultural Property in Armed Conflict; the so-called World Heritage Convention of 1972, and Protocol II additional to the 1949 IV Geneva Convention relating to the protection of victims.[13]

Another issue concerns the competing claims and interests that are playing out in the context of globalization, the tensions that may occur between the uses of cultural heritage as economic resources on the one hand and as cultural practices from the involved individuals and communities on the other hand. These claims are also discussed in the context of the UN Declaration on the Rights of Indigenous Peoples (DRIPS) and the caucus in WIPO circles on intellectual property rights to cultural expressions from indigenous communities and the safeguarding of rights of minority communities to their tangible and intangible cultural heritage. Limitations to access to cultural heritage may occur in line with the right of source communities to grant or withhold prior consent for access to and use of their cultural heritage.[14]

The Access Report concludes that the right of access to and enjoyment of cultural heritage is part of human rights law, in particular the right to

---

[11] Ibid., p. 233.

[12] A.F. Vrdoljak, 'Cultural heritage in human rights and humanitarian law', in O. Ben-Naftali (ed.), *International Human Rights and Humanitarian Law* (OUP 2011), p. 250.

[13] Mali ratified the 1999 Second Protocol additional to the 1954 Hague Convention in November 2012, which was after the attacks.

[14] Access Report, para. 16. See on the issue of the representation of communities Chapter 2 by Lotte Hughes.

the enjoyment of cultural life, the right of minorities to enjoy their own culture, and the right of indigenous peoples to self-determination.

This means that individuals and communities have the right to access to, provide meaning for, know, enter, visit, exchange and develop cultural heritage, as well as to benefit from the cultural heritage of others. This includes the right to identification of cultural heritage and the right to participate in the protection of cultural heritage. However, the diverse interests of individuals and communities make it necessary to accept a variety of levels of access and enjoyment, dependent on the relationship between individuals and communities and the heritages of choice.[15]

3. COMMENTARY

3.1 Cultural Rights in the Global Society

Cultural rights and its interpretations are part of the body of public international law that is designed to set normative standards, see to its administration, and provide for a system of enforcement. The traditional view is that states are the main actors in human rights law in a vertical relation between state and citizen. But discussing cultural rights as only a state responsibility is a limited exercise. If we understand law as a means to regulate public good objectives, we must also recognize that law is part of a system of global governance: 'a system of formal and informal institutions, mechanisms, relationships, and arrangements among states, their constituent markets, and private organisations, groups and individuals which through collective interests in the global sphere are articulated, rights and obligations established, and differences mediated'.[16] In today's multi-layered legal order a focus on hard law alone makes us forget to look at the potential of realizing its objectives by making use of the effects of soft law or other instruments of governance. Indeed, a more functional approach sees human rights as part of the relation between state and citizen that is increasingly regulated by soft

---

[15] Access Report, paras 77–79.

[16] B.K. Woodward, *Global Civil Society in International Lawmaking and Global Governance* (The Hague: Martinus Nijhoff 2010), p. 15.

law instruments, instruments of co-regulation and self-regulation, codes of conduct, ethical codes and voluntary agreements.[17]

The renewed attention on the full spectrum of regulation instead of only focussing on hard law reflects new points of view on the organization of societies in the age of internet, digital media, migration and globalization as formulated by scholars from the humanities and social sciences like Leon Castells, Saskia Sassen and Arjun Appadurai. Castells was one of the first to recognize the important implications of the introduction of the internet and digital media in a global society. The image of the network is a symbol for the interconnections between people, institutions and societies. The far-reaching effects are not only that the means and ways of communication have changed, but also that the relations between people, and between people and institutions, are constantly changing. We are now part of system of networked connections that reach beyond the traditional framework of nation states and their institutions.[18]

As a cultural anthropologist active in globalization studies, Appadurai favours an even more organic model and presents nation states as 'vertical' or 'vertebrate' structures that are based on hierarchies and rules. If we view human rights as the international legal standard on obligations on nation states, we can easily picture them as part of the spinal column of the international legal order. Since the late 1980s these vertebrate structures are in constant interaction with smaller 'horizontal', 'cellular' organized entities that are, through the use of digital media, connected on a global scale.[19] Sassen notes similar developments in transnational human rights networks involving NGOs and local communities.[20] She describes this as part of a process which enables those who are the subjects of human rights decisions, such as indigenous peoples, immigrants and refugees, to become actors in global politics. By making use of new information and communication technologies individuals and collectives can access international institutions that used to be reserved

---

17 A. Reinish, 'The Changing international legal framework for dealing with non-state actors', in P. Alston, *Non-State Actors and Human Rights* (OUP 2005), pp. 38–42.

18 M. Castells, 'The network society: from knowledge to policy', in M. Castells, G. Cardoso (eds), *The Network Society: From Knowledge to Policy* (Washington, DC: Johns Hopkins Center for Transatlantic Relations 2005), pp. 3–23; M. Castells, *Communication Power,* (OUP Oxford 2009), p. 7.

19 A. Apadurai, *Fear of Small Numbers* (Duke University Press 2006), p. 176.

20 S. Sassen, 'The global city: introducing a concept' (2005) 11(2) *Brown Journal of World Affairs* 32.

for nation states, thereby building networks that circulate information and gain political power.[21] This in itself means that non-state actors are taking part in the process of the governance of human rights.

However, the basic rule of international treaty law is that the obligations are to be met by states parties, and we do, indeed, see that most of the recommendations in the Access Report are addressed to states. At first instance, it is the state that is responsible for the protection of cultural rights. The recommendations in this Report, however, also provide for a principle of responsibility connected to other public and private actors. I will return to this later, but first, I want to offer a few observations on the normative content of the right to access of cultural heritage as presented in the Access Report in the context of the earlier UN General Comment 21 of 2009.

3.2 The Normative Content of Cultural Rights

The initial aim of the ICESCR was to consolidate the obligation of 'taking steps which should lead to achieving progressively the full realisation of the rights by all appropriate means'.[22] After a first period of developing guidelines and schemes for monitoring these steps, the 1986 Limburg Principles developed the doctrine of a 'minimum core content' of cultural rights.[23] The 1997 Maastricht Guidelines emphasized that 'a failure to perform any of the obligations to respect, protect or fulfil any of these rights' would constitute a violation of these rights.[24] In that same period, the Vienna Declaration of 1993 had affirmed that all human rights are universal, indivisible and interdependent and interrelated.[25]

The Global Compact Program of 1999 marked the start of the development of the UN Millennium Goals and signalled a new approach to operating human rights – no longer a top-down process involving only state obligations, but a call for a mainstreaming of human rights which not only addressed nation states but all institutions, including private corporations. In September 2015 the UN announced the Sustainable Development Agenda, containing 17 Goals. Of note is the call on the

---

[21] S. Sassen, 'Local actors in global politics' (2004) 52(4) *Current Sociology* 649.

[22] ICESCR, art. 2.1.

[23] UN Doc. E/CN.4/1987/17, Committee General Comment No 3: The Nature of State Parties Obligations (art. 2.2), 5th Session 1990, paras 7–10.

[24] 'Maastricht Guidelines on Violations of Economic, Social and Cultural Rights' (1997) *15 Netherlands Quarterly of Human Rights*, p. 244.

[25] UN Doc. A/ Conf.157/ 23, para. 5.

website that everyone is to do their part: 'governments, the private sector, civil society and people like you'.[26]

The 2009 General Comment No. 21 explains ICESCR Article 15(1) on the right of everyone to the enjoyment of cultural life as a 'freedom', which includes the obligation of the state to withhold from infringement (respect and protect bound obligations), but also to 'fulfil' it by ensuring the conditions that will safeguard cultural rights.[27]

How do these requirements play out in the context of the right of everyone to access cultural heritage? The obligation of the state to ensure access to one's own culture and to those of others implies that the state is responsible for the design of cultural policies that pay respect to the diversity of cultural practices and traditions. Moreover, this also means that it is required to create the conditions to ensure the participation of a diversity of cultural groups in the decision-making processes that shape cultural heritage policies.[28] The necessary conditions are enclosed in the five As providing a framework for positive action that is expected of states in the aforementioned 2009 General Comment 21. **A**ccessibility for everyone, including minorities and disabled persons, is to be ensured within a framework of conditions in which **A**vailability implies the protection of cultural and natural heritage, as well as cultural policies aimed at providing the conditions for the production of cultural goods and services and the means of the communication thereof. **A**cceptability sees to it that everyone has the right to be represented in the decision-making processes. Likewise, **A**daptability regards the necessary flexibility to respect the cultural diversity within and between communities, and **A**ppropriateness adds a moral condition to ensure the respect for the sensitivities of other cultures and the balancing of the rights of individuals with those of communities, minorities and indigenous peoples.[29]

---

[26] http://www.un.org/sustainabledevelopment/sustainable-development-goals/, last accessed 1 November 2015.

[27] A. Chapman (ed.) *Core of Obligations: Building a Framework for Economic, Social and Cultural Rights* (Sage Russell, 2002), pp. 11–12; General Comment 21, *supra* note 6, para. 48.

[28] S. Hansen, 'The right to take part in cultural life', pp. 279–303, in Chapman, ibid.

[29] General Comment No. 21, *supra* note 6, para. 16, See also L. Belder (ed.) *Cultivate! Cultural Heritage Institutions, Copyright and Cultural Diversity in the European Union and Indonesia* (Amsterdam, Delex 2014), p. 280.

3.3 Normative Content in the Report

The Access Report relies on the work done by the Committee on Economic, Social and Cultural Rights by referring to the '4A' scheme of conditions necessary for the full realization of cultural rights: Availability, Accessibility, Acceptability and Adaptability.[30] This scheme was developed in the framework of the right to education, and it may be noted that the ICESCR Committee's 2009 General Comment No. 21 on the right of everyone to take part in cultural life added a 5th A, Appropriateness, as a necessary condition. The Report makes no reference to this particular aspect.[31]

The Access Report's interpretation of 'Accessibility' in the context of cultural heritage implies: (a) physical access; (b) economic access; (c) access to information, and (d) access to decision-making and monitoring procedures, with the emphasis that all this is subject to the principle of non-discrimination, and that special attention must be given to disadvantaged groups.

A specific feature of cultural rights is that both individuals and communities can be rights holders, with the understanding that individuals should be free to choose their communities. As was also explained in the General Comment, there are many stakeholders in cultural heritage who have rights of access to varying degrees. Originators and 'source communities', who distinguish themselves as custodians, should not be considered along the same lines as those individuals and communities that understand a specific cultural heritage to be a part of their cultural life even though they are not actively involved. Other important groups are scientists and artists, and the general public.[32]

Shaheeds' Access Report affirms that the state obligations in cultural rights consist of the obligation to respect, protect and fulfil as considered in the 2009 General Comment 21 on Article 15. The first two core obligations are often taken together as in 'the obligation to respect and protect cultural heritage in all its forms, in times of war and peace …'.[33] The obligation to fulfil refers to obligations to facilitate, promote and provide an enabling environment for the protection rights.

Part of the state obligations also are the positive obligations in the UNESCO Culture Conventions and its Operational Guidelines and Directives, as in the 2005 Diversity of Cultural Expressions Convention stating

---

30 Access Report, *supra* note 1, paras 58–60, and footnote 32.

31 General Comment No. 21, *supra* note 6, para. 16.

32 Ibid., para. 62–63.

33 Ibid., para. 50.

that nation states are to develop policies facilitating access to a rich and diverse cultural life.[34]

The Access Report ends with a list of recommendations that are mainly addressed to states. Regarding the 'respect and protect' obligations in cultural rights, states must recognize and value the diversity as well as respect the free development of cultural heritage. States should furthermore be active in including relevant communities and individuals in the governance of cultural heritage. The last requirement of the threesome, 'to fulfil', leads to the positive obligation to design active policies.

It is worth noting that the Access Report formulates a Recommendation that is the standard rule in the UNESCO inscription procedures: The right of free, prior and informed consent of the communities involved in the preparation of new inscriptions on the UNESCO Lists.[35] The same right is also articulated in the DRIPS and in the Reports of the WIPO Intergovernmental Committee on Intellectual Property and Genetic Resources, Traditional Knowledge and Folklore.[36]

States must ensure that no cultural heritage policy will harm the communities involved, that peaceful and democratic societies will be built and that cultural diversity will be promoted. At a more practical level the Access Report encourages states to develop inventories and impact assessments.

In view of the following, it is important to note that the recommendations in the Access Report are not addressed to states only. Some of them explicitly involve private parties like the tourism and entertainment industries. These must act in accordance with cultural rights, especially when remedies for claims by the communities or peoples regarding the management of their cultural heritage are involved. The Access Report also singles out professionals who are expected to build stronger relationships with source communities and peoples, as well as to consider in good faith requests for repatriation (Recommendation sub g.). Likewise, scholars must also improve their relationships with communities and

---

[34] Ibid., pp. 51–2.

[35] On the right of free, prior and informed consent in UNESCO documents, see the 2008 Operational Guidelines to the UNESCO World Cultural and Natural Heritage Convention, para. 64, and para. 79 of the Operational Directives of the UNESCO Convention on the Safeguarding of Intangible Cultural Heritage, and its Criterion R.4 of the Nomination File for inscription on the Representative List. See also UN Doc. A/61/L.67, Declaration on the Rights of Indigenous Peoples, arts 28 and 31.

[36] See e.g., WIPO Doc WIPO/GRTKF/IC/17/INF/8, 'Note on the Meanings of the 'public domain', November 2010.

secure the latter's free, prior and informed consent (Recommendation sub h.). In addition, under Recommendation sub i. the tourism and entertainment industry must take into consideration the claims of local communities regarding misuse, misrepresentation, and misappropriation.

3.4 Access to and Enjoyment of Cultural Heritage as a Cultural Right

What is the added value of the Access Report? The Report gives centre stage to the issues that are the result of the system of protection of cultural heritage as developed under the aegis of UNESCO. Given the human rights angle of the Report that is no surprise. Along with the increasing awareness of the importance of cultural heritage to all the stakeholders involved comes the understanding of the power structures that are at play and the diversity of interests that are involved.

This analysis confirms the views expressed in various critical comments on UNESCO's ambiguity in building a cultural heritage 'regime'. That it is a system which on the one hand claims to be of 'transnational' importance, while on the other hand confirms the essential role of the nation state, emphasizing the important role of communities but weakening their position by dominating the legal framework in which heritage protection is to take place.[37]

Coombe and others have highlighted how a neoliberal ideology regulates governmental institutions and structures in a globalizing world order and the effects of neoliberalism on the operations of cultural heritage institutions that provide access to cultural heritage.[38] One effect is the understanding of cultural heritage governance in terms of its potential to generate economic and social benefits by attracting tourism, by adding value to regional activities and by contributing to social and cultural identity building.[39]

---

[37] De Cesari, 'Thinking through heritage regimes', in R.Bendix et al. (eds), *Heritage Regimes and the State* (Gottingen, Universitätsverlag Gottingen 2014), p. 400.

[38] R. Coombe and L.Weiss, 'Neoliberalism, Heritage Regimes, and Cultural Rights', in L. Meskell (ed.), Global Heritage: A Reader (Hoboken, N.J.: Wiley-Blackwell 2015), pp. 43–69; N. Brenner, J. Peck and N. Theodore, 'Variegated neoliberalization: geographies, modalities, pathways' (2010) 10(2) *Global Networks* 10 (2), pp. 182–222; De Cesari, ibid.; S. Labadi and C. Long (eds) *Heritage and Globalisation* (Oxford, Routledge 2010).

[39] D. Throsby, *Economics and Culture* (Cambridge University Press 2001), pp. 110–33.

Granted, the position of the individual as rights holder is central in neoliberal thinking; he or she is to be empowered to improve their conditions, to be able to make independent choices and to enjoy the benefits. A similar focus on the individual as the subject of human rights was core to the human rights system from the start – in part as a response, at the time of the draft of the UN Declaration on Human Rights in 1948, to the events of the Second World War. The focus on the individual is also prominent in the Access Report and in particular, its emphasis on individual choice. The Access Report does recognize, though, how the post-colonial world order also brings in the perspectives from indigenous communities and their claims to their cultural heritage. The Report reflects the concerns that are the result of these claims on access to cultural heritage for others. The solution to this conflict is the adoption of a 'flexible approach', in which respect for the distinctive interests should lead to distinctive levels of access for stakeholders in cultural heritage.[40]

Of note is the fact that the states parties' obligations to observe the 'free prior and informed consent of communities' in the procedure for enlisting specific cultural heritage in the Operational Guidelines of UNESCO Culture Conventions are now included in the Recommendations in the Access Report. Indeed, the underlying argument of this chapter is that the recommendations in Shaheed's Report contribute towards turning the responsibility for access to cultural heritage into a fundamental principle of law which makes these recommendations binding also on non-states-actors.[41]

3.5 A Principle of Responsibility for the Access to and Enjoyment of Cultural Heritage?

The International Bill of Human Rights is the codification of general principles, a statement of leading principles for all people and all nations.[42] If we understand cultural rights and the right to access to

---

40 See also Y. Donders 'A right to cultural identity in UNESCO' in F. Francioni (ed.) *Cultural Human Rights* (Nijhoff, Leiden 2008), pp. 317–40.

41 See on principles in international law, as in art. 38 of the statute of the International Court of Justice, the ILA Report of the Working Group on Non State Actors in International law, 2010.

42 Crawford (ed.) *Brownlies Principles of International Law* (8th ed., Oxford University Press 2012), p. 20, R.C. Blitt, 'Beyond Ruggie's Guiding Principles on Business and Human Rights: charting an embracive approach to corporate human rights compliance' (2011) 48(1) *Texas Law Journal* p. 38.

cultural heritage as the reflection of a general principle, we can also recognize a principle of responsibility for non-state actors for the 'progressive implementation' of cultural rights in general and the right to access to and enjoyment of cultural heritage in particular.[43] This question is not at the core of the Report, but I will argue in the following that the Report clarifies a principle of responsibility for the access to cultural heritage which includes public and private actors in addition to states.

It should be mentioned, first, that the important position given in the Guidelines and Directives to the UNESCO Culture Conventions to communities and civil society in the implementation of the Culture Conventions already implies a responsibility on the part of non-state actors.[44] This would imply that together with the right to take part in the decision-making process comes the responsibility and the accountability for the results thereof.[45]

Secondly, recent developments in international human rights law instruments demonstrate a wider tendency towards including non-state actors among those who must take responsibility for the protection of human rights. This comes as part of the rapid expansion of the circle of actors for whom human rights norms are considered to provide a minimum standard of behaviour.[46]

The UDHR states in its Article 29 for example, that every individual and every organ of society, '... shall strive ... to promote respect for these rights and ... to secure their universal and effective recognition and observance'.[47]

Likewise, the preamble of the ICESCR mentions that, 'Realizing that the individual, having duties to other individuals and to the community to

---

43 For the purpose of this chapter responsibility sets the norm for actions of the responsible entity itself, accountability includes the system of administration and monitoring by others, and liability involves a system of enforcement and judicial action.

44 Operational Guidelines of the World Natural and Cultural Heritage Convention, para. 64; arts 11 and 15 of the UNESCO Convention on the Safeguarding of Intangible Cultural Heritage, and paras 79 and 80 of its operational directives. See also arts 28 and 31 of the Declaration on the Rights of Indigenous Peoples.

45 See also the International Law Association; The Hague Conference 2010; Non State Actors, First Report of the Committee, 2010, p. 4.

46 Blitt, *supra* note 42, p. 38.

47 Reinish *supra* note 17, pp. 71–3; See also M. Ssenyonjo, 'Non-state actors and economic, social and cultural rights' in M. Baderin and R. McCorquodale (eds), *Economic, Social and Cultural Rights in Action* (OUP 2007), pp. 109–23.

which he belongs, is under a responsibility to strive for the promotion and observance of the rights recognized in the present Covenant'.

The ICESCR General Comment No. 14 on the right to health furthermore states that:

> While only states are parties to the Covenant and thus ultimately accountable for compliance with it, all members of society – individuals, including health professionals, families, local communities, intergovernmental and non-governmental organizations, civil society organizations, as well as the private business sector – have responsibilities regarding the realization of the right to health. State parties should therefore provide an environment which facilitates the discharge of these responsibilities.[48]

A recent important step was taken on the 'governance gap' in relation to acts of multinational corporations (MNCs). The simultaneous lack of governmental control over the compliance of these MNCs with human rights standards and the granting of protection to them under the system of human rights law was addressed in a comprehensive investigation by John Ruggie, the Special Representative of the UN Secretary General on the Issue of Human Rights and Transnational Corporations and other Business Enterprises. The resulting Guiding Principles are now known as the Ruggie Framework.[49] It is a three-pillar framework which builds on:

(1) the state duty to respect, protect and fulfil human rights;
(2) the corporate responsibility to respect human rights; and
(3) the need for effective remedies for victims of human rights abuses.

The mere fact that MNCs are now required to respect human rights (including, as a minimum, the International Bill of Human Rights and therefore also cultural rights) as a global standard is a milestone in itself. Although the wording of the principles related to corporations centre on 'respect' only, this does not mean that the obligations involved are less important. Principle 11 states that business enterprises should not only avoid infringement of human rights, but also address whatever adverse human rights impacts they cause. This includes a policy commitment,

---

48 ICESCR GC No 14, UN Doc. E/C/12/2000/4 para. 42.

49 UN Office of the High Commissioner, *Guiding Principles on Business and Human Rights, Implementing the United Nations 'Protect, Respect and Remedy' Framework* (New York, Geneva 2011). HR/PUB/11/04, endorsed by Resolution 17/4 of 16 June 2011.

and implementation of a due diligence process, and instate processes to enable the remediation of human rights impacts.[50]

So, if we understand access to cultural heritage as part of the right to the enjoyment of cultural life and as closely linked to the right to access to information and the right to privacy, the responsibility for the protection of access to cultural heritage is not that of the state, or of the states involved in particular expressions of cultural heritage, only. The responsibility is that of both state and non-state actors in a networked society. Or, to put it in a more 'organic' way, the operationalization of access to cultural heritage is to be realized by connecting the 'vertebrate organism' of states with the cellular organisms or entities presented by networks of non state actors like cultural heritage institutions.

The next section will discuss how this relates to museums as public institutions holding cultural heritage collections.

4. THE ROLE OF PUBLIC MUSEUMS AND COLLECTIONS

Museums are institutions that define, determine and present objects and expressions as cultural heritage to the public. This public can be both local and global. In today's perspective, access to cultural heritage comes hand in hand with the availability of information. Digital technology has been embraced to create new means for disclosing information about cultural heritage institutions and their collections, and for contributing this information to interconnected databases.[51] The issues related to the local and global reach of museums are addressed by the new UNESCO Recommendation on the protection and promotion of public museums and collections, their diversity and their role in society, that was adopted in the 38th Session of the General Conference in November 2015.[52] The

---

[50] Jan Wouters and Anna-Luise Chané, 'Multinational corporations in international law', in M. Noortmann, A. Reinisch and C. Ryngaert (eds), *Non-state Actors in International Law* (Hart Publications 2015), pp. 239–42.

[51] Belder, *supra* note 29.

[52] UNESCO Doc. 38 C/25, 27 July 2015. The Recommendation Paragraph 4 presents the ICOM definition of museums as *a public or private non-profit agency or institution*: 'non-profit, permanent institution in the service of society and its development, open to the public, which acquires, conserves, researches, communicates and exhibits the tangible and intangible heritage of humanity and its environment for the purpose of education, study and enjoyment'. Para. 5 on the definition of Collections is also based on the ICOM interpretation as: 'an

Recommendation defines a public museum as a place open to the public, which can be either a public or private non-profit agency or institution.

The reference in the Recommendation to both museums and collections is the result of debates in the preparatory phase in which collections as such were not considered as important to the overall ambition of the instrument, which was to focus on the value of museums as institutions especially in non-Western states. During the expert meeting in May 2015 however, it was accepted that collections of public institutions like universities or hospitals equally merit the recognition of their fundamental importance to the dissemination of cultural heritage and their contribution to the enhancement of cultural rights.[53] The result of this change in perspective is that the text of the final draft is sometimes ambiguous as it is not always clear why some provisions refer to museums and collections and others only to museums.

As we have seen in the Access Report, one of the major human rights issues is the relation between museums and collections and source communities in a post-colonial world. Major cultural heritage projects like Europeana, focused on the digitization of objects in public museums and collections, including those with a non-Western origin, aim to provide a maximum of access to the cultural heritage in the collections of cultural heritage institutions.

However, this may clash with claims of source communities. They may find that the presentation of their cultural heritage and the context in which this takes place constitute an infringement of their cultural rights.

Another concern is the differences in resources and objectives between Western museums and collections, and heritage collections in states with a history of colonization. China and Brazil, both major players in the global economy, take the lead in vocalizing the ambitions of upcoming economies, and also bring these issues to the table in UNESCO circles and the international museum community like ICOM, the International Committee on Museums. Increasingly aware of the value of the recognition and the institutionalization of national or regional cultural heritage, the non-Western world deliberately attacks the traditional 'old world' view of preserving and presenting tangible cultural heritage as something of universal and outstanding cultural value, no matter where its origins lie. This cannot be fully understood without realizing that museums and collections not only contain access to tangible heritage objects but also

---

assemblage of natural and cultural properties, tangible and intangible, past and present'.

[53] See the Considerations in the draft Recommendation.

present and provide access to information on the context of these objects, as well as to intangible cultural expressions representing intangible processes and values.

In view of the concept of a principle of responsibility for non-state actors, it is interesting to note how the UNESCO Recommendation sees the responsibility of museums. The chapter on policies clearly aims at making museums co-responsible for the realization of its objectives. Paragraph 21 of the Recommendation states that member states are to ensure that 'museums implement principles of applicable international instruments. Museums are committed to observe the principles of international instruments for the protection and promotion of cultural and natural heritage, both tangible and intangible. (...) Museums must also take into account the ethical and professional standards established by the professional museum community'. States are to encourage a network of actors in the realization of these objectives, as in paragraph 24: '... collaborative and participative efforts between museums, communities, civil society and the public should be strongly encouraged'.

The ethical standard for the work of museums is to be provided by the code of ethics for museums as the most widely shared standard adopted by Council of ICOM.[54] The same paragraph encourages member states to promote the adoption and dissemination of these and other codes of ethics and good practices and 'to use them to inform the development of standards, museum policies and national legislation'.

The code of ethics demonstrates an inclusive approach of human rights issues.[55] In general, museums are expected to work in close collaboration with the communities from which their collections originate as well as with those they serve.[56] Museum professionals are expected to be professional and act in line with all the major culture conventions. With regard to culturally sensitive or sacred objects and human remains, the code states that these materials are to be housed securely and cared for respectfully, while taking into account 'the interests and beliefs of members of the community, ethnic or religious groups from which the

---

54 UNESCO Museums Recommendation, para. 26.

55 The first version of the ICOM Code of Professional Ethics was adopted unanimously by the 15th General Assembly of ICOM in Buenos Aires (Argentina) in 1986. It was amended by the 20th General Assembly in Barcelona (Spain) on 6 July 2001, retitled ICOM Code of Ethics for Museums, revised by the 21st General Assembly in Seoul (Republic of Korea) on 8 October 2004.

56 ICOM Code of Ethics, principle 6.

objects originated, where these are known'.[57] It is important to note, however, that this code does not provide for a system of monitoring compliance, or even reporting; neither is there any mechanism for addressing breaches of the code.

The UNESCO Recommendation, which is in essence a recommendation to states, refers to the authority of the ICOM Code of Ethics, that is, whose latest version dates from 2004. This instrument of self-regulation in the museum world binds all museums who by being a member of ICOM subscribe to the provisions in the Code.

All of this demonstrates the networking effect of a multi-layered system of laws, principles and codes that involves the recognition of a principle of responsibility for the protection of access to cultural heritage. The Recommendation presents international law as binding for states, while at the same time, referring to the authority of the ICOM Code of Ethics. So, while the principle of responsibility for the access to cultural heritage that is part of international law makes museums and collections objects of protection, at the same time museums and collections are regarded as actors that are responsible for upholding principles in international law and for contributing to the development of new standards to be taken into account in the development of national laws.

5. CONCLUDING REMARKS

This commentary on the Access Report by independent expert Fareedah Shaheed provided a short summary and discussed the normative content of the right to access and enjoyment of cultural life in a human rights based approach. Although the Report's main focus is on the responsibility of states to ensure the conditions in which these rights may be protected, it recognizes the principle of responsibility for other public or private actors, including cultural heritage institutions, civil society, industry and individual professionals and researchers. As cultural heritage is increasingly identified as something with a specific use value, as an economic and social resource, cultural heritage institutions may be considered as important actors in providing access to cultural heritage and the realization of cultural rights.

The clear and concise outline of the normative framework together with the recommendations to strengthen the right to access cultural heritage provide a solid base for the work that lies waiting for Shaheed's

---

57 Ibid., para. 2.5, see also paras 3.7 and 4.3.

successor Karima Bennoune. Her assignment may rely on a concept of a principle of responsibility for the protection of cultural rights in general, and the protection of access to and the enjoyment of cultural heritage in particular that is not only related to states but also to other public and private actors.

4. The right to enjoy the benefits of scientific progress and its applications – Report 2012 (A/HRC/20/26)

Helle Porsdam and Matthias Mann

'Addressing science through a human rights lens is both novel and potentially significant,' wrote Audrey Chapman and Jessica Wyndham in the journal *Science* in 2013.[1] Both Chapman and Wyndham have attempted to draw the attention of scientists as well as the general public to this particular corner of human rights for many years, but what prompted their *Science* article was the publication in May 2012 of Farida Shaheed's report, 'The right to enjoy the benefits of scientific progress and its applications' (hereafter 'The right to science').[2]

'The right to science' was Shaheed's third thematic report. It followed closely after her first report on 'Implementing cultural rights' in 2010[3] and her 2011 report on 'Access to cultural heritage,' both dealing with core issues relating to the very implementation of and access to culture and cultural heritage. This shows the importance of 'the right to science' – its high priority on the list of 'Issues in focus' that Shaheed (and the experts who advised her) put together upon becoming the first UN Special Rapporteur in the field of cultural rights.

Shaheed starts her third thematic report, which grew out of a series of seminars and meetings, by stressing the strong link between the right to science and other human rights, especially the right to participate in cultural life. She then states that the right to science includes the following normative content: (a) access by everyone without discrimination to the benefits of science and its applications, including scientific

[1] Chapman and Wyndham, 2013.

[2] Shaheed, 2012a.

[3] The full title of the 2010 report is 'Implementing cultural rights: Nature, issues at stake and challenges.'

knowledge; (b) opportunities for all to contribute to the scientific enterprise and freedom indispensable for scientific research; (c) participation of individuals and communities in decision-making and the related right to information; and (d) an enabling environment fostering the conservation, development and diffusion of science and technology. She ends the report by making a number of recommendations, and by proposing the adoption of a public good approach to knowledge innovation and diffusion.

This normative content and the recommendations made in 'The right to science' will form the point of departure for the four sections of the present chapter. In the first section, we will focus on the link Shaheed makes between the right to science and the right to culture. The second section will discuss 'the access perspective': the need to ensure that science and technology will be of benefit to everyone, not least the most vulnerable groups around the world. Then we will turn, in section 3, to 'the protection perspective': the need to foster an environment that protects the individual researchers and enables them to produce scientific knowledge and subsequently disseminate it, alone or together with their group.

Finally, section 4 will analyze and comment upon Shaheed's 'areas for further consideration': the right to science and intellectual property (IP); the equitable sharing of benefits and transfer of knowledge; and third-party actors and their obligations (the private-public divide). We will end by suggesting a fourth area that, in our opinion, merits further consideration – namely, the possible clash between (fundamentalist) religion and science. Along the way we will also offer other suggestions for topics or areas that we think need attention and/or clarification.

1. THE LINK BETWEEN SCIENCE AND CULTURE

The human right to science has been explicitly enshrined in the 1948 Universal Declaration of Human Rights (UDHR, art. 27) and in the 1966 International Covenant on Economic, Social and Cultural Rights (ICESCR, art. 15). In addition, it is referred to in a number of regional instruments.

As Shaheed sees it, the underlying premise of 'The right to science' is this: 'The scope, normative content and obligations of the State under this right … remain underdeveloped while *scientific innovations are changing human existence in ways that were inconceivable a few decades ago*' (emphasis added).[4] The topic is urgent. Precisely because many of the changes we are experiencing are due to science and technology, we need to see the right to science as a right which is important in and of itself. Most often, it has been viewed as merely a right which supports other rights such as e.g. the rights to health, the environment, development, housing, and education, and this has tended to lessen its value.

Likewise, it is important to view the right to science as a right which is strongly linked to the right to participate freely in the cultural life of the community, Shaheed argues. The link between the rights to science and culture is written into the very mandate on cultural rights. In the resolution renewing that mandate, 'the right of everyone to take part in cultural life and to enjoy the benefits of scientific progress and its applications' was reaffirmed.[5]

Both rights relate, first of all, to the pursuit of knowledge and understanding as well as to human creativity. Just as the right to participate in cultural life enables people to continuously be creative and contribute to society's cultural meanings and manifestations, so the right to science gives people the possibility to engage in critical thinking and to investigate and contribute new knowledge in the field of science, 'understood as knowledge that is testable and refutable, including revisiting and refuting existing theorems and understandings'.[6]

Secondly, the link between science and culture enables people to think of a better future for themselves – to 'aspire,' Shaheed writes, borrowing a term from social-cultural anthropologist Arjun Appadurai.[7] The ability to 'aspire' is a cultural one (a 'cultural capability'), and it can lead to improvements in socio-economic situations, but beyond that also to a life with self-realization, dignity, and meaningful participation in the community. It reflects who people choose to be and *could* be. The important thing, Shaheed writes, again following Appadurai, is that such aspiration also becomes realistic. Access to science and culture is a major, transformative tool for realizing and making these dreams come true.[8] We shall come back to Appadurai during our discussion of 'the access perspective'.

The link between science and culture is explicit in both article 27 UDHR and article 15 ICESCR. Repeating much of the wording of the

---

4 Shaheed 2012a, para. 1.

5 Ibid., para. 16.

6 Ibid., para. 18.

7 Ibid., para. 20.

8 A good example is the Hole-in-the-Wall Education Project: http://www.hole-in-the-wall.com/.

former, article 15.1 ICESCR talks about the rights of everyone to take part in cultural life, to enjoy the benefits of scientific progress and its applications, and to benefit from the protection of the moral and material interests resulting from any scientific, literary or artistic production. Parts 2–4 of article 15 furthermore demand that States Parties promote the conservation, development and diffusion of science and culture (art. 15.2); respect the freedom indispensable for scientific research and creative activity (art. 15.3); and recognize the benefits to be derived from the encouragement and development of international contact and cooperation in the scientific and cultural fields (art. 15.4).

As Lea Shaver reminds us, this link was already present in the 1945 UNESCO Constitution which established the Organization with the mission 'to contribute to peace and security by promoting collaboration among the nations through *education, science and culture*'. Indeed, throughout the UNESCO Constitution, the notion of 'culture' should be understood to refer, very broadly, to science as well as the arts (emphasis added).[9] The connection of both science and culture with education is furthermore worth noting. Education is often seen as a fundamental human right which is essential for the exercise of all other human rights, and taking normative action for realizing this right has always been very important in the UNESCO context. This is something that we shall return to.

In an interview that we conducted with her in November 2015 in Copenhagen, Farida Shaheed stressed how learning to appreciate the connection between science and culture had been one of the most useful lessons she has learned as UN Special Rapporteur.[10] This is especially interesting in light of the general assumption that the domains of science and technology are very different from the domains of the arts and humanities. In the Introduction to this book, the famous 'two cultures' debate between the two Cambridge, UK colleagues, C.P. Snow and F.R. Leavis about higher education and core curricula was brought up. This debate has surfaced, since the 1960s, in various contexts, most recently in debates concerning the digital humanities and the future, in general, of

[9] Shaver, 2010, 142–3.

[10] 'UCPH Talking About – Negotiating Cultural Rights', Helle Porsdam interviewing Farida Shaheed, November 13, 2015 – available at http://video.ku.dk/secret/12446221/64f4083b0fdbbbde433687327261b013. See further Ch. 1 this volume, in which Shaheed also reflects on this issue.

the humanities. For many digital humanists, the promise of the comparatively new field, Digital Humanities, is precisely that it can bridge the gap between the 'two cultures'.[11]

For Shaheed, there really no longer seem to be two, but only one culture or 'cultural capability'. Does this mean that science IS, in fact, culture – and if so, what are the implications for the way in which we perceive the scientific process, its methodologies and tools? Her definition of science as testable and refutable knowledge includes 'all fields of inquiry, including social sciences, and encompassing all research'. Whereas the social sciences are singled out for mention, we notice, the humanities – an area of inquiry just as, if not more often associated with the arts, culture and cultural heritage – are not. The humanities relate well, though, to Shaheed's notion of 'scientific progress' as 'convey[ing] the idea of a positive impact on the well-being of people and the realization of their human rights'.[12]

In terms of research, in other words, the extent to which culture and the humanities are also protected by the right to science is somewhat unclear – as is the question of whether or not science and scientists are protected in the same way artists are. One of Shaheed's other reports concerns 'The right to artistic freedom.' Later, we shall argue that the rights of the individual scientist ought to be highlighted in much the same way as those of the individual artist.

2. 'THE ACCESS PERSPECTIVE'

Early on in the report, in the paragraph concerning the recognition in international law of the right to share in scientific advancement and its benefits, Shaheed notes that the rights to science and culture should not only be read together; they should also be read 'in conjunction with, in particular the right of all peoples to self-determination and the right of everyone to take part in the conduct of public affairs'.[13]

A human rights approach automatically adds a focus on the disadvantaged. Applied to the right to the benefits of scientific progress, as Audrey R. Chapman has argued, 'this requires a form of affirmative action, that is, specific investments in science and technologies likely to benefit those at the bottom of the economical and social scale'.[14] In

[11] Porsdam, 2013.
[12] Shaheed, 2012a, para 24.
[13] Ibid., para 7.
[14] Chapman, 2009.

Shaheed's statement on the normative content of the right to benefit from scientific progress and its applications, access by all without discrimination accordingly takes up by far the major part. Points (a) and (c) directly concern access and the opportunity for all to participate in decision-making. Even in points (b) and (d), which are the ones that most directly address the need to protect the rights of scientists, the most import issue is the diffusion of science as a precondition for public participation in decision-making.

Normative point (a) concerns access by everyone without discrimination to the benefits of science and its applications, including scientific knowledge. Out of the four normative points, this is the one on which Shaheed spends most space and energy, thereby signalling that this is the most essential for the realization of the right to science. 'Access', she writes, 'must be to science as a whole, not only to specific scientific outcomes or applications'.[15] There is an educational element to this, just as there is an element of access to scientific information as well as to its applications and technologies. The right to gain scientific knowledge, that is, to get a science education overlaps with both the right to education and the right to information. It is a right, Shaheed explains, that exists inside as well as outside the classroom proper. Inside the classroom, students should learn about the latest scientific discoveries and their applications. But popularizing science outside the classroom, for example in science cafés or in science museums dedicated to a more popular dissemination of scientific knowledge, is also important.[16]

In terms of access to scientific information, Shaheed stresses the need for making the latest scientific discoveries and discussions available to everyone. Not only is it important that scientists around the world get access to such information, and that scientists in richer countries share with their colleagues in less well-off parts of the world. It is also essential that public access to such information be available. Today, this primarily involves the digital media – making public digital versions of new research by means, for example, of open-access journals and repositories and mandatory open-access policies which especially enable publicly funded research to be shared across the world.

Ensuring access to information to communication technologies and the Internet is therefore a crucial obligation for States, Shaheed argues. Significant digital divides exist today; not everyone around the world can afford access to the Internet, and when it comes to the use of digital

[15] Shaheed, 2012a, para. 26.
[16] Ibid., para. 27.

media gender still seems to be a major factor. Intellectual property furthermore constitutes a barrier to digital access, and 'the right to science and intellectual property rights' is the first of three areas for further consideration that Shaheed outlines toward the end of her report on 'the right to science.' The importance that she attaches to this topic is also evident from the fact that her last two reports from 2015 are dedicated to IP issues. We shall return to IP in more detail later but will just note here that the topic is equally relevant with regard to access to scientific applications and technologies. It is a core principle, writes Shaheed, that 'innovations essential for a life with dignity should be accessible to everyone, in particular marginalized populations'.[17] Patented medicine for illnesses suffered especially by people in developing countries such as HIV-AIDS or malaria is often prohibitively expensive, and this is something that we must look more into.[18]

Normative point (c) also chiefly concerns the importance of democratic access. From a human rights perspective, participation must ensure decision-making. Public consultations on scientific advances and their implications are necessary for two reasons. First, all persons, not least marginalized populations such as indigenous peoples, must be protected from 'the negative consequences of scientific testing or applications on, in particular, their food security, health or environment'.[19] Scientific research cannot be completely free, but must be conducted in a socially and ethically responsible manner – especially when the human research subjects are vulnerable and/or poor and uneducated so that they cannot give their consent.[20]

Seeing access to scientific research as an essential capacity for democratic citizenship, Shaheed comes close to sharing Appadurai's call for a right to research. In his 2006 article, 'The right to research,' Appadurai famously links the capacity to do research with the cultural capacity to 'aspire,' mentioned above:

> Without aspiration, there is no pressure to know more. And without systematic tools for gaining relevant new knowledge, aspiration degenerates into fantasy or despair. Thus, asserting the relevance of the right to research, as a human right, is not a metaphor. It is an argument for how we might revive an old idea, namely, that taking part in democratic society requires one to be informed. One can hardly be informed unless one has some ability to conduct research, however humble the question or however quotidian its inspiration.

---

17 Ibid., para. 29.
18 Helfer and Austin, 2011.
19 Shaheed, 2012a, para. 43.
20 Ibid., para. 52.

> This is doubly true in a world where rapid change, new technologies and rapid flows of information change the playing field for ordinary citizens every day of the week.[21]

It is worth noting in this context that an overly cautious approach to consent and undue inducement to act as a research subject may, however, lead to a different set of problems: it may exclude vulnerable populations from research, and, consequently, from medicines that work *for them.*[22]

Ensuring the participation of individuals and communities in decision-making is important, secondly, for the promotion of appropriate research that can address vital societal needs, e.g. in the areas of public health and the environment.[23] 'Major decisions regarding funding and research priorities, science policies, emerging areas of research, and new technological applications should entail a participatory process,' writes Shaheed and mentions the ways in which some States have initiated consensus conferences, dialogues and other consultative mechanisms with the participation of the general public.[24]

While the wish to make sure that the views of the public are heard – especially when we are talking about research that is publicly funded and from which the public should benefit – is entirely understandable, we think Shaheed may be going too far in her wish to link scientific research to societal needs. As we see it, such directed research risks damaging the kind of free and curiosity-driven basic research that often is the prime motivational source for researchers. The 2009 'Venice Statement on the Right to Enjoy the Benefits of Scientific Progress and its Applications,' one of the few other recent attempts at clarifying the cultural right to science that we have, talks about the freedom of inquiry of each individual researcher and reminds us that such:

> Freedom of inquiry is a vital element in the development of science in its broadest sense. *Science is not only about advancing knowledge of a specific subject matter, nor merely about procuring a set of data and testing*

---

[21] Appadurai, 2006, 176–7.

[22] For more on the controversy over 'vulnerable populations' in clinical research, see e.g. Denny and Grady, 2007. For more on undue inducement, see e.g. Emanuel, 2005 and for more on informed consent, see e.g. Rhodes, 2005 – We wish to thank Dr. Sebastian Porsdam Mann for this valuable insight.

[23] Shaheed, 2012a, para. 33.

[24] Ibid., para. 43.

> *hypotheses that may be useful for some practical purpose*. It is also, at the same time, about enhancing the conditions for further scientific and cultural activity.[25]

Subject to the same ethical standards based on human rights as the research that originates on the basis of societal needs, such free and basic research – research that does not come about because of some strategic goals set by specific political actors in response to perceived societal goals – is very important, we think.

We are not arguing in favour of replacing all societal goal-inspired research with free and basic research; we are saying, instead, that both kinds of research are needed and that one supports the other. If all research becomes strategic in the sense that public funding is only given to certain topics, defined by politicians in response to the perceived needs of the general public – and this is a trend that we see in many Western countries for the time being – then we risk going against the freedom of inquiry and the interests of the individual researcher whose scientific work forms the backbone of much societal growth. Furthermore, past experience shows that counter-intuitively, it is often the curiosity-driven research that later becomes the basis of solving real-world problems.

While public consultation is a good thing, moreover, it may not be appropriate in cases where there is a total lack of understanding among the public of the relevant risks and benefits (cf, the MMR vaccine scare, for example). Just as we do not ask judges to consult the public before they make controversial decisions, information and outreach ought to take the place of consultation in cases involving difficult issues such as the MMR vaccine.

This takes us to Shaheed's normative points (b) and (d) that concern the protection of research scientists themselves.

3. 'THE PROTECTION PERSPECTIVE'

Normative points (b) and (d) concern the 'freedom indispensable for scientific research and opportunities for all to contribute to the scientific enterprise' and 'an enabling environment for the conservation, development and diffusion of science', respectively. Among the issues mentioned by Shaheed as being especially important for securing the scientific freedom of scientists are freedom from political and other interference, the right freely to communicate and publish research results without any

---

25 UNESCO (2009).

kind of censorship, the right to join any professional association and to collaborate with colleagues all around the world. Likewise, scientists must be free to come and go as they please in their own countries but also abroad, just as they must be able to express their scientific opinion without fear of repression by the State or any other actor.[26]

It is furthermore essential that everyone around the world, regardless of gender, race, religion, and language, can participate in scientific research – that is, can enter the scientific profession – just as the dissemination of scientific results must be within reach of everyone, including the less well-off and disadvantaged of this world. As previously mentioned, even in the sections dedicated to the protection of scientific inquiry and freedom, it is the access perspective that is stressed the most by Shaheed. Ultimately, the individual interests and rights of scientists, scholars and researchers are seen as subordinate to the core ideal of public access to knowledge and science. 'The diffusion of science,' she sums up, 'is a precondition for public participation in decision-making and essential for fostering further research, development and applications'.[27]

Shaheed's position seems to be pretty much in line with that of the drafters of the UDHR who saw science as a means to combat prejudice of various kinds, as Aurora Plomer has demonstrated. Examining, in her very interesting 2015 book *Patents, Human Rights and Access to Science*, the challenges posed by the modern patent system to the right of everyone to access to the benefits of science in international law, Plomer traces the drafting history of article 27 UDHR and UNESCO's activities in relation to article 15 ICESCR. Her analysis shows:

> that from the very beginning, the elaboration and implementation of UNESCO's mission had to straddle the vision of (Western) liberal economies which envisaged UNESCO to play a minimalist role in facilitating scientists' free exchange of ideas and the more proactive role favoured by others who envisaged that UNESCO would facilitate science and technology transfer from industrialized to less advanced countries.[28]

These tensions are still ongoing, Plomer argues. Shaheed's choice of strategic priorities in her 'right to science' report shows her to be on the side of those who believe in the importance of science and technology transfer from the Global North to the Global South. What Plomer's analysis also shows, however, is that for the drafters of the UDHR and

---

26 Shaheed, 2012a, para. 40.
27 Ibid., para. 48.
28 Plomer, 2015, p. 165.

the ICESCR, there was no inherent contradiction between the wish to enable free and public access to the benefits of science and the wish to protect the creative efforts of the individual scientist:

> The two ideas are two faces of the same coin. Free and public access to science is required to facilitate the creative efforts of individual scientists whose creations, in turn, require protection to facilitate scientific progress and the advancement of science for the benefit of society. In this way, the right to access the benefits of science reflects the public and the private transformative power of science and knowledge.[29]

Thus, the drafters were well aware that without first nurturing the freedom of inquiry of scientists and scholars, we will not get the kind of path-breaking scientific developments that may lead to collective economic, social and cultural progress.

Towards the end of their *Science* piece on ‘A Human Right to Science’, mentioned above, Chapman and Wyndham refer to a new report by the American Association for the Advancement of Science (AAAS) which would be published shortly.[30] This report, of which Wyndham was herself one of the authors, was entitled ‘Defining the Right to Enjoy the Benefits of Scientific Progress and Its Applications: American Scientists’ Perspectives’.[31] The AAAS report, published toward the end of 2013, builds on and repeatedly refers to Shaheed’s report, just as it refers to the 2009 Venice Statement.

The Venice Statement specifically calls for the participation of the scientific and academic communities in clarifying the meaning of the right to science, as set out in article 27 UDHR and article 15.1(b) ICESCR. And as the title of the 2013 AAAS report shows, its authors are especially interested in the perspectives of American scientists’ themselves. ‘The scientific and human rights communities need to provide input,’ Chapman and Wyndham write in their *Science* article.[32] We do not think that we will get such important input – or that we will get scientists and scholars interested in, let alone feel any sense of ownership to, the right to science – unless we change the balance somewhat in favour of the freedom of scientific inquiry. We need to focus more on the human rights of scientists and scholars, on how we create the sort of academic freedom under ethical responsibility that is conducive to doing good research.

---

29 Ibid.

30 See note 1.

31 AAAS, 2013.

32 See note 1.

One way to do so is to pursue the link between science and culture to its logical conclusion. In addition to her report on the cultural rights of women Shaheed's 'right to science' report was followed by the report on 'The right to artistic freedom' in 2013. In her fifth thematic report, Shaheed writes of her conviction 'that freedom of artistic expression and creativity cannot be dissociated from the right of all persons to enjoy the arts, as in many cases restrictions on artistic freedoms aim at denying people access to specific artworks'.[33] We would like to suggest that the right to science be the subject of a new report. Such a report on 'The right to scientific freedom' could be modelled on the 2013 report on the right to artistic freedom and could focus, in more detail than does Shaheed's 'right to science' report, on the right to freedom of scientific expression and creation.

There are a number of international Civil Society Organizations dedicated to documenting, monitoring and defending freedom of artistic expression. *Freemuse*, based in Copenhagen and headed by Ole Reitov, is one example. It has published country and thematic reports and books on the mechanisms and effects of censorship of music, documented and monitored violations of artistic freedom, engaged in court cases and prison visits, and provided advice to artists at risk around the world. *Freemuse* has consultative status with the UN and was consulted by Farida Shaheed for the report on artistic freedom. In his chapter, 'Challenges of Artistic Freedom,' for the first UNESCO Global Report on the Monitoring of the 2005 Convention on the Protection and Promotion of the Diversity of Cultural Expressions (2015), Reitov writes how 'the right of artists to express themselves freely are under threat worldwide, *especially where artistic expressions contest or critique political ideologies, religious beliefs, and cultural and social preferences*' (emphasis added).[34]

Something similar is the case with regard to scientific freedom. There are a few organizations who do for science what *Fremuse* does for the arts. Scholars at Risk (SAR), based at New York University, is one such organization or network of higher education communities and their members which responds to attacks aimed at controlling access to information and restricting research, publication, teaching and learning. Other examples are the AAAS Program for Scientific Freedom, Responsibility and Law and the New York-based Committee for Concerned Scientists, dedicated to the promotion of academic freedom throughout

---

[33] Shaheed, 2013, para. 5.
[34] Reitov, 2015, p. 193.

the world, free travel of scientists and academics, and the public's right to the benefit of science.

We think the promotion of what could be called a 'science commons' is every bit as important as the work presently going into promoting a 'cultural commons'. A report on 'The right to scientific freedom' could investigate publication strategies (i.e. gold or green open-access policies for journals and repositories for research) and funding policies (public as well as private). It could furthermore address laws and regulations restricting scientific freedoms as well as economic and financial issues significantly impacting on such freedoms, e.g. IP. It could analyze the underlying motivations for such restrictions – whether they may be ascribed to political, religious, cultural or moral reasons, or merely to interests of an economic kind. It could examine the issue of the role of the scientist as a public intellectual and his/her moral obligations toward sharing his/her knowledge with the rest of society. And much like the report on 'The right to artistic freedom,' it could end with a study of the international framework on possible limitations to scientific freedom, and also stress positive obligations of States (and possibly other actors) in support of the right of people to enjoy science and their scientific freedoms.[35]

4. AREAS FOR FURTHER CONSIDERATION

The three areas singled out by Shaheed for further consideration are the relation of the right to science to IP rights, to the equitable sharing of benefits and transfer of technologies, and to third-party actors and their obligations, respectively. These are excellent choices on Shaheed's part, all three areas being in urgent need of attention, not least because they overlap and interact with each other in sometimes very problematical ways.

Right to Science and IP

Shaheed starts by emphasizing that the IP regime is 'a temporary monopoly' and that 'the rights of authors protected by human rights instruments are not to be equated with 'intellectual property rights'.[36] At issue is especially part (c) of article 15.1 ICESCR which concerns the right to benefit from the protection of the moral and material interests

35 Compare Shaheed, 2013, Summary.
36 Shaheed, 2012a, para. 57.

resulting from any scientific, literary or artistic production. This part of article 15 is often seen as being in conflict with its two other parts (the rights to culture and to science), and is increasingly claimed by people in favour of strong IP rights as 'proof' that these rights are human rights.[37] That Shaheed so forcefully puts down this claim, here as in her two last thematic reports on copyright and patents, is extremely valuable.

In the context of the right to science, patents are very important – especially when the rights to health and food, or climate change are involved. A good deal of research is available on the right to health,[38] but also the right to food and climate change are currently receiving more attention. Following this research, Shaheed points to possibilities of adding access to e.g. medicines at affordable costs such as 'patent pools' that give patent holders the possibility of licensing their patents to third parties, and 'generic competition' that allows significant reductions in the cost of drugs. She also mentions the use of exceptions and flexibilities in international treaties as a way of ensuring compatibility with the right to science.[39]

Equitable Sharing and Third-party Actors and their Obligations

The issue of IP protection overlaps with both the equitable sharing of benefits/transfer of technologies and the third-party actors and their obligations. Over the past decade or so legal scholars have exposed the tension between IP rights and public goods.[40] In her analysis of the right to science and IP rights as the foremost area that calls for further consideration, Shaheed accordingly proposes the adoption of a public good approach to the creation of knowledge and its dissemination.

In her 2014 thematic report on copyright, Shaheed mentions the so-called 'fair use' exception or limitation.[41] 'Fair use' is an American term that allows limited use of copyrighted material without requiring permission from the rights holders, such as use for scholarship or review. It is based on a First Amendment right to free speech. 'Fair dealing' is the term used for a similar principle in certain other common-law countries. Though similar, there are certain important legal differences between fair dealing and fair use. Generally speaking, fair use is broader and a number of scholars have argued that it is more beneficial to users.

---

37 See Helfer and Austin, 2011.
38 See e.g. Donders, 2015.
39 Shaheed, 2012a, paras 61, 62.
40 Shaver, 2010, pp. 121–84.
41 Shaheed, 2014, para. 73.

Together with 'patent pools' and 'generic competition' the 'fair use' and 'fair dealing' exceptions lead to what Shaheed calls, in her right to science Recommendations, 'a minimalist approach to IP protection'.[42]

Such a minimalist approach to IP can also protect against the increasing privatization (and commercialization or commodification) of knowledge. The relationship between human rights and science is complicated by the fact that private and non-State actors are increasingly the principal producers of scientific progress and technological advances. Cuts in public spending for scientific research are one reason for this; the possibility of making money from copyrighted or patented knowledge is another. Shaheed points, in her Recommendations, to corporate social responsibility as a way for the private sector to contribute to the realization of the right to science.[43]

States, for their part, she furthermore advises, should undertake more scrutiny of research methods and knowledge creation in the private sector.[44] States should also adopt mandatory open-access policies for journals and repositories for research and strengthen publicly funded research in order to secure the dissemination of scientific knowledge and applications – across the scientific community, but also more broadly in society and within the international community. This is not least important vis-à-vis the obligation according to article 15.2–4 ICESCR for developed countries to 'comply with their international legal obligations through the provision of direct aid, financial and material, as well as the development of international collaborative models of research and development for the benefit of developing countries and their populations'.[45] But it is also important in relation to the various support policies by universities to publish open access, instigated in part to comply with the conditions now in place for major research grants from e.g. the European Union.

Shaheed notes how several scholars have questioned both the economic effectiveness of IP regimes and the familiar terms of 'incentives-for-creation,' the traditional theory of copyright according to which there would be insufficient incentives to invent, create, and build commercial goodwill without intellectual property law. The documentation and conservation of traditional knowledge is interesting in this context.

---

42 Shaheed, 2012a, Recommendations (o).
43 Ibid., Recommendations (b).
44 Ibid., para. 54.
45 Ibid., para. 68.

Further discussion is needed, Shaheed correctly argues, 'on the modalities and conditions under which others should benefit from such accumulated knowledge while safeguarding the moral and material interests of the individual or collective creators'.[46]

What Shaheed may be referring to here is the fact that some indigenous communities and other minorities have begun to invoke IP rights in their fight for the distinctive rights to their intangible cultural heritage, forcing the international human rights system to articulate the principles through which traditional knowledge and traditional cultural expressions may best be recognized and protected. Indigenous claims for IP are voiced in terms of identity politics, cultural survival and human rights and 'these new claims for intellectual property understand rights not just in the familiar terms of incentives-for-creation, but also as tools for both recognition and redistribution'.[47] The potential clash between the wish of indigenous populations to expand their IP rights for the protection of their traditional knowledge and the wish for open access and access to knowledge on the part of other individuals and groups is an area that truly needs more attention.

Science, Religion and Education

There is a second clash involving the conservation of traditional knowledge in relation to the right to science that needs clarification. We are thinking of the possible clash between (fundamentalist) religion and science. Under normative point (b), when talking about the freedom that is indispensable for scientific research, Shaheed mentions the importance of the scientific enterprise remaining 'free of political and other interference'.[48] The 'other interference' alluded to here presumably includes religious interference. In her fourth thematic report on the cultural rights of women, Shaheed argues for the elimination of 'the justification for direct discrimination against women by reference to culture or religion – which, according to information provided to the Special Rapporteur, continues …'.[49] But religion is never mentioned directly in the report on the right to science.

We would like to end by proposing this clash between religion/tradition and science as a fourth area that merits further consideration. At stake is not only scientific freedom of expression (cf. Reitov's remark,

46 Ibid., para. 64.
47 Sunder, 2006, p. 273.
48 Shaheed, 2012a, para. 39.
49 Shaheed 2012b, para. 62.

quoted above, about artistic freedom of expression being under threat worldwide when it is perceived to be critical of 'political ideologies, religious beliefs, and cultural and social preferences'). At stake is also the right to a scientific education which, as we have seen, is so important in relation to the cultural capability of 'aspiring'. Do students in public school science classes around the world have a right to be scientifically enlightened? Does the right to science for their parents and fellow citizens entail a right to know – even if such a right is fundamentally at odds with their religious views? And what about indigenous groups for whom religion is closely related to vital questions of identity, tradition, even survival?

In the United States, creationism, creation science, intelligent design and other religious theories challenge widely held scientific explanations about the origin of the universe, for example. The U.S. Constitution guarantees the rights of Americans to believe the religious theories of creation (as well as other theories), but the Supreme Court has held that these theories may not be taught in public school science classes. Religious theories of creation may be included in classes on comparative religion as an example of how some religious groups believe human life began. However, creationism may never be taught as scientific fact. Nevertheless, there is ongoing debate in several school districts as to whether creationism should be taught as a 'competing scientific theory' in high school science classes.[50]

Creationism also seems to play an expanding role in public debates about science policy and school curricula in Europe.[51] And in parts of the Arab world, the schism between science and Islam seems to widen with time, making the philosophical implications of relativity, quantum mechanics, chaos theory, strings, or stem cells, just to mention a few examples, unacceptable not only to the political/religious power structure but also to high school or university students and the general public.[52] A related problem are the public and private schools in other parts of the world with a fundamentalist religious agenda that are free of charge for students and financed by fundamentalist states from the Arab world.

---

[50] See the Anti-Defamation League, 'Religion in the Science Class? Why Creationism and Intelligent Design Don't Belong' – available at http://archive.adl.org/issue_religious_freedom/create/creationism_qa.html#.V0M9nL5KVdA.

[51] See Blancke, Hjermitslev, and Kjærgaard, 2014; and Blancke and Kjærgaard, 2016.

[52] Hoodbhoy, 2006, see also Hoodbhoy, 1991.

5. CONCLUDING REMARKS

In summary, we propose as a topic for a new report the protection of the right to scientific freedom – a report that could be modelled on Shaheed's report on 'The right to artistic freedom' from 2013. We also suggest that a fourth area, the possible clash between (fundamentalist) religion and science, be added to the three areas for further consideration on which Shaheed focuses: the right to science and IP; the equitable sharing of benefits and transfer of knowledge; and third-party actors and their obligations (the private-public divide).

For all these topics and areas for further discussion, the right to education plays a major role. As early as 1968, in one of the first meetings on 'Cultural Rights as Human Rights' at UNESCO Headquarters, Professor B. Boutros-Ghali of Cairo University, who went on to become Secretary-General of the UN between 1992 and 1996, linked cultural rights to the right to education, as set forth in article 26 UDHR: 'There is no right to culture without a minimum of education. The person who can neither read nor write and who has not received the most elementary instruction is impervious to any true culture'.[53]

This focus on the importance of education for the enjoyment of cultural rights was one that was shared by all participants at the UNESCO meeting. 'There was no disagreement about the supreme importance of education: *in the developing world the right to culture is in substance the right to education*,' as the Report of the meeting, published in 1970 and adopted by all participants, succinctly stated (emphasis added). The report summed up the battle between tradition and the right to know in relation to cultural rights in this very thought-provoking way:

> This problem could be summed up as the conflict between the right to culture and the rights of cultures. The first is the right of individuals to access to culture, of which they can be deprived by poverty or political oppression. The second is the right of cultures to survive in face of a radical transformation of the modern world. The first right requires modernization, the second has much to fear from it.[54]

The importance of the right to education and its relation to the rights to science and culture runs like a red thread through the 1970 UNESCO report – and through most reports dealing with cultural rights that have

---

[53] UNESCO, 1970, p. 73. For a longer and more thorough discussion of this, see Porsdam, 2016, 87–104.

[54] UNESCO, 1970, p. 115.

followed it, including those authored by Shaheed. If we take seriously this link between the rights to culture, science and education, then we need to clarify the relationship of these three core rights to the right to freedom of thought, conscience and religion.[55]

REFERENCES

AAAS (2013) 'Defining the Right to Enjoy the Benefits of Scientific Progress and Its Applications: American Scientists' Perspectives' (Report prepared by Margaret Weigers Vitullo and Jessica Wyndham, Science and Human Rights Coalition). DOI: 10.1126/srhrl.aaa0028 – available at http://www.apa.org/topics/human-rights/scientific-progress.pdf.

Anti-Defamation League, 'Religion in the Science Class? Why Creationism and Intelligent Design Don't Belong' – available at http://archive.adl.org/issue_religious_freedom/create/creationism_qa.html#.V0M9nL5KVdA.

Appadurai, Arjun, 'The Right to Research' (2006) 4(2) *Globalisation, Societies and Education* 167–77.

Bennoune, Karime (2017) Report of the UN Special Rapporteur in the field of cultural rights, 'The Impact of Fundamentalism and Extremism on the Enjoyment of Cultural Rights', A/HRC/34/56, 16 January – available at https://documents-dds-ny.un.org/doc/UNDOC/GEN/G17/007/43/PDF/G1700743.pdf?OpenElement.

Bennoune, Karima (2016) Introductory Report, A/HRC/31/59, 3 February – available at https://documents-dds-ny.un.org/doc/UNDOC/GEN/G16/016/97/PDF/G1601697.pdf?OpenElement.

---

[55] In her first introductory report, Shaheed's successor as UN Special Rapporteur in the field of cultural rights, Karima Bennoune, highlights priority areas in which she believes further advances should be made. One of these concerns the 'diverse forms of fundamentalism and extremism, which have now reached devastating proportions in many regions of the world and have had grave repercussions on cultural rights …' (Bennoune 2016, para. 35). As this volume goes to print, Bennoune has indeed just published a report on 'The impact of fundamentalism and extremism on the enjoyment of cultural rights', A/HRC/34/56, 16 January 2017. This report and the work that goes into it are extremely important, and Bennoune does express concerns that overlap with those expressed in the present chapter. However, most of her concerns relate, more concretely, to artistic freedom and attacks against artists (paras 62–69), intellectuals and cultural rights defenders (paras 70–73), and the right to take part in cultural life without discrimination (paras 74–89). In paras 90–92, Bennoune talks about attacks against educational institutions, personnel and students – and it is here that she comes closest to the right to science-related issues outlined in our chapter. On the whole, though, she seems more interested in the devastating effects of fundamentalism and extremism on the culture – than the science-related parts of cultural rights.

Blancke, Stefaan and Peter C. Kjærgaard, 'Creationism Invades Europe: An Antiscience Movement Once Limited Mostly to the U.S. is Gaining Ground on the Eastern Side of the Atlantic' (2016) 315(4) *Scientific American* – available at https://www.scientificamerican.com/magazine/sa/2016/10-01/.

Blancke, Stefaan, Hans Henrik Hjermitslev and Peter C. Kjærgaard (eds) (2014) *Creationism in Europe* (Baltimore, MD: Johns Hopkins University Press).

Boutros-Ghali, B. (1970). 'The Right to Culture and the Universal Declaration of Human Rights,' in UNESCO 1970.

Chapman, Audrey R., 'Towards and Understanding of the Right to Enjoy the Benefits of Scientific Progress and Its Applications, (2009) 8(1) *Journal of Human Rights* 1–36.

Chapman, Audrey R. and Jessica Wyndham, 'A Human Right to Science' Policy Forum, (2013) 340(6138) *Science* 1291.

Denny, Colleen C. and Christine Grady, 'Clinical Research with Economically Disadvantaged Populations' (2007) 33(7) *Journal of Medical Ethics*, 382–5 – available at http://www.ncbi.nlm.nih.gov/pmc/articles/PMC2598135/.

Donders, Yvonne, 'Exploring the Cultural Dimensions of the Right to the Highest Attainable Standard of Health' (2015) 18(2) *Potchefstroom Electronic Law Journal/Potchefstroomse Elektroniese Regsblad (PELJ/PER)* – available at http://www.saflii.org/za/journals/PER/2015/16.pdf.

Emanuel, Ezekiel J., 'Undue Inducement: Nonsense on Stilts?' (2005) 5(5) *The American Journal of Bioethics* 9–13.

Helfer, Laurence R. and Graeme W. Austin (2011). *Human Rights and Intellectual Property: Mapping the Global Interface*. Cambridge: Cambridge University Press.

Hoodbhoy, P. (2006) 'Islam and Science – Unhappy Bedfellows' Islamic Science, Global Agenda, 1–2 – available at http://eacpe.org/content/uploads/2014/02/Islam-and-Science-unhappy-bedfellows.pdf.

Hoodbhoy, P. (1991) *Islam and Science: Religious Orthodoxy and the Battle for Rationality*. Zed Books.

Leavis, F.R. (1962), *Two Cultures? The Significance of C.P. Snow.* The Richmond Lecture, London: Chatto & Windus.

Plomer, Aurora (2015), *Patents, Human Rights and Access to Science,* Cheltenham UK, Northampton MA: Edward Elgar.

Porsdam, Helle (2016). 'Education, cultural rights and digital communication in the 'long 1970s,' in Villaume, Poul, Rasmus Mølgaard Mariager & Helle Porsdam (eds), *The 'Long 1970's: Human Rights, East-West Détente and Transnational Relations*, Routledge, 87–104.

Porsdam, Helle (2013). 'Digital Humanities: On Finding the Proper Balance between Qualitative and Quantitative Ways of Doing Research in the Humanities,' *Digital Humanities Quarterly* 7.2/2013 – available at http://www.digitalhumanities.org/dhq/vol/7/3/000167/000167.html.

Reitov, Ole (2015). 'Challenges of Artistic Freedom,' in UNESCO (2015), 189–201.

Rhodes R., 'Rethinking Research Ethics' (2005) 5(1) *American Journal of Bioethics* 7–28.

Shaheed, Farida (2014). Report of the Special Rapporteur in the field of cultural rights, 'Copyright policy and the right to science and culture', A/HRC/28/57, 24 December.

Shaheed, Farida (2012a). Report of the Special Rapporteur in the field of cultural rights, 'The right to enjoy the benefits of scientific progress and its applications', A/HRC/20/26, 14 May.

Shaheed, Farida (2012b). Report of the Special Rapporteur in the field of cultural rights, 'The enjoyment of cultural rights by women on an equal basis with men', A/67/287, 10 August.

Shaheed, Farida (2013). Report of the Special Rapporteur in the field of cultural rights, 'The right to artistic freedom and creativity,' A/HRC/23/34, 14 March.

Shaver, Lea (2010). 'The Right to Science and Culture.' 2010 *Wisconsin Law Review* 121–84.

Snow, C. P. (1998), 'The Two Cultures. The Rede Lecture, 1959,' in *C.P. Snow The Two Cultures*. Cambridge: Cambridge University Press.

Sunder, Madhavi, 'IP3' (2006) 59(20 *Stanford Law Review* 257–332.

UNESCO (2015), UNESCO Global Report on the Monitoring of the 2005 Convention on the Protection and Promotion of the Diversity of Cultural Expressions, entitled 'Re Shaping Cultural Policies. A Decade Promoting the Diversity of Cultural expressions for Development' – available at https://www.unesco.de/fileadmin/medien/Dokumente/Kultur/GMR_Re_Shaping_Clt_Policies_256p_EN.pdf.

UNESCO (2009), 'Venice Statement on the Right to Enjoy the Benefits of Scientific Progress and its Applications'– available at http://unesdoc.unesco.org/images/0018/001855/185558e.pdf.

UNESCO (1970), '*Cultural* Rights as *Human* Rights,' Studies and Documents on Cultural Policies – available at http://www.unesco.org/ulis/cgibin/ulis.pl?catno=1194&set=50533209_1_0&gp=1&lin=1&ll=1.

5. The enjoyment of cultural rights by women on an equal basis with men – Report 2012 (A/67/287)

Yvonne Donders

1. INTRODUCTION

For a long time, cultural rights were considered the 'Cinderella of the human rights family';[1] neglected by States, academics and other stakeholders. The establishment of the mandate of the Special Rapporteur on Cultural Rights formed an important catalyst for the further elaboration of these human rights. One of the reasons why cultural rights were neglected or addressed with a considerable amount of reserve or skepticism was that these rights were considered to protect and promote, apart from the positive dimensions of cultures, also cultural activities and practices that are very questionable from a human rights perspective. Many of such harmful cultural practices particularly affect women. Examples are female genital mutilation (FGM), widow cleansing, forced marriage and forced prostitution.[2]

[1] H. Niec, 'Casting the Foundation for the Implementation of Cultural Rights' in H. Niec (ed.), *Cultural Rights and Wrongs, A Collection of Essays in Commemoration of the 50th Anniversary of the Universal Declaration of Human Rights* (Paris: UNESCO Publishing, 1998) 176; P. Meyer-Bisch (ed.), *Les Droits Culturels, une catégorie sous-développée de droits de l'homme, Actes du VIIIe Colloque interdisciplinaire sur les droits de l'homme* (Editions Universitaires Fribourg Suisse 1993).

[2] Joint General Recommendation No. 31 of the Committee on the Elimination of Discrimination against Women/General Comment No. 18 of the Committee on the Rights of the Child on Harmful Practices (UN Doc. CEDAW/C/GC/31-CRC/C/GC/18 14 November 2014).

In other words, culture is often seen as an obstacle to the enjoyment of human rights by women.[3] The report by the Special Rapporteur called 'Enjoyment of cultural rights by women on an equal basis with men'[4] shows that, but it also focuses on a more positive role of culture for women. Culture is not only an impediment to, but also an important instrument for, the realization of their human rights.[5] This report thereby fits in the more general approach taken by the Special Rapporteur to emphasize the importance of cultural rights for the enjoyment of other human rights.

The title of the report suggests that it is mainly about the equal enjoyment of cultural rights by women and men.[6] The report deals, however, with much more than that, notably it elaborates on the *role of women* in the development, preservation and decision-making in relation to culture. In other words, the report is not only about the (cultural) rights of women, but about the complex and dynamic relationship and interaction between cultural rights and gender.

Paragraph 3 of the report of the Special Rapporteur seems to capture the crux of the matter:

> Gender, culture and rights intersect in intricate and complex ways. The tendency to view culture as largely an impediment to women's human rights is both over simplistic and problematic. By attributing self-propelling agency to 'culture' independent of the actions of human beings, it diverts attention from specific actors, institutions, rules and regulations, keeping women subordinated within patriarchal systems and structures. It also renders invisible women's agency in both reproducing and challenging dominant cultural norms and values. Nevertheless, many practices and norms that discriminate against women are justified by reference to culture, religion and tradition, leading experts to conclude that 'no social group has suffered greater violation of its human rights in the name of culture than women' and that it is

---

[3] Susan Moller Okin, 'Is Multiculturalism Bad for Women?' (1999) *Boston Review*; Yvonne Rafferty, 'International Dimensions of Discrimination and Violence against Girls: A Human Rights Perspective' (2013) 14(1) *Journal of International Women's Studies* 1–23.

[4] Report of the Special Rapporteur in the field of cultural rights, Farida Shaheed, 'The enjoyment of Cultural Rights by Women on an Equal Basis with Men' (UN Doc. A/67/287 10 August 2012).

[5] This is also the approach in the book by Rikki Holtmaat and Jonneke Naber, *Women's Human Rights and Culture – From Deadlock to Dialogue* (Antwerp: Intersentia, 2010).

[6] It could be noted that on the website of the Office of the High Commissioner for Human Rights the report is announced as 'Cultural Rights for Women'.

> 'inconceivable' that a number of such practices 'would be justified if they were predicated upon another protected classification such as race'. The use of discourses of cultural relativism to challenge the universal legitimacy and applicability of human rights norms is a serious concern.

In the following sections, different parts of this statement are discussed and placed in the broader context of the advancement of cultural rights within international human rights law.

2. 'THE USE OF DISCOURSES OF CULTURAL RELATIVISM TO CHALLENGE THE UNIVERSAL LEGITIMACY AND APPLICABILITY OF HUMAN RIGHTS NORMS IS A SERIOUS CONCERN'

When the mandate of the Special Rapporteur (then independent expert) was established, there were many States (among which was The Netherlands) that were hesitant about a mandate on cultural rights. They feared that this mandate would promote cultural relativism at the expense of the idea of the universality of human rights. One of the main achievements of the Special Rapporteur is that with her country visits and reports she has shown that it is possible to reconcile the universality of human rights with the promotion and protection of cultural rights and cultural diversity.

This report rightly emphasizes that respect for cultural rights or cultural diversity may not undermine the universality of human rights (para. 57) and that (respect for) cultural diversity is not to be confused with cultural relativism (para. 70). Indeed, respect for cultural diversity can be consistent with the notion of the universality of human rights. Cultural relativism, in the sense of asking for respect for cultural diversity, not of challenging the legitimacy of international human rights norms as such, and universality do not have to mutually exclude each other. The dichotomy can be overcome by making a distinction between formal universality and substantive universality, between universality of application and universality of implementation and between universality of the subjects (beneficiaries) and universality of the norms (content).[7]

---

[7] Yvonne Donders, *Human Rights: Eye for Cultural Diversity*, Inaugural lecture delivered upon appointment to the chair of Professor of International Human Rights and Cultural Diversity (29 July 2012 University of Amsterdam) available at http://dare.uva.nl/record/1/373400.

The idea that human rights should be universally enjoyed – by all persons on the basis of equality – is not very controversial. In general, formal universality, or the universality of the subjects of human rights, does not present problems. No one will seriously argue that some people in the world do not *have* human rights. International human rights instruments clearly endorse this universal approach. The Universal Declaration of Human Rights (UDHR), for example, not only refers to universality in its title, but also states in Article 1 that 'all human beings are born free and equal in dignity and rights'. The UDHR as well as the international human rights treaties speak of 'everyone', 'all persons' or 'no one', affirming that *all* human beings have these rights and freedoms, no matter where they were born or to which (cultural) community they belong.

The universal value and application of human rights does, however, not necessarily imply the *uniform implementation* of these rights. In other words, while human rights apply universally to everyone on the basis of their human dignity, the implementation of these rights does not have to be uniform. The European Court of Human Rights (ECtHR) has adopted this approach by stating that, while the purpose of the European Convention on Human Rights (ECHR) was to lay down international standards, 'this does not mean that absolute uniformity is required'.[8] Scholars have called this the 'relative universality of human rights',[9] 'inclusive universality'[10] or the 'culturalization of human rights';[11] the main idea being that while human rights apply universally, they do not have to be implemented in a uniform way. Human rights promotion and protection imply respect for and advancement of cultural diversity. Such diversity should be determined in close cooperation with different stakeholders and their interests have to be balanced. The report by the Special Rapporteur also endorses this approach by stating that universality should be understood as a transformative dialogue (para. 65).

---

[8] ECtHR, *Sunday Times v. United Kingdom*, Appl. No. 13166/87, decision of 26 November 1991, para. 61.

[9] Jack Donnelly, 'The Relative Universality of Human Rights' (2007) 29 *Human Rights Quarterly* 281–306, 281, 300.

[10] Eva Brems, 'Reconciling Universality and Diversity in International Human Rights: A Theoretical and Methodological Framework and Its Application in the Context of Islam' (April–June 2004) 5(3) *Human Rights Review* 5–21, 11–12; Eva Brems, 'Reconciling Universality and Diversity in International Human Rights Law', in Andras Sajo (ed.) *Human Rights with Modesty: the Problem of Universalism* (Koninklijke Brill 2004) 213–30, 223–5.

[11] Federico Lenzerini, *The Culturalization of Human Rights Law* (Oxford: OUP, 2014).

3. 'GENDER, CULTURE AND RIGHTS INTERSECT IN INTRICATE AND COMPLEX WAYS'

The complex intersection or interface between gender, culture and rights is highlighted in several parts of the report. There is indeed important interaction between gender and cultures; gender identities and gender relations are crucial aspects of cultures and cultures are (partially) shaped by gender. In other words, gender 'functions as an organizing principle for society because of the cultural meanings given to being male or female'.[12]

The concept of gender concerns more than the rights of women. It is a social concept referring to the social meanings given to biological sex differences. Gender 'refers to socially constructed identities, attributes and roles for women and men and society's social and cultural meaning for these biological differences resulting in hierarchical relationships between women and men and in the distribution of power and rights favouring men and disadvantaging women'.[13]

While people are born either male or female (biological sex), they are taught appropriate behaviours for males and females (gender norms) – including how they should interact with people of the same or opposite sex within households, communities and workplaces (gender relations) and which functions or responsibilities they should assume in society (gender roles).[14]

Gender roles and especially gender stereotypes play an important role in the (lack of) advancement of women's cultural rights and in the defense of cultural practices harmful to women. A gender stereotype is 'a generalised view or preconception about attributes or characteristics that are or ought to be possessed by, or the roles that are or should be performed by, men and women'.[15] Gender stereotyping refers to:

---

[12] Johanna Schalkwyk, 'Culture, Gender Equality and Development Cooperation', paper prepared for the Canadian International Development Agency (Cida) (June 2000) available at www.oecd.org/social/gender-development/1896320.pdf, p. 1.

[13] CEDAW Committee, General Recommendation No. 28 on the core obligations of States parties under article 2 of the Convention on the Elimination of All Forms of Discrimination against Women (UN Doc. CEDAW/C/GC/28 16 December 2010) para. 5.

[14] World Health Organisation, 'Fact sheet N°403, Gender' (August 2015).

[15] Rebecca J. Cook and Simone Cusack, *Gender Stereotyping: Transnational Legal Perspectives* (Philadelphia: University of Pennsylvania Press, 2010) 20; as

> the *practice* of applying a stereotypical belief to an individual member of the subject group; that is to say, the practice of ascribing to an individual woman or man specific attributes, characteristics, or roles by reason only of her or his membership in the social group of women or men.[16]

A gender stereotype is harmful when it limits women's or men's capacity to develop their personal abilities and make choices about their lives; gender stereotyping is wrongful when it results in a violation of human rights.

Sex and gender are both important factors determining personal cultural identity, but they play a different role. Sex is certainly part of one's personal identity, but it is less self-evident what role it plays in the development of one's *cultural* identity. Sex may be an important factor in the personal perception and interpretation of culture, but such perception seems to refer more to and be determined by *gender*. It concerns not merely objective differences between biological sexes, but in particular the roles assigned to the different sexes, the interrelationships with other individuals and communities and power structures in these relationships. Gender and culture have a multi-dimensional relationship. A crucial feature of any culture is the way a culture perceives the different characteristics of the two biological/physical male and female sexes resulting in ideas and constructs relating to gender, possibly leading to gender stereotypes.[17]

Gender is moreover a complex and dynamic notion. Unlike sex, which is for most people an un-chosen and un-changeable factor, gender is context and time-specific and changeable. Gender expectations vary between cultures and can change over time.[18] The report rightly emphasizes that it is of vital importance that individuals are not forced to identify themselves in terms of a singular aspect of their identity, such as being female, or of a particular ethnic, religious or linguistic background. Gender aspects, including possible stereotypes, are important factors informing the development of cultural identities of individuals as well as communities.

---

referred to in OHCHR commissioned report, *Gender Stereotyping as a Human Rights Violation* (2013) 8.

16 Cook and Cusack, ibid., 20; OHCHR, ibid., 9.

17 Holtmaat and Naber, note 5, 52; Schalkwyk, note 12, 1–2.

18 World Health Organisation, note 14, Introduction.

The Special Rapporteur rightly indicates in this report that many different factors inform the development of personal cultural identity. Cultural identity is not a simple, uniformly consisted entity given from birth. Cultural identity is not homogeneous; it is not created within bounded areas, but within spaces of interaction. According to the report, important factors include, for instance, 'values, beliefs, convictions, languages, knowledge and the arts, institutions and ways of life, but equally by other aspects of human life, such as professional training; economic, social and political engagements; urban or rural environments; wealth or poverty; or, more generally, the particular geographical, socio-economic and cultural context of a person's life' (para. 11). Indeed, personal cultural identities are made up of participation (or non-participation) in different (cultural) communities.

4. 'BY ATTRIBUTING SELF-PROPELLING AGENCY TO 'CULTURE' INDEPENDENT OF THE ACTIONS OF HUMAN BEINGS, IT DIVERTS ATTENTION FROM SPECIFIC ACTORS, INSTITUTIONS, RULES AND REGULATIONS, KEEPING WOMEN SUBORDINATED WITHIN PATRIARCHAL SYSTEMS AND STRUCTURES. IT ALSO RENDERS INVISIBLE WOMEN'S AGENCY IN BOTH REPRODUCING AND CHALLENGING DOMINANT CULTURAL NORMS AND VALUES.'

The report by the Special Rapporteur naturally pays a lot of attention to equality and non-discrimination. In paragraph 6 it is stated that the principle of non-discrimination has, according to some, attained the status of *jus cogens*.[19] Although equality and non-discrimination are recognized as crucial human rights principles and as such cut across the whole spectrum of human rights, it is more doubtful whether they are norms of *jus cogens*. Although some authors have strongly advocated for the

[19] Report of the Special Rapporteur in the field of cultural rights, para. 6, p. 5.

recognition of the prohibition of sex discrimination as *jus cogens*,[20] others have just as strongly expressed that currently it is not.[21]

Jus cogens is a norm 'accepted and recognized by the international community of States as a whole as a norm from which no derogation is permitted'.[22] Non-discrimination on the basis of race has indeed been accepted as a norm of *jus cogens*,[23] but it is more doubtful that non-discrimination on the basis of sex has also gained that status. It does not seem that the 'international community of States' has 'accepted and recognized' it as a norm from which no derogation is permitted. Although most States have formally outlawed discrimination on the basis of sex, there continues to exist widespread discrimination of women in many States. The fact is also that while almost all States have ratified the Convention on the Elimination of all Forms of Discrimination Against Women (CEDAW), many of them have filed reservations to this treaty precisely on issues related to sex equality and the equal enjoyment of rights by women and men.[24]

Some authors have rightly pointed at the necessity to take women's experiences more into account in the development of *jus cogens* norms, eventually leading to the recognition of sex discrimination as *jus cogens*.

---

[20] The report of the Special Rapporteur refers to Christine Chinkin, Marsha Freeman and Beate Rudolf (eds) *The UN Convention on the Elimination of All Forms of Discrimination Against Women: A Commentary* (Oxford: OUP 2012). See, also, Christine Chinkin, 'The Gender of *Jus Cogens*' (February 1993) 15(1) *Human Rights Quarterly* 63–76, 70; Bruno Simma and Philip Alston, 'The Sources of Human Rights Law: Custom, Jus Cogens and General Principles' (1992) 12 *Australian Yearbook of International Law* 82–94, 95.

[21] Alain Pellet, 'Comments in Response to Christine Chinkin and in Defense of Jus Cogens as the Best Bastion against the Excesses of Fragmentation' (2006) XI/II *Finnish Yearbook of International Law* 84–90, 85. He argues that:

> the condemnation of gender discrimination is still limited to certain parts of the world … which prevents it to be considered as 'a norm accepted and recognized by the international community of States as a whole as a whole as a norm from which no derogation is permitted'.

[22] Vienna Convention on the Law of Treaties, art. 53. Done at Vienna on 23 May 1969. Entered into force on 27 January 1980. United Nations, Treaty Series, vol. 1155, p. 331.

[23] Ian Brownlie, *Principles of Public International Law* (6th edn, Oxford: OUP 2003), 488–9.

[24] Yvonne Donders, 'Cultural Pluralism in International Human Rights Law: The Role of Reservations' in A. Vrdoljak (ed.) *The Cultural Dimension of Human Rights*, Collected Courses Volume, European University Institute (Oxford: OUP, 2013) 205–39.

An indication of this development is an advisory opinion by the Inter-American Court of Human Rights in which it held that 'at the existing stage of the development of international law, the fundamental principle of equality and non-discrimination has entered the realm of *jus cogens*'. In the same opinion it stated that the principles of equality and non-discrimination, without specifying the prohibited grounds, belong to *jus cogens* 'because the whole legal structure of national and international public order rests on it and it is a fundamental principle that permeates all laws'.[25] However, this is a non-binding advisory opinion and the court does not seem to have given this more concrete substance. It seems that the court has used the concept of *jus cogens* as a tool to make a choice between conflicting principles.[26] It may therefore be too early to consider non-discrimination on the basis of sex an accepted norm of *jus cogens*. This does however not diminish the importance of equality and non-discrimination as principles of human rights and binding treaty norms.

Cultural rights, by promoting and preserving cultural differences, have often been accused of being against the idea of equality. This statement is however based on an incomplete interpretation of the rights to equality and non-discrimination. The right to equality namely also means the right to be different and accordingly, respect for cultural differences can be fully in line with the principle of equality. This is because having equal rights is not the same as being treated equally. Indeed, equality and non-discrimination not only imply that equal situations should be treated equally, but also that unequal situations should be treated unequally. The Human Rights Committee (HRC) has underscored that 'the enjoyment of rights and freedoms on an equal footing ... does not mean identical treatment in every instance'.[27] Consequently, not all difference in treatment constitutes discrimination, as long as the criteria for differentiation are reasonable and objective and serve a legitimate aim.[28] Difference in

---

[25] IACtHR, Juridical Condition and Rights of the Undocumented Migrants, Advisory Opinion OC-18/03 of September 17 2003, Series A No.18, para. 101.

[26] Pellet, note 21, 88.

[27] Human Rights Committee, General Comment No. 18, Non-Discrimination, 10 November 1989, para. 8. The ECtHR has reaffirmed this in many cases, including the cases of *Thlimmenos v. Greece* Appl. No. 34369/97 6 April 2000, para. 44 and *D.H. and others v. the Czech Republic* Appl. No. 57325/00, 7 February 2006, para. 44.

[28] Legal doctrine generally distinguishes between differentiation, distinction and discrimination. Differentiation is difference in treatment that is lawful; distinction is a neutral term which is used when it has not yet been determined

treatment may also involve affirmative or positive action to remedy historical injustices, social discrimination or to create diversity and proportional group representation.[29] Accordingly, States may have to take special measures for individuals and cultural communities, such as minorities and indigenous peoples, to promote diversity.

The report by the Special Rapporteur validly addresses the different forms of discrimination – direct, indirect and structural – that may affect women. The report stresses that structural discrimination 'is the most difficult to bring to the surface and to combat' (para. 44). It is often structural discrimination that prevents women from participation in certain aspects of life, thereby sustaining their underrepresentation in politics, but also in culture, media and science. This problem exists not only in underdeveloped countries, but also in developed countries. For instance, the structural underrepresentation of women in science in a developed country can be well-illustrated by a survey concerning women participation in Dutch universities. The study highlights that, broadly speaking, the higher the scientific position in the academic hierarchy, the smaller the number of women. With every step on the academic ladder the number of women decreases. For instance, in 2014, about 53 per cent of the graduates were female. In the next step of an academic career, the PhD candidates, the percentage of women was lower than men (about 43

---

whether difference in treatment is lawful or not; and discrimination is difference in treatment that is arbitrary and unlawful. Consequently, only treatment that results in discrimination is prohibited. See M. Bossuyt, 'Prevention of Discrimination – The Concept and Practice of Affirmative Action' (17 June 2002 UN Doc. E/CN.4/Sub. 2/2002/21) para. 91, p. 20.

[29] See, also, art. 1(4) of the International Convention on the Elimination of Racial Discrimination, adopted by General Assembly resolution 2106 (XX) of 21 December 1965, entry into force on 4 January 1969:

> Special measures taken for the sole purpose of securing adequate advancement of certain racial or ethnic groups or individuals requiring such protection as may be necessary in order to ensure such groups or individuals equal enjoyment or exercise of human rights and fundamental freedoms shall not be deemed racial discrimination, provided, however, that such measures do not, as a consequence, lead to the maintenance of separate rights for different racial groups and that they shall not be continued after the objectives for which they were taken have been achieved.

The Human Rights Committee has further stated that the principle of equality under art. 26 ICCPR may sometimes require States parties to take affirmative action to diminish or eliminate conditions which cause or help to perpetuate discrimination prohibited by the ICCPR. Human Rights Committee, General Comment No. 18, Non-Discrimination, 10 November 1989, para. 10.

per cent). In every following functional step, the percentage of women decreased. One out of three assistant professors was female; one out of four associate professors and one out of six professors.[30]

In the report the Special Rapporteur notes that it is hard to find good data on women's participation and representation. There are, however, some interesting initiatives. EurActiv has analysed the participation of women in politics and concluded that in 2015 only 22 per cent of national parliamentarians worldwide are female. If we look at Europe specifically, the Nordic countries do rather well with 41 per cent, but the rest of Europe together does not do better than 23 per cent. As regards participation of women in decision-making in relation to culture, the Compendium on Cultural Policies and Trends in Europe is of good use for data of individual countries as well as good practices at national levels, albeit for European countries only.[31]

Underlying discrimination, in particular its structural form, is often based on persistent gender stereotypes and patterns in societies sustaining the subordinate position of women. There is a tendency to see gender as a purely *cultural* construction and consequently to 'blame culture for bad behaviour',[32] including the subordination or oppression of women.[33] As described above, gender may certainly be reaffirmed in cultural practices, beliefs and values in society, as well as in societal and cultural institutions and practices, such as legislation and government policies, education, the media, health care, housing, land ownership, etc.[34] Gender 'affects the distribution of resources, wealth, work, decision-making and political power, and enjoyment of rights and entitlements within the family as well as public life'.[35]

Whether this can all be blamed merely on culture is however questionable; it seems to be more complex. For instance, there is an important power element in the construction and reproduction of (unequal) gender

[30] 'Monitor Female Professors in The Netherlands' 2015, to be found at http://www.lnvh.nl/monitor2015/.

[31] The compendium is sponsored by the Council of Europe and can be found at: http://www.culturalpolicies.net/web/index.php.

[32] Leti Volpp, 'Blaming Culture for Bad Behaviour' (2000) 12 *Yale Journal of the Humanities* 89–115.

[33] Yvonne Rafferty, 'International Dimensions of Discrimination and Violence against Girls: A Human Rights Perspective' (January 2013) 14(1) *Journal of International Women's Studies* 1–23, 7–8.

[34] Holtmaat and Naber, note 5, 7–8, 52–3.

[35] '1999 World Survey on the Role of Women in Development' (United Nations New York 1999) ix as cited in Holtmaat and Naber, ibid., 53.

relations.[36] The topic of power or power relationships is addressed by the Special Rapporteur at several places in the report. Power is indeed also determinant in relation to cultures and cultural communities. It is broadly recognized, and the report notes it as well, that cultures are not static, homogeneous entities. They are dynamic and heterogeneous. Cultures are as much about products as they are about processes.[37] The question is, who are the initiators and who are the decision-makers in these processes? For instance, who decides what the cultural values and practices of a community are and which of these should be preserved or changed and how? Often such processes are not inclusive but decided by power elites, thereby sustaining existing power relations. The report also addresses the issue of communities and their representation (para. 36). It asks several crucial questions to be taken into account, including: which groups are recognized and who within these groups is accepted as the legitimate voice of the community, by States as well as the international community, and to be added, by the community itself and members of that community? Whose power is preserved and who is challenging practices and norms or existing power structures (para. 68)?

Indeed, as the Special Rapporteur notes in her report (para. 22), women are often not part of decision-making processes in relation to culture, education, religion or politics.[38] The UN working group on discrimination against women also confirmed that stereotypes of women's gender roles negatively affecting women's effective participation in political and public life persist around the world. Stereotypes of female inadequacy or less capability continue to be used as a basis for their marginalization and segregation in decision-making positions. While topics such as education, health care and social welfare are allocated to women, men are assigned to economic and defence affairs.[39] 'Women's full participation requires that women be integrated into positions with

---

[36] Bronwyn Winter, 'Religion, Culture and Women's Human Rights: Some General Political and Theoretical Considerations' (2006) 29 *Women's Studies International Forum* 381–96, 382; Yvonne Rafferty, note 33, 7–8.

[37] Winter, ibid., 382; Schalkwyk, note 12.

[38] Rafferty, note 33, 2; Winter, ibid., 383; Overseas Development Institute (ODI), Pilar Domingo, Rebecca Holmes, Tam O'Neil, Nicola Jones, Kate Bird, Anna Larson, Elizabeth Presler-Marshall and Craig Valters, *Women's Voice and Leadership in Decision-making – Assessing the Evidence* (April 2015) available at http://www.odi.org/sites/odi.org.uk/files/odi-assets/publications-opinion-files/9627.pdf.

[39] 'Report of the UN Working Group on the Issue of Discrimination against Women in Law and in Practice' (UN Doc. A/HRC/23/50 19 April 2013) para. 69.

decision-making power across the spectrum of issues dealt with by the institutions to which they have been elected or appointed.'[40]

It is important to emphasize that participation in decision-making is a right in itself, and also a right of women, but it is also a prerequisite for the enjoyment of other human rights, such as the right to take part in cultural life or freedom of religion, expression, movement or assembly. The Special Rapporteur rightly stresses in her report that representation of women at all levels of decision-making, in general affairs as well as specific cultural affairs, is a crucial step in strengthening their role in shaping and enjoying cultural rights (para. 37).

5. 'MANY PRACTICES AND NORMS THAT DISCRIMINATE AGAINST WOMEN ARE JUSTIFIED BY REFERENCE TO CULTURE, RELIGION AND TRADITION'

Although international human rights law aims to respect and promote cultural diversity, it should not be blind to the challenges posed by it. Culture may have negative effects as well. Culture can for instance be used as a justification for harmful practices that are in conflict with or limit the enjoyment of human rights. In general, it cannot be over-emphasized that respect for cultural diversity cannot be an argument to systematically or grossly deny international human rights law. In the UNESCO Convention on the Protection and Promotion of the Diversity of Cultural Expressions (2005, art. 2(1)) it is formulated as follows:

> cultural diversity can be protected and promoted only if human rights and fundamental freedoms … are guaranteed. No one may invoke the provisions of this Convention in order to infringe human rights and fundamental freedoms as enshrined in the Universal Declaration of Human Rights or guaranteed by international law, or to limit the scope thereof.

Cultural practices are very diverse, which makes it impossible but also undesirable to make general, abstract statements about their acceptability in relation to human rights. But it is important not to see cultural and religious practices as per se against women's rights, as if it is always a choice between one of the two. 'The struggle for women's human rights

---

[40] Ibid., para. 41.

is not *against* religion, culture, or tradition.'[41] The critical issue is to empower women to own their culture, religion and traditions, as well as to enjoy their human rights and take part in decision-making.[42]

The starting point is, as laid down in the Universal Declaration on Cultural Diversity (2001), that 'all persons have the right to ... conduct their own cultural practices, subject to respect for human rights and fundamental freedoms' (art. 5). In other words, cultural practices that are clearly in conflict with international human rights law cannot be justified as a reflection of cultural diversity and harmful practices affecting women and girls are not protected by cultural rights. Examples of such practices, as identified by the UN Committee on the Elimination of All Forms of Discrimination Against Women (CEDAW Committee) and the UN Committee on the Rights of the Child (CRC Committee), are FGM, child and/or forced marriage, polygamy and crimes committed in the name of so-called honour.[43]

While some practices thereby fall outside the scope of protection of cultural rights, others may fall within the scope of protection, but be prohibited or restricted under a legitimate limitation of cultural rights. Cultural rights, just as other human rights, cannot be enjoyed unlimitedly. The general framework of such limitations is outlined in article 29(2) UDHR, in which it is stated that:

> in the exercise of his rights and freedoms, everyone shall be subject to only such limitations as are determined by law solely for the purpose of securing due recognition and respect for the rights and freedoms of others and of meeting the just requirements of morality, public order and the general welfare in a democratic society.

Similar limitation clauses can be found in most human rights instruments. Sometimes they apply to the instrument as a whole, sometimes they are linked to a particular provision. These provisions allow States to limit the enjoyment of the right in question for reasons of morality,

---

41 Marsha Freeman, 'Article 16 and the Right to Practice Ones Beliefs', in Rikki Holtmaat and Ineke Boerefijn (eds) *Women's Human Rights and Culture/ Religion/Tradition: International Standards as Guidelines for the Discussion?* Proceedings of the Colloquium in the Peace Palace, The Hague 12 May 2009 (Utrecht: SIM Special nr. 32 2010) 63–65, 63, 64.

42 Ibid.; Bronwyn Winter, Denise Thompson and Sheila Jeffreys, 'The UN Approach to Harmful Traditional Practices' (2002) 4(1) *International Feminist Journal of Politics* 72–94.

43 Joint General Recommendation No. 31 General Comment No. 18, see note 2, section IV, pp. 6–9.

security, health, public order and the rights and freedoms of others. Cultural and religious particularities may well be part of these reasons. Such limitation measures are meant to prevent the unlimited exercise of cultural rights seriously endangering the rights of others or of society as a whole. For example, freedom of expression can be limited in that creative expressions should not harm the cultural life of society as a whole or of specific groups, such as children. The right to take part in cultural life can be limited in cases where cultural activities use or promote racist or discriminatory expressions.

In other words, States, including the legislator, executive and judiciary at all different levels, have an important role to play in promoting cultural diversity with respect for human rights, including weighing and balancing the different interests of different communities and individuals. They also have a role in *changing* harmful cultural practices. Harmful practices are often prohibited by law, but still they are practiced. Changes in cultural practices are most successful if they arise within the cultural community itself and are not imposed from outside, by law or by the State. But this does not relieve States from the responsibility of finding ways to promote such changes. Several treaties emphasize this role of the State in eradicating harmful cultural practices. The CEDAW, for example, states in article 5 that:

> States Parties shall take all appropriate measures: (a) To modify the social and cultural patterns of conduct of men and women, with a view to achieving the elimination of prejudices and customary and all other practices which are based on the idea of the inferiority or the superiority of either of the sexes or on stereotyped roles for men and women.[44]

The CRC contains in Article 24(3) that 'States Parties shall take all effective and appropriate measures with a view to abolishing traditional practices prejudicial to the health of children'.

---

[44] A similar provision can be found in art. 2(2) of the Protocol to the African Charter on Human and Peoples' Rights on the Rights of Women in Africa (2005):

> States Parties shall commit themselves to modify the social and cultural patterns of conduct of women and men … with a view to achieving the elimination of harmful cultural and traditional practices and all other practices which are based on the idea of the inferiority or the superiority of either of the sexes … .

See, also, Holtmaat and Naber, note 5.

Although 'traditional practices' are not defined, it can be inferred from the drafting documents that this provision was targeted against FGM.[45]

Several UN treaty-monitoring bodies have also emphasized the role of States in abandoning cultural practices that are against human rights. The CEDAW Committee has adopted a specific recommendation on female circumcision, urging States to eradicate this practice harmful to the health of women.[46] In its General Comment on the equal enjoyment of rights, the HRC has also stated that 'States Parties should ensure that traditional, historical, religious or cultural attitudes are not used to justify violations of women's rights to equality before the law and to equal enjoyment of all Covenant rights.'[47] It has also listed a number of harmful cultural practices as violations of human rights. It maintains that female infanticide, widow burning and dowry killings are violations of the right to life, that forced abortion, forced sterilization and FGM are violations of the right not to be subjected to inhumane and degrading treatment, and that forced male guardianship is a violation of the freedom of movement.[48]

More recently the CEDAW and CRC Committees have jointly adopted a General Recommendation on harmful practices.[49] In this document they have established the following criteria for the determination of harmful practices:

a) they constitute a denial of the dignity and/or integrity of the individual and a violation of the human rights and fundamental freedoms enshrined in the two Conventions;
b) they constitute discrimination against women or children and are harmful insofar as they result in negative consequences for them as individuals or groups, including physical, psychological, economic and social harm and/or violence and limitations on their capacity to participate fully in society or develop and reach their full potential;

---

45 Sonia Harris-Short, 'International Human Rights Law: Imperialist, Inept and Ineffective? Cultural Relativism and the UN Convention on the Rights of the Child' (February 2003) 25(1) *Human Rights Quarterly* 130–81, 136–7.

46 Committee on the Elimination of All Forms of Discrimination Against Women, General Recommendation No. 14, Female Circumcision, ninth session, 1990.

47 Human Rights Committee, General Comment No. 28, Equality of Rights Between Men and Women (art. 3) (UN Doc. CCPR/C/21/Rev.1/Add. 10 29 March 2000) para. 5.

48 Ibid., paras 10, 16.

49 Joint General Recommendation No. 31 General Comment No. 18, see note 2.

c) they are traditional, re-emerging or emerging practices that are prescribed and/or kept in place by social norms that perpetuate male dominance and inequality of women and children, on the basis of sex, gender, age and other intersecting factors; and
d) they are imposed on women and children by family members, community members or society at large, regardless of whether the victim provides, or is able to provide, full, free and informed consent.[50]

Several practices are specifically labelled as harmful, including FGM, child and/or forced marriage, polygamy and crimes committed in the name of honour.[51] The CEDAW and CRC Committees further advocate a holistic approach to eradicate such practices, including data collection and monitoring, legislation and enforcement, prevention and protection and response.[52] Such a holistic approach requires mainstreaming and coordination vertically and horizontally. 'Horizontal coordination requires organization across sectors, including education, health, justice, social welfare, law enforcement, immigration and asylum and communications and media. Similarly, vertical coordination requires organization between actors at the local, regional and national levels and with traditional and religious authorities.'[53] Women are certainly actors and stakeholders who should be part of this process.

UN treaty bodies further systematically encourage States to promote changes in harmful cultural practices in their dialogue with States under the periodic reporting procedure. Studies have shown that States during this dialogue often – at least formally – agree on the harmfulness or unacceptability of such practices, which is why they are prohibited by law. These States point out, however, that changing the deeply-rooted cultural convictions of certain communities is difficult and requires time and patience. Formal legislation prohibiting harmful practices and culturally motivated violence is not sufficient to eliminate the practice altogether.[54] What becomes clear is that the adoption of laws prohibiting harmful cultural practices may be necessary, but that it is not the only

---

50 Ibid., para. 16.
51 Ibid., paras 19–30.
52 Ibid., s. VII.
53 Ibid., para. 34.
54 Harris-Short, note 45, 140–45, 164; Michael Ado, 'Practice of United Nations Human Rights Treaty Bodies in the Reconciliation of Cultural Diversity with Universal Respect for Human Rights'(August 2010) 32(3) *Human Rights Quarterly* 624–5, 631–5.

and not always the most effective way to get rid of them: a holistic approach including education and awareness raising is needed.[55]

What is the role or responsibility of cultural communities themselves in this regard? How should cultural communities protect and promote their collective interest as well as the rights of their individual members? Cultural communities are important for individuals, but at the same time it is necessary to stress that individuals should remain autonomous and free to develop their own cultural identity. Cultural communities may have a certain amount of freedom to arrange their internal structure and institutions and they may also put limited pressure on their members to follow the cultural norms of the community. However, cultural communities should always guarantee and respect the rights and freedoms of their individual members. They should not only refrain from cruel, inhuman and degrading treatment of their members, but communities should also respect the right of their members to take part in the decision-making processes that determine and develop the community's cultural life. Moreover, the community should be based on non-coercive membership and respect the individual's right and freedom to leave the community. In order to be able to make informed choices about membership and participation in the community, communities should also respect the rights of their members to participate in society at large, e.g. through education, expression, information, election processes and labour.[56] Or as the report by the Special Rapporteur notes: 'To enjoy equal cultural rights, women must become equal participants and decision makers in all the cultural affairs of their own specific communities, and in the wider 'general' society.' (para. 37)

---

[55] Joint General Recommendation No. 31 /General Comment No. 18, see note 2, section VII, pp. 10–22; Winter, Thompson and Jeffreys, note 42, 72–94.

[56] Ado, note 54, 624–5; Brems, note 10, 18; Brems in Sajo (ed.), note 10, 227, 229; Yvonne Donders, *Towards a Right to Cultural Identity?* (Antwerp Intersentia 2002) 103–5, 338; Laura Reidel, 'What are Cultural Rights? Protecting Groups with Individual Rights' (2010) 9(1) *Journal of Human Rights* 70–74, 78; Leighton McDonald 'Can Collective Rights and Individual Rights Coexist?' (1998) 22 *Melbourne University Law Review* 372; Ch. Kukathas 'Are there any Cultural Rights?' (February 1992) 20 *Political Theory* 117, 128, 133–4.

6. RECOMMENDATIONS AND CONCLUDING REMARKS

This report by the Special Rapporteur is a well-elaborated and very comprehensive document on cultural rights and women, addressing issues of gender, discrimination and harmful practices, but also stressing the importance of culture for women. It provides an important contribution to the discussion on these issues by not painting a mere negative picture of the relationship between cultural rights and women, but by emphasizing the importance of cultural rights to empower women and to transform cultures. Of course, there are still many obstacles to tackle, including systemic discrimination of women and gender stereotypes of (the role of) women that underlie their subordinate position or cultural practices harmful to their health and dignity. Women in many parts of the world do not enjoy their human rights, including their cultural rights. The Special Rapporteur emphasizes in her report that cultural rights can be empowering and transformative rights. They should also be participatory rights, giving women the opportunity to fully participate and contribute to cultures and decision-making processes. The report ends with a large set of recommendations that cover a wide range of issues. While this does indeed reflect the broadness and complexity of the issues described in the report, it may also overwhelm States and other stakeholders which may not see the forest for the trees. The reports of the Special Rapporteur are, however, not meant as mere checklists for compliance with human rights treaties, but as helpful tools for States and other stakeholders to better understand and implement cultural rights. It may in that regard perhaps be interesting to add in future reports an analysis of other vulnerable groups. Indigenous peoples, minorities and migrants would perhaps be 'usual suspects' for a report on cultural rights. These groups however have specific instruments on their rights and have their own mandate holders.[57] This is also true for people with disabilities.[58] One group that comes to mind that may be interesting in relation to cultural rights are children. The CRC includes many cultural rights and children

[57] UN Declaration on the Rights of Persons Belonging to National or Ethnic, Religious and Linguistic Minorities (1992) and the Special Rapporteur on Minority Issues; UN Declaration on the Rights of Indigenous Peoples (2007) and the Special Rapporteur on Indigenous Peoples.

[58] Convention on the Rights of Persons with Disabilities (2006), and Special Rapporteur on Persons with Disabilities.

are important stakeholders in culture.[59] Perhaps a future report could deal with our future generations and their cultural rights.

[59] There is a Special Rapporteur on the sale of children, child prostitution and child pornography, but not on the full spectrum of children's rights.

6. The right to freedom of expression and creativity – Report 2013 (A/HRC/23/34)

Shahira Amin

Special Rapporteur Farida Shaheed's report on cultural rights addresses the different ways the right of freedom has been curtailed, stifling artistic expression and creativity and silencing artists. She cites the motives for the restrictions as often being 'religious, political, cultural or moral or economic interests – or all combined'.

In Egypt's case, this is certainly true: in the past year, we have seen the space for artistic expression and creativity – and freedom of expression in general – shrink dramatically in the name of either 'public morality', 'religion' or 'national security'. Journalists, bloggers, artists and photographers have been imprisoned for no crime other than their work although the charges against them are often 'terrorism related'. They are often falsely accused of having links to the outlawed Muslim Brotherhood or spreading lies to harm the state. This is a dangerous precedent as in the restrictive climate, the fear that dissipated during the 18-day uprising in 2011 has been reinstated, forcing many artists to practice self-censorship or stop working altogether. Artists face heavy censorship of their work but also risk detention, threats on their lives, and sometimes – in the mass hysteria and nationalistic fervour sweeping the country – they also face mob assaults (by citizens who perceive themselves as more 'patriotic') or accusations of treason and espionage.

The examples are many. Let me cite a few: 27-year-old Shawkan Zeid, a young photographer has spent more than two years behind bars since his arrest in August 2013 as he took pictures of pro-Muslim Brotherhood protests and their violent dispersal by security forces. He has been accused of weapons' possession (when his only weapon was his camera), illegal assembly, murder and attempted murder and his detention has been repeatedly extended by the Public Prosecutor. He has contracted Hepatitis C in prison and his health is deteriorating. His lengthy detention is in violation of the Constitution which guarantees freedom of artistic expression and which limits pretrial detention to two years.

Esraa El Taweel, another young photographer, has also been detained without charge since early June. She was one of several hundred citizens who have 'forcibly disappeared' in recent months, but was found two weeks later at a detention facility operated by security forces where she was held for 16 days for interrogation. Her detention has been extended several times. She is unable to walk without a crutch after having been shot in the leg by security forces while taking pictures at a Muslim Brotherhood protest. It is not just photographers who suffer such a fate, in the summer of 2014, 19-year-old cartoonist and graffiti artist Hisham Rizk disappeared for a week. His body was found in a Cairo morgue and according to an autopsy report, the cause of death was 'drowning in the Nile'.

More recently, two belly-dancers were sentenced to six months in prison each for a music video posted on YouTube, deemed 'too sexy' by critics. They were charged with 'debauchery and promoting immorality'. This is shocking and comes hot on the heels of the banning of 'raunchy' music videos from Egyptian TV channels (because the performers show too much skin or the lyrics express sexual connotations).

This is a classic example of state censorship with combined 'political, religious and economic interests' motives. President Abdel Fattah El Sisi who was Defence Minister under the ousted Muslim Brotherhood Government and who is now President has been perceived by many as the 'saviour or guardian of the revolution'. Millions of Egyptians took to the streets to topple the Islamist regime for fear that the Muslim Brotherhood would try to impose strict Islamic values and alter Egypt's 'moderate' nature. The 'secular' government now in place has been trying to woo the radical Salafis to get their votes in the legislative election. It has also been trying to appease Saudi Arabia and other Gulf states that have generously donated money to help shore up the ailing Egyptian economy since Sisi came to power. Saudi Arabia has been exporting Wahhabism, a stricter or more rigid form of Islam to Egypt for decades. This started with the Gulf oil boom in the 1970s when millions of Egyptians moved to the Gulf seeking better livelihoods and returned home with new, hitherto alien traditions such as the face veil or burka and other stances.

Last month while on a visit to Sweden, I received a call from Ramy Essam, known as 'the Singer of Tahrir Square'. He gained popularity among the Tahrir activists during the 18-day uprising with his 'revolutionary' songs and anti-regime lyrics, some of them composed and written on the spot in Tahrir Square. One of the songs *Irhal* or *Leave* became the anthem of the revolution. In 2011, it was selected by *Time*

Out as the third most world-changing song of all time. In March 2011, just a few short weeks after Mubarak had stepped down, Essam was arrested by soldiers and tortured by the military. In October 2014, he moved to Sweden at the invitation of the Malmo Municipality, which gave him a residence permit for two years. He is studying music there and was happy to share the news with me of the release of his new album.

The restrictive climate in Egypt, post revolution has forced many young artists to leave the country. Those who have been unable to leave are either behind bars or have had their work censored and been forced into silence.

In June 2013, Egyptian author Karam Saber was sentenced to five years in prison for his book – a collection of short stories – titled 'Where is God?' The court found his writings insulted religion, the first case of blasphemy following the 2011 Revolution.

The prosecution of writers and artists sends a chilling message to others and can only serve to further stifle artistic expression and creativity. The underlying motivation in many of these cases is political, aimed at crushing dissent and allowing only the official narrative. Karam's case signals the return of Hesbah, which basically means that any citizen can file a legal complaint against another citizen seen as violating Islamic morals even if the work does not harm the person directly.

In the Report's recommendations, the Special Rapporteur encourages states to review their legislation and practices imposing restrictions on freedom of artistic expression taking into consideration their obligation to respect, protect and fulfil this right. In Egypt's case, it is not the legislation as there are laws in place that protect and guarantee freedom of artistic expression, it is rather the huge gap that exists between constitutional protection for expression and the reality as faced by Egypt's artists on the ground. The 2011 Revolution had raised hopes for increased freedom of expression for decades constrained by strict censorship, but a culture of repression still prevails today. Art that addresses politics, religion and sex continues to be censored in the name of protecting public order, morals and state interests. The new Constitution passed with overwhelming support in early 2014 states that 'public morals, ethics, traditions, customs, values, culture and heritage determine society's evolution and guarantee the rights and liberties of all individuals'. The reality however, is different. The effects of censorship on the arts and the unjustified restrictions on artistic expression are stifling artists. The General Directorate for the Censorship of Artistic Works continues to censor artists, restricting film makers by either cutting scenes from their films, changing titles and even banning films altogether. Al Azhar, the oldest Islamic institution is often consulted by the directorate and has a final say on the works of art – whether films, drama serials or books.

Musicians too have been asked to submit the lyrics of their songs for review and approval before performances at the Sawy Cultural Wheel, a venue that is meant to promote art and culture but which has instead been censoring musicians and artists.

Last but not least, the wall of the American University in Cairo's Science Building on Mohamed Mahmoud Street in downtown Cairo – one of the last symbolic emblems of the Revolution – is being pulled down. This wall depicts revolutionary slogans and murals painted by the graffiti artists – many of them women – after the fall of Mubarak. Under Mubarak, graffiti was illegal but after he stepped down, there was an outburst of creativity with the then little-known artists joining the new movement to paint their revolutionary murals and messages for the public to see. These included Bahia's collection of Nos, rejecting sexual harassment and gender-based violence to oppression and dictatorship as well as artist Ganzeer's work touching on the themes of civic responsibility and social justice. Now both these artists have taken their work outside the country because of the restrictive atmosphere and the high risks involved.

What is happening in Egypt is a classic example of challenges to freedom of expression where a repressive regime attempts to block, limit and inhibit journalists, bloggers, artists and writers – indeed, an entire population in an effort to crush dissent. We all know how important freedom of expression is: not only is it a fundamental human right, it also underpins most other rights, allowing them to flourish. The right to express oneself freely on important issues in society whether through art, drama, film or writing, plays a vital role in the healthy development of any society. And here I quote Amartya Sen from his book *Development as Freedom* in which he argues that 'expansion of freedom is both the primary end and principal means of development'.[1]

In Egypt, where cultural and religious customs are often used to clamp down on artists' rights to free expression, basic human rights are undermined in the process. Access to freedom of expression is made all the more difficult by the rampant poverty, the high illiteracy rate (estimated at over 25.5 per cent of the population) and inadequate

[1] https://www.cmi.no/publications/file/953-a-balanced-view-of-development-as-freedom

education (affecting women and girls the most because of the high level of poverty among women in particular and because women make up the majority of those who are illiterate). Poverty and discrimination stop people participating fully in society, hindering their ability to read, write and fully engage. This is why it is important not only to amend laws that restrict freedom of artistic expression and creativity, but it is also vital to tackle other barriers such as poverty, discrimination (whether it is against religious /ethnic minorities or women or both) and fear – all of which choke creativity.

Besides the big challenges mentioned above, there are also other obstacles such as lack of encouragement, negative feedback or even worse, no feedback at all. We all know that creative people thrive on having others impacted by their work but when a cartoonist is labelled a 'traitor' by the public for depicting President Sisi in his caricature, this will deter him/her from continuing the work.

Egypt is a diverse society with many different social groups of varying ideologies. This is fertile ground for creativity but the lack of acceptance of anything new or different is another deterrent. Children should be taught at a young age to accept and respect different views and ideas. This is a society where sadly, too often, new ideas are not welcome.

I end with the quote from Einstein who said, 'Everybody is a genius but if you judge a fish by its ability to climb a tree, it will live its whole life believing that it is stupid.'[2] Artists need to feel comfortable in their role and not live in a constant state of creativity-crushing panic. With the right circumstances, training, encouragement and feedback for their work but most important, the freedom to express themselves, they can flourish and better themselves while enriching their society.

2 https://www.quora.com/What-did-Albert-Einstein-mean-when-he-said-Everybody-is-a-genius-But-if-you-judge-a-fish-by-its-ability-to-climb-a-tree-it-will-live-its-whole-life-believing-that-it-is-stupid

7. Corporate interests and artistic voices: the *Plesner* case

Stina Teilmann-Lock

Among the motivations for imposing restrictions on, or creating obstacles for the freedom of artistic expression and creativity, the Special Rapporteur in the field of cultural rights, Farida Shaheed, lists in her Report a number of political and ideological factors. As she points out, in the past, as today, artists have typically been censored for the sake of suppressing political dissent in the context of, notably, 'the quest for nation-building and pursuit of hegemonic policies'.[1] Thus, criticism of governments and unpatriotic expression continues to be banned in numerous states around the world. Furthermore, there is a long history of the outlawing of blasphemous or immoral expression. Blasphemy laws that prohibit art that does not 'show respect' for a religion are to be found in many countries, with a stifling impact on freedom of artistic expression. These laws (and others regarding nudity and questions of gender) are often enforced by popular opinion; violence and threats of violence lead cultural institutions (and even artists) to avoid controversial topics and abstain from presenting works that might provoke protest and controversy.

INTELLECTUAL PROPERTY LAW AND THE FREEDOM OF EXPRESSION

Yet another – and sometimes overlooked – motivation that Shaheed identifies is the 'protection of corporate interests'.[2] There is a desire to silence criticism of corporate activities by artists, and to protect a specific

[1] United Nations Human Rights Council (2013), Report of the Special Rapporteur in the Field of Cultural Rights, Farida Shaheed, 'The Right to Freedom of Artistic Expression and Creativity', A/HRC/23/34, 10.

[2] Ibid., 11.

logo or brand from mockery or parodic use.[3] Indeed in a world where branding has become a major generator of cultural significance[4] there is likely to be a conflict of interest between corporations that aim to control the meanings associated with their brands and artists who aim to critique the cultural significance of such brands.[5] In disputes of this type corporations have been seen to invoke their intellectual property rights as a means to curb artistic expression of which they disapprove on economic grounds.

One such clash between a corporation and an artist is mentioned by Shaheed (in a footnote), that of *Nadia Plesner* v. *Louis Vuitton*.[6] This case was the result of a controversy involving the Danish-born Nadia Plesner, a visual artist, and the holders of the right to use the luxury brand 'Louis Vuitton'. The case is an example of how legislation – whose intended purpose was obviously not to impose censorship – can turn out to be one of the 'multi-faceted ways in which the right to the freedom indispensable for artistic expression and creativity may be curtailed'.[7] Intellectual property law is designed to protect the rights of creators and innovators so as to stimulate investments in commerce and arts that will be beneficial to society. However, the way in which intellectual property rights are enforced may, in effect, transform them into an instrument of censorship to be invoked by corporations or other private actors.[8]

In recent years a series of intellectual property infringement cases (especially copyright) have been heard by various national and supranational courts over the issue of how to weigh the freedom of expression – in particular the freedom of artistic expression – against the protection of the exclusive rights of intellectual property owners.[9] Traditionally, copyright and other intellectual property rights have not been seen as a problem for the exercise of freedom of expression; the consensus has been that intellectual property rights may sometimes afford a legitimate

---

3 Ibid., 12.

4 Lury 2011.

5 See Klein, 2000 and Coombe, 1998.

6 *Nadia Plesner Joensen* v. *Louis Vuitton Malletier SA*, Case number 389526/KG ZA 11-284, Court of The Hague, 4 May 2011.

7 Supra n. 1, 1.

8 See also United Nations Human Rights Council (2014); United Nations General Assembly (2015) and Geiger, 2016.

9 Torreman, 2008.

exception to the wider principle of freedom of expression.[10] Moreover, there is case law in which it has been maintained that there are limitations and constraints built in to the definitions of intellectual property law that already serve to protect the space for freedom of expression.[11]

However, the traditional stance has been challenged recently. Courts have started to address and reappraise the legal frameworks which have given rise to potential conflicts between intellectual property rights and freedom of expression.[12] In order to understand the implications of such legal activity for the freedom of artistic expression, and for creativity, it is worth studying in detail the *Plesner* case to which Shaheed draws our attention.

THE *PLESNER* CASES

The 2011 legal case that involved Nadia Plesner, who was then residing in the Netherlands, was brought by the fashion house Louis Vuitton and heard by the District Court of The Hague. The court's verdict found in favour of the plaintiff and prohibited Plesner's use of Louis Vuitton's protected designs. A few months later, when Plesner counter-sued, the Court of The Hague ruled in favour of Plesner. The latter ruling by the Court of The Hague has become fundamental to the question of balancing intellectual property rights and the freedom of artistic expression. Controversy between Plesner and Louis Vuitton had begun some years earlier. In 2007, bedridden after an accident, Plesner had been appalled by the juxtaposition, in a newspaper, of a small notice about the humanitarian crisis in Darfur and a full-page story about the escapades of the celebrity Paris Hilton. As she related in court, this lack of proportion in the mass media incited her to find some artistic expression to communicate its absurdity. Figuring that 'wearing designer bags and small dogs dressed in pink apparently is enough to get you in the news, maybe it is worth a try for people who actually deserve and need

[10] See e.g. the European Human Rights Convention, art. 10(2) which states that the exercise of the freedom of expression may be subject to restrictions necessary for the protection of the 'rights of others'.

[11] See for example the ruling of the United States Supreme Court *Harper & Row Publishers, Inc* v. *Nation Enterprises*, 471 U.S. 539 (1985) where it was stated that: 'the Framers intended copyright itself to be the engine of free expression.' See also the case *Eldred* v. *Ashcroft*, 537 U.S. 186 (2003).

[12] For a recent overview of legal developments and debates see Lee, 2015.

attention'[13] she got the idea for the 'Simple Living' work. 'Simple Living' is a depiction of the artist's vision in the shape of a drawing of a starving boy in Darfur with nothing on except two particular attributes associated with Paris Hilton: a designer hand-bag and a Chihuahua dog. As to the artistic intention of the drawing, Nadia Plesner explained to the court:

> I mixed the cruel reality with showbiz elements in *Simple Living* and had the drawing printed on T-shirts and posters, which I sold to raise money for the organisation *Divest for Darfur*. I was hoping that the drawing would raise awareness about Darfur and start a debate about mass media language and the sometimes distorted relationship between small and big world news.[14]

In 2008, the T-shirts and posters with the 'Simple Living' motif that Plesner was selling came to the attention of Louis Vuitton. The fashion house contacted the artist to demand financial compensation, claiming that the image was an infringement of the copyright and trademark rights in their bag labelled 'Audra'. There is no doubt that the designer bag carried by the boy on Plesner's drawing is very similar to Louis Vuitton's Audra bag, though there is one difference: on the bag drawn by Plesner the V of the LV-logo on Louis Vuitton's bag had been replaced by an S (for 'simple'). Following an *ex parte* order by a French court,[15] in 2008, Nadia Plesner thought it wise to stop the sale of the T-shirts.

Even so, at this point Plesner launched another 'Simple Living' art project. In Simple Living, part 2, she included the boy with the handbag and the Chihuahua in an oil on canvas painting. Her legal counsellor had advised her that working in such a traditional artistic medium would make her legal position against Louis Vuitton safer.[16] This resulted in the oil painting 'Darfurnica', the title being a calque on Picasso's celebrated oil painting 'Guernica' wherein Picasso protested against the bombing of the Basque village of Guernica in 1937. Plesner's 'Darfurnica', at 32 square metres exceeding even the monumental dimensions of 'Guernica', replicates many of its motifs and compositional elements. Plesner's work was completed in 2010 and was shown at an exhibition in Copenhagen in 2011. By this time the District Court of The Hague had accepted Louis Vuitton's claim that 'Darfurnica' also constituted an infringement of Louis Vuitton's rights; included in 'Darfurnica' is part of the 'Multicolor

13 Plesner, undated.
14 Ibid.
15 Tribunal de Grande Instance de Paris, 25 May 2008.
16 *Supra* n. 13.

Canvas Design' that makes the decoration of the Audra bag, and that had been legally registered as a design. On 27 January 2011 the court had issued an *ex parte* injunction against Nadia Plesner and the Copenhagen gallery where Darfurnica was exhibited, prohibiting the use of Louis Vuitton's registered design in the painting. However, as mentioned, Nadia Plesner counter-sued with the result that the Court of The Hague, in a judgment of 4 May 2011, quashed the order of 27 January retroactively. This judgment and its reasoning have come to set a precedent for subsequent cases where intellectual property rights have come into conflict with freedom of expression and artistic creativity.

COURT OF THE HAGUE RULING

The fashion house Louis Vuitton complained that Nadia Plesner had once again in her painting made use of the Audra bag; in particular Plesner had included it in the Darfurnica painting as well as on T-shirts and posters. Furthermore, as Louis Vuitton pointed out, the boy with the bag had been used as an 'eye-catcher' for the art exhibition where works by Plesner were on sale. As Louis Vuitton had not permitted this use they claimed that it infringed their design right; they accordingly requested that Plesner cease and desist the use of the design.

In her explanation to the court Nadia Plesner pointed out that she had used the picture of the handbag because she 'wished to draw attention to the poignant difference between luxury and affluence on the one hand, and poverty and famine in Darfur on the other hand'.[17] She had been successful in achieving this goal insofar as her art had contributed to raising awareness in the media about the situation in Darfur. Moreover, the 'Simple Living' picture had also been effective in establishing Plesner's reputation as an artist.

In their claims, both parties, Louis Vuitton as well as Nadia Plesner, were relying on rights set out in the European Convention on Human Rights. Plesner maintained that she was entitled to use the picture of the bag on the basis of article 10 of Convention, which defines the right to freedom of expression, while Louis Vuitton invoked article 1 of the first protocol of the Convention, which relates to the protection of property

---

17 *Nadia Plesner Joensen* v. *Louis Vuitton Malletier SA*, *Nadia Plesner Joensen* v. *Louis Vuitton Malletier SA*, Case number 389526/KG ZA 11-284, Court of The Hague, 4 May 2011, at 2.3. English translation by, Kennedy Van der Laan attorneys in Amsterdam, the firm that represented Nadia Plesner, is available at www.nadiaplesner.com.

rights including intellectual property rights. Thus as the Court of The Hague spelled out in its verdict, the case concerned 'rights that are on an equal footing but conflicting' and therefore 'a fair balance should be sought between the general interest and the interests of the parties involved'.[18] The court noted that Louis Vuitton had a 'right to peaceful enjoyment of its exclusive right of the design'.[19] Yet contradicting this fundamental right, Nadia Plesner, as an artist, had a fundamental right that was even weightier. Thus the court stated:

> There is, according to established case law of the European Court of Human Rights, the fundamental right of Plesner that is high in a democratic society's priority list to express her opinion through her art. In this respect it applies that artists enjoy a considerable protection with regard to their artistic freedom, in which, in principle, art may 'offend, shock or disturb' (cf. European Court of Human Rights 25 January 2007, RvdW 2007, 452 *Vereinigung Bildender Künstler* v. *Austria* [...]). In this respect it is furthermore important that the use by Plesner is to be regarded for the time being as functional and proportional and that it does not serve a mere commercial purpose. Under preliminary judgment it is plausible that Plesner's intention with '*Simple Living*' is not (or was not) to free ride with Louis Vuitton's reputation in a commercial sense. She rather uses Louis Vuitton's reputation to pass on her society-critical message.[20]

The court then went on to say that, in Plesner's use of the picture of the handbag, there was nothing that could suggest or imply that Louis Vuitton was in any way involved in the humanitarian crisis in Darfur. And it was emphasised that Louis Vuitton in its use of celebrities for advertising had exposed itself to this sort of conflict:

> The circumstance that Louis Vuitton is a very well-known company, the products of which enjoy a considerable reputation, which it also stimulates through advertising [with] famous people, moreover implies that Louis Vuitton must accept critical use [such] as the present one to a stronger degree than other right-holders.[21]

On this basis the Court of The Hague ruled against Louis Vuitton, ordering the firm to pay the costs of the proceedings. In this way Plesner's use of the illustration 'Simple Living' on the painting Darfurnica and on promotion material was found to be a lawful statement of her

---

[18] Ibid., at 4.3.
[19] Ibid., at 4.8.
[20] Ibid., at 4.8.
[21] Ibid.

artistic opinion and we may add a lawful expression of her artistic creativity. The use of the boy with the handbag as an eye-catcher for an exhibition in which Plesner's works were for sale was justified by the fact that the motif occupied a central position in Plesner's artistic œuvre.

CORPORATE INTERESTS AND ARTISTIC VOICES

Plesner's use of the picture of Louis Vuitton's Audra handbag was first banned with reference to the exclusive right of Louis Vuitton to the 'peaceful use' of their registered design. No discrimination was made by the court between the use of the design for artistic expression and any other purposes or types of use of the design. However, in the judgment of 4 May 2011 such a distinction was made: artistic use of intellectual property was to be treated quite separately from any other uses, even when the artistic use had an element of commercial value as in the poster for the exhibition. As the court argued, it is of the greatest importance in a democratic society that artistic freedom should be preserved, and accordingly that artists should be enabled to contribute to social debates, and not prevented by the law from so doing; artistic expression is therefore comprehended as within the interests of society, and these therefore outweigh the interests of individual right-holders. In this way the judgment confirmed that where there is a type of cultural significance attached to brands and other forms of intellectual property to which protection may be given, it is precisely there that such protection may be limited, suspended or abrogated in the interests of cultural critique and artistic expression.

The *Plesner* case illustrates the potential of a branch of law, which was never intended to serve as an instrument of censorship, to be transformed into such by conflicts of interests arising between different sets of actors, neither set representing the state. Where such transformation or distortion has occurred, or is threatened, it is the obligation of the state through its courts of law courts to prevent censorship by recognizing that rights may seem absolute or 'exclusive' but that there is a hierarchy, and that within a democracy the right to freedom of expression is possibly a superior right to that of intellectual property. The right to freedom of expression is reckoned by the state to be fundamental to the interests of society, whereas the right to intellectual property is of benefit mainly to its holders. The *Plesner* judgment creates a precedent in asserting that the courts must adjudicate between conflicting rights not only in terms of plaintiff and defendant as individuals but in accordance with the value of each right to society as a whole.

BIBLIOGRAPHY

Coombe, Rosemary (1998), *The Cultural Life of Intellectual Properties: Authorship, Appropriation, and the Law*, Durham NC: Duke University Press.

Geiger, Christophe (ed.) (2016), *Intellectual Property and Access to Science and Culture: Convergence or* Conflict? CEIPI/ICTSD Publications Series, Issue 3, Strasbourg.

Klein, Naomi (2000), *No Logo: Taking Aim at the Brand Bullies*, Toronto: Knopf.

Lee, Yin Harn (2015) 'Copyright and Freedom of Expression: A Literature Review', CREATe Working Paper 2015/04 https://zenodo.org/record/18132/files/CREATe-Working-Paper-2015-04.pdf, accessed on 10 January 2017.

Lury, Celia (2011), *Consumer Culture*, 2nd ed., Cambridge: Polity Press.

Plesner, Nadia (undated) 'Simple Living and Dafurnica' http://www.nadiaplesner.com/simple-living–darfurnica1 accessed on 10 January 2017.

Torreman, Paul (ed.) (2008), *Intellectual Property and Human Rights*, Alphen an den Rijn: Kluwer Law International.

United Nations Human Rights Council (2013), 'Report of the Special Rapporteur in the Field of Cultural Rights, Farida Shaheed, 'The Right to Freedom of Artistic Expression and Creativity', A/HRC/23/34.

United Nations Human Rights Council (2014), Report of the Special Rapporteur in the Field of Cultural Rights, Farida Shaheed, 'Copyright Policy and the Right to Science and Culture', A/HRC/28/57.

United Nations General Assembly (2015), Report of the Special Rapporteur in the Field of Cultural Rights, Patent Policy and the Right to Science and Culture, A/70/279.

8. History, memory and memorialization processes[1] – Reports 2013–2014 (A/68/296, 2013 and A/HRC/25/49, 2014)

Hanne Hagtvedt Vik

Travelling the world in her capacity as United Nations Special Rapporteur in the field of cultural rights, Farida Shaheed frequently witnessed intense disagreement over events of the past. Although history is one of the few mandatory curriculum subjects in education systems the world over,[2] Shaheed's work nevertheless convinced her that, in most societies, people cannot access historical narratives and cultural heritage in a way that fosters critical thinking and the understanding of alternative realities and perspectives.[3] Historical research and its presentation to a popular audience are 'about identity, about who we are and where we came from', Richard J Evans argues.[4] We are living through a 'memory boom': David Lowenthal has noted that the past, 'once certified by experts and reliant on written texts, has become a fragmented, contested history

[1] I would like to thank the editors of this volume for their suggestions on how to improve the manuscript, and the participants of the 2015 Copenhagen conference that led to this collection for comments on an earlier version of this chapter. I also thank Maja Gudim Burheim and Marte Heian-Engdal for their guidance in fields they know much better than I; Lotte Hughes, Elisabeth Teige and the members of the University of Oslo Research Group on Contemporary History for helpful comments; and Maria Merkling for superb editorial work.

[2] General Assembly, UNGA A/68/296, 9 August 2013, Report of the Special Rapporteur in the field of cultural rights Farida Shaheed, 'Writing and Teaching of History', para. 2, p. 4 (hereafter *History*).

[3] Intervention by Farida Shaheed at the conference 'Negotiating cultural rights' in Copenhagen, 15 November 2015. See also *History*, para. 2, p. 4.

[4] Richard J. Evans, 'Prologue: What is History? – Now' in David Cannadine (ed.), *What is History Now?* (New York: Palgrave Macmillan, 2002).

forged by us all'.[5] The power of historical narratives to shape identities, arouse emotions and motivate and legitimate political action are a source of both inspiration and worry for states, groups and individuals and therefore also for international organizations like the UN. How should the past be researched, taught and remembered? The past is a battlefield. George Orwell famously posited that 'who controls the past controls the future: who controls the present controls the past'.[6] Interpretations and distortions of history are potent political tools; states and non-state actors alike try to impose particular versions on their own and other populations. Narratives of the past are important legitimizers of political and social structures; they carry the power of suppression and may even pave the way for violence and war. The genocides in Rwanda and Bosnia of the 1990s are dramatic examples of situations where violence was 'buttressed and to some degree caused by particularly hateful national memories and interpretations of history'.[7]

Shaheed's reports 'Writing and Teaching of History' (2013 – hereafter *History*) and 'Memorialization Processes'[8] (2014, hereafter *Memorialization*) stand on the observation that international human rights treaties proclaim the right of all humans to their cultural heritage, and that this includes knowing the past.[9] But to *which* cultural heritage and history does that right pertain? And what would characterize truly human rights-based approaches to the past? The reports deal primarily with post-conflict and divided societies but have relevance for all. They offer

---

[5] Quote from web page referring to the new edition of David Lowenthal's 1984 book *The Past is a Foreign Country,* at <http://www.geog.ucl.ac.uk/about-the-department/news/news-archive-2013/april-2013/david-lowenthal-at-90> accessed 7 September 2016.

[6] George Orwell, *1984* (London: Secker & Warburg 1949) 249.

[7] Elazar Barkan, 'Introduction: Historians and Historical Reconciliation' (2009) 114(4) *American Historical Review* 908.

[8] UN General Assembly, A/HRC/25/49, 23 January 2014, Report of the Special Rapporteur in the field of cultural rights, Farida Shaheed, 'Memorialization Processes' (hereafter *Memorialization*).

[9] The most prominent provision on this right is art. 15 of the UN Covenant on Economic, Social and Cultural rights of 1966, cited in *History*, para. 10, p. 5. For a legal discussion see P.Y.S. Chow 'Culture as Collective Memories: An Emerging Concept in International Law and Discourse on Cultural Rights' (2014) 14(4) *Human Rights Law Review* 611–46. For a discussion of the notion of 'cultural heritage and the politics of memory in an African context, see L. Hughes, A.E. Coombes and Karega-Munene, 'Introduction' (2011) 70(2) *African Studies* 175–80.

normative statements and guidance mainly for state actors but also for others involved in historical research, teaching and the processes of memory.

Shaheed's principal objective is the advancement of 'multi-voiced narratives' of the past. This and other propositions stem from concerns and commitments such as ensuring that history teaching and memorialization not lead to or escalate conflict; that victims be recognized; that history teaching not fortify nationalist identity; that historical narratives not be manipulated; and that teaching and memorialization build on the principles of right to freedom of opinion and expression, and the right to information and academic freedoms. These aims, however, reflect inherent tensions, some of which may be irreconcilable. In this chapter I summarize the reports and reflect on some main propositions and assumptions, and suggest a future path for the current Special Rapporteur in the fields of history and memory.

THE REPORTS

The reports on historical and memorial narratives in divided and post-conflict societies are based on country visits and consultations with governments, experts and civil society actors by the Special Rapporteur for cultural rights and her team. Academic literature informs their work and is broadly cited in the main body of the reports as well as footnotes. The reports thus reflect their accumulated insights into the contemporary conditions and practices of history writing, teaching and public memorialization.

What do these reports contribute? *History* and *Memorialization* stand as official UN statements on the scope of the international obligations of states under existing human rights instruments. The reports have broad, wide-ranging implications for defining and securing this particular aspect of cultural human rights in all societies. The reports call on states to review how they intervene – directly or indirectly – in the research and teaching of history and public memorialization processes and to report this to the UN, thereby further embedding these activities into frameworks of international policy fields. Following the view that international human rights instruments uphold the right of all to know their past, each of us has this right regardless of whether we live in relatively peaceful or in conflict-ridden societies. The challenges of realizing these rights are similar across the spectrum, although war and violent conflicts render them acute. For these reasons, the reports should be read as challenges to politicians, government officials, historians, educators and cultural workers to engage critically in discussions, nationally and internationally, on the long-term aims and conditions of historical investigations and dissemination.

The *History* report deals with historical research and education, with a special focus on textbooks for primary and secondary schools. It takes as its point of departure that all children have a right to develop a historical perspective through their education.[10] Inverting von Clausewitz, the report notes wryly that history teaching can serve as 'a continuation of war by other means'[11] – perpetuating conflict ideology and creating an atmosphere that sustains acute or chronic conflicts within and between states.[12] This may involve excluding, minimizing and justifying particular events or time periods in the teaching of history,[13] or communicating stereotypes of minorities or marginalized groups.[14] It may also involve presenting a historical narrative of a repeated, chronic conflict between two or more states or collectives, while excluding from the story examples of cooperation and friendly relations.[15] Notwithstanding, the Special Rapporteur finds the teaching of history to represent the best hope for dealing with a recent, painful past.[16] Essentially, Shaheed suggests replacing undesirable, instrumental perspectives – narratives aimed at shaping national or regional identities or fostering loyalties to the state – with 'multi-voiced narratives' to emphasize the complexities of the past and nurture comparative, transnational and multi-perspectival approaches.[17]

The teaching of history is – or should be – inextricably linked to historical research. The *History* report expresses concern with the lack of academic freedom in many states.[18] States may control almost all aspects of the work of historians – from access to sources, to cooperation with colleagues, to how or even whether texts are published. The report cites many examples of unlawful state interference with academic freedoms,

---

10 *History*, para. 87, p. 22; ref. *Convention on the Rights of the Child* 28(3).

11 Ibid., para. 27, p. 9. In his seminal 1832 book *On War*, Carl von Clausewitz famously held that 'war is merely the continuation of politics by other means' (Princeton: Princeton University Press 1984) 87.

12 *History*, para. 30, p. 10.

13 Ibid., para. 20, p. 8, and para. 25, p. 9.

14 Ibid., para. 31, p. 10.

15 Ibid., para. 30, p. 10.

16 Ibid., para. 26, p. 9.

17 Ibid., para. 58, p. 16.

18 Ibid., Ch. 4.

including how states seek to control universities and research institutes by reviewing courses and curricula, and deciding what topics are permitted for study. The report also emphasizes positive obligations of states, such as securing sufficient autonomy for institutions for higher education and research and ensuring these have institutional rules and procedures that are as fair, transparent and participatory as possible.[19]

Into the already crowded field of national and international practices, Shaheed in *Memorialization* advances the cultural-rights approach as a specific, prioritized concern, emphasizing its potential to foster a cultural landscape 'reflective of cultural diversity'.[20] Following conflicts, states often engage in what Shaheed calls 'active memorial policies' either on their own initiative or that of other stakeholders. Where traumatic events have taken place, sites – be they torn down, altered, or left unchanged – carry meaning and need to be discussed and interpreted.[21] Remembrance, the report holds, is not a neutral process. Like history, it is 'never immune from political influence and debate'.[22] Public sites of memory may constitute 'entire cultural and symbolic landscapes' which shape human identities and social interactions.[23] These can be physical places or commemorative activities that focus on a specific event or a person.[24] The sites may be authentic places of trauma (mass graves, camps, prisons) or symbolic (monuments, museums, squares) or even virtual (internet sites).[25]

Borrowing a phrase from the South African judge and human rights advocate Albie Sachs, *Memorialization* recommends that a memorial culture based on human rights be 'broadly located, mobile, multi-layered and interactive dialogical truth'.[26] The report also defines the most important obligation of the state as securing 'a plurality of complementary viewpoints on the past'.[27] There are always many views within a group, and when traumatic events are to be remembered, it is vital to

---

19 Ibid., para. 44, p. 13.

20 *Memorialization*, para. 48, p. 12. See also para. 47, p. 11.

21 Ibid., para. 63, p. 14; para. 65, p. 15; para. 81, p. 18.

22 Ibid., para. 3, p. 4.

23 Ibid., Summary, p. 1.

24 Ibid., para. 5, pp. 4–5.

25 Ibid., para. 6, p. 5. Following the lead of French historian Pierre Nora, historians have sought to document the 'realms' or 'sites' of memory. See Pierre Nora 'Between Memory and History: Les Lieux De Mémoire' (1989) 26 *Representations* 7–24.

26 *Memorialization*, para. 20, p. 7.

27 Ibid., para. 76, p. 17. See also para. 99, p. 20; para. 103, p. 21.

avoid simplistic representations of the past.[28] States and actors should promote critical thinking and broad civic participation and ensure that the locations of pivotal events become sites of knowledge, not solely trauma.[29] Furthermore, they must make available sites for public acts of remembrance, to which end artists and curators may work without interference from states.[30]

From a historian's perspective, the reports are themselves historical documents – historical sources attesting to the state of affairs in international cooperation in the social and cultural fields as well as in the protection of international human rights at the time of their writing. The reports embody interpretations of the past and are inscribed with contemporary concerns. As with human rights documents before them, they cannot be detached from the context in which they are written. Both the UN Charter and the UN Universal Declaration of Human Rights encapsulated the experiences and ideas of the inter-war years, the Second World War and fast-developing situations in the contemporary world, such as the Palestinian refugee crises.[31] Similarly, the UN convention on racial discrimination came out of the historical experience of de-colonization and reflected the quondam concern with apartheid as well as with discrimination in many other states, most prominently the USA. A series of anti-Semitic attacks also informed part of the background.[32]

The reports reflect a set of partly interrelated historical trends. On the one hand the world saw the surge of social movements in the 1960s and the cultural revival they brought, and the rise of multi-culturalism, including new international norms for the rights of indigenous peoples in the 1980s. On the other, the world struggled with aftermath in the many attempts to deal with past historical injustices after the Cold War, as well as efforts international and national to deal with post-conflict societies following the internecine strife and civil wars of this period. Together, the reports on history and memory reflect a contemporary concern and interest in remembrance of the past, sometimes labelled 'memory boom'

---

28 Ibid., para. 50, p. 12.

29 Ibid., paras 64–65, pp. 14–15.

30 Ibid., para. 75, p. 17.

31 Johannes Morsink, *The Universal Declaration of Human Rights: Origins, Drafting and Intent* (University of Pennsylvania Press 1999); Mary Ann Glendon, *A World Made New: Eleanor Roosevelt and the Universal Declaration of Human Rights* (Random House 2001).

32 Steven L.B. Jensen, *The Making of International Human Rights: The 1960s, Decolonization and the Reconstruction of Global Values* (Cambridge University Press, 2016).

or 'memory fever'.[33] Historian Jay Winter has noted that 'just as we use words like love and hate without ever knowing their full or shared significance, so we are bound to go on using the term "memory", the historical signature of our own generation'.[34]

Related to the observation that the reports reflect certain trends and concerns of a particular present, we note issues relating to the historical experience of colonialism raised in several places. Here, Shaheed and her team seem to have had only European overseas colonialism in mind – not Russian/Soviet, or Japanese, or North-American.[35] We may also discern a particular mobilization of the past in how the reports take for granted the notion of 'indigenous peoples' and be mindful that the reports form part of international and local dynamics of establishing hierarchies of minority status. The concept of 'indigenous peoples' is an identity construct as well as a political and legal one, and it has undergone significant changes along its various dimensions over time, with the current notion dating from the late 1960s. Today it is used to distribute rights and benefits within states and in the international system.[36]

Furthermore, the reports focus on divided and post-conflict societies which have experienced international or internal conflicts in 'the recent and less recent past'.[37] The historical experience of slavery is singled out for special attention.[38] Historically, slavery has been a multifaceted phenomenon with many geographic locations and disparate victims. The UN differentiates between historical and contemporary slavery, but 'slavery' is not defined in the reports, and therefore it is not clear who the 'victims' of slavery are. In light of the recommendation to enhance

---

33 The term 'memory fever' was coined by Andreas Huyssen in *Twilight Memories: Marking Time in a Culture of Amnesia* (New York/London: Routledge 1995).

34 Jay Winter, *Remembering War: The Great War Between Memory and History in the Twentieth Century* (New Haven: Yale University Press 2006) 51.

35 See *History*, para. 32, p. 10; *Memorialization*, para. 19, p. 7 and para. 34, p. 10.

36 Ronald Niezen, *Origins of Indigenism, Human Rights and the Politics of Identity* (Berkeley: University of California Press, 2003); Einar Niemi, 'Kategoriene etikk og minoritetene i nord: Et historisk perspektiv' in Samisk forskning og forskningsetikk (Oslo: Forskningsetiske komiteer, Nr. 2, 2002) 22–44; Hanne Hagtvedt Vik, 'Indigenous Internationalism' in Glenda Sluga and Patricia Clavin (eds), *Internationalisms: A Twentieth Century History* (Cambridge University Press 2016) 315–339.

37 *History*, para. 2, p. 4.

38 Ibid.

memorialization efforts for victims of slavery, it is reasonable to assume that Shaheed had the trans-Atlantic slave trade in mind.[39]

Therefore read with an eye to how they reflect the past, both reports are, like other international documents, themselves sites of memory.

ON THE RELATIONS BETWEEN HISTORY AND MEMORY

Social scientists and historians have long engaged in lively global discourse on issues of history and remembrance that has yielded both empirical and theoretical insights.[40] Academic studies of how we memorialize emerged in the latter half of the nineteenth century and lasted to the first quarter of the twentieth.[41] A new wave of scholarly interest in memorialization hit in the 1960s and 1970s, partly connected to Holocaust remembrance, but the take-off period for academic memory studies was the 1980s. Since then, memory studies has become a mature academic field, with its own journals, landmark publications, conferences

---

[39] *Memorialization*, para 105 (h), p 22. On UN efforts on contemporary slavery, see <http://www.ohchr.org/EN/Issues/Slavery/SRSlavery/Pages/SRSlaveryIndex.aspx> accessed 15 May 2016.

[40] Alon Confino, 'History and Memory' in Axel Schneider and Daniel Wolff (eds), *The Oxford History of Historical Writing: Volume 5 Historical Writing Since 1945* (New York: Oxford University Press 2011) 36–51.

[41] Winter, note 34, 20–25. For an overview of the developments, concepts and debates in the field until the late 1990s, see Jeffrey K. Olick and Joyce Robbins, 'Social Memory Studies: From "Collective Memory" to the Historical Sociology of Mnemonic Practices' (1998) 24 *Annual Review of Sociology* 105–140. For more recent interventions, see Susannah Radstone and Bill Schwarz (eds) *Memory: Histories, Theories, Debates,* (New York: Fordham University Press, 2010); Marek Tamm, 'Beyond History and Memory: New Perspectives in Memory Studies' (2013) 11(6) *History Compass* 458–73; and Patrick Finney, 'The Ubiquitous Presence of the Past? Collective Memory and International History' (2014) 36(3) *The International History Review* 443–72. Sociologist Maurice Halbwachs was a pioneering theorist of memory: see his *Collective Memory* (first published 1925, New York: Harper & Row 1980) 48.

and an online discussion group.[42] It also has a high profile in major history journals.[43]

Historians and other scholars of memory trace discourses, pinpointing the shapes and significance of the past at later times and in various contexts. The mobilization of the past for contemporary purposes has often been studied from the scholarly fields of nationalism, ethnic identities and the recent 'politics of recognition', which aims to rectify the wrongs of the past.[44] The scope of such studies has been broadened to encompass a wide range of topics, with studies of post-conflict societies a major interest. In brief, historians of memory identify dominant narratives of the past, including their biases and silences, and consider 'who wants to remember what and why, and how memory is produced, received, and rejected'.[45]

The UN reports use the notion of 'collective memory' without defining it, but noting that while the discipline of history represents critical thinking, memorialization is inextricably emotional.[46] This chapter does not address the many competing and overlapping academic definitions of the phenomenon of 'collective memory'; however, the distinction between history and memory is critical. These different phenomena share close, complex relations; they overlap in various ways and cannot always be separated. Historian Jay Winter has emphasized that while history is narratives of the past 'backed up by the authority of direct experience' to be gleaned from written and oral sources, memory by contrast is how individuals retrieve a personally encountered event. The space between them (a 'field of force', he has argued) is the historical memory – the way we give meaning to the past.[47]

---

[42] A Google Ngram search reveals a sharp increase in the frequency of the term 'collective memory' starting from 1980. The journal *History and Memory* has been published since 1989, the journals *Memory Studies* and *The Holocaust in History and Memory* since 2008.

[43] See for example A.H.R. Forum 'Collective Memory and Cultural History: Problems of Method' (1997) 102(5) *American Historical Review* 1371–412; and 'Special Issue: Social Memory and Historical Justice' (2011) 44(4) *Journal of Social History* 1007–138.

[44] Jan Werner Müller, *Memory and Power in Post-War Europe* (Cambridge, UK: Cambridge University Press 2002) 2.

[45] Confino, 'History and Memory', 41.

[46] *History*, para. 5, p 4–5.

[47] Jay Winter, 'Foreword: Historical Remembrance in the Twenty-First Century' in Martin O Heisler, 'Introduction: The Political Currency of the Past: History, Memory, and Identity', *The Annals of the American Academy of Political and Social Science* Vol. 617, The Politics of History in Comparative Perspective

Ultimately, only individuals can remember. But remembrance is normally a social process involving the sharing of memories within a group, small or large. Families, for example, are transmitters of knowledge across generations of major, formative experiences or ways of looking at the world. The same is true for religious and ethnic communities – even national public arenas. Power relations shape remembrance; yet collective memories are a phenomenon more complex than simply the result of power relations. Focusing on how memories are shaped, some elect to use 'social memory' or 'cultural memory' over 'collective memory'; others limit their studies to phenomena of the public domain, employing the concept of 'public memory'. Focusing on agency and the collective acts of remembrance at public sites or spaces, Jay Winter makes a case for using the analytical term 'remembrance' rather than 'memory'.[48]

The surge of interest in memory studies has stripped away any illusions about historians being the sole or even the central proprietors of the past.[49] The *History* report points out that history is only one of many factors contributing to collective memory.[50] A wide variety of actors are shaping the dominant narratives of the past in different contexts. The UN reports employ the notion of 'memorial entrepreneurs' and draws attention in particular to the agencies of states but also to historians, curators and others involved in acts of public remembrance. To this we may add the makers of film and computer games, novelists, musicians, journalists, leaders and members of religious communities, interest groups, think tanks and other private organizations, among many others.[51]

However, even though there is an obvious need for continued and expanded reflection on the relations between history and memory, Shaheed gives no direction to historians in terms of prioritizing how we remember and represent the past. This is rightly an important part of the

---

(May 2008) 9, 12. See also Winter, 'Sites of Memory' in Susannah Radstone and Bill Schwarz (eds), *Memory: Histories, Theories, Debates* (New York: Fordham University Press 2010).

48 Jay Winter, 'Historical Remembrance', 9, 12. See also J.V. Wertsch and H.L. Roediger III 'Collective Memory: Conceptual Foundations and Theoretical Approaches' (2008) 16(3) *Memory* 318–26.

49 Winter, 'Sites of Memory', 314.

50 *History*, para. 5, p. 4.

51 For a review of examples drawn from five genres/media types of historical representations that significantly impacts contemporary historical culture, see the 2009 issue themed 'Historical representation and historical truth' edited by Christoph Classen and Wulf Kansteiner for the journal *History and Theory* (2009).

historian's work, as is the obligation to work on un(der)studied events and trends and to re-evaluate the studied and contested ones.

THE HISTORIAN'S CRAFT

How do – and should – historians work when seeking to understand the events, ideas and processes of the past? Both Shaheed's reports strongly defend the virtues of history as a discipline, and many of the assertions and recommendations go to the core of methodological and theoretical problems central to the discipline, particularly relations between sources, perspective and interpretation.

To me, Shaheed's defense of the principles of academic freedom is by far her most important contribution concerning historical research. This includes the freedom to choose a specific research subject, to have access to archives, to publicize potentially controversial synthetic works and to cooperate with historians of other countries. In Eastern Europe during the Cold War, many historians who 'wanted to be truthful to their craft often worked on more remote periods of the past or on histories of distant locations'.[52] The same is true in many places in the world today, where historians work under tight government control, making contemporary political history particularly difficult.

Professional historians muster as much evidence and careful arguments as possible about the past they study. Many work in several languages and consult documents and other sources of multiple origins. This enables them, again quoting Winter, to 'establish the boundary conditions of possibility' of what happened in the past they study.[53] Their narratives establish with as much certainty as possible the chronology of past events, the ideas and motivations of the main actors, and the social, economic and cultural landscapes of which they were a part. This forms the basis for careful arguments about causes and contingencies, and of the significance of that particular (aspect of the) past. Meticulously researched historical narratives of a contested historical event may unearth and document facts that make it impossible to refute they happened, or how and why they did.

---

[52] Patryk Babiracki's review of Adam Daniel Rotfeld and Anatoly Vasilyevich Torkunov (eds) *White Spots–Black Spots: Difficult Matters in Polish-Russian Relations, 1918-2008*. H-Diplo, H-Net Reviews <https://www.h-net.org/reviews/showrev.php?id=44893> accessed 15 May 2016.

[53] Winter, *Remembering War*, 10.

Arriving at such narratives presupposes the existence of rich, relevant sources and the historian's access to the same. Archives remain at the core of historical investigations. It is a grave and ongoing problem that many collections are destroyed, go missing, or are otherwise made unavailable for research. The French army, for example, destroyed and shipped between 53 000 and 200 000 cartons of documents from Algeria to France in 1961–62, some of which were later repatriated.[54] Even when documents are preserved, historians may still be unable to access archives. After a period of disclosure following the end of the Cold War, today many Russian archives are closed. Furthermore, although private institutions and international organizations like many states are dedicated to principles of freedom of information and have laws and regulations granting researchers access to documents, this is often no guarantee. In Norway, for example, a government official has held the only copies of documents on secret negotiations between Israeli and Palestinian representatives during the Oslo Peace Process and refused to release these records, leaving historians to guess what these might add to the official story.[55] Private papers of members of the elite are often kept, but these too may be destroyed. Kwame Nkrumah decided to burn his private papers, for example, again leaving historians to guess at important aspects of his role during the early history of the independent state of Ghana.[56] As a nationalist leader and his country's first prime minister and president, Nkrumah's insights could have provided unique glimpses into a crucial period and his role in Ghana's formative years.

The preservation of archives and the access of researchers to these and other sources must be a priority in a human rights-based approach to cultural heritage. What is kept in state and private archives results from decisions by multiple actors, and what has been considered worth keeping has changed. In the late 1950s, for example, archival practices broadened in many contexts to include materials of private associations

---

[54] Todd Shepard, 'Of Sovereignty: Disputed Archives, "Wholly Modern" Archives, and the Post-Decolonization French and Algerian Republics, 1962–2012' (2015) 120(3) *American Historical Review* 869–83. For a discussion of the problem in a Middle Eastern context in the same issue, see Omnia El Shakry, 'History without Documents: The Vexed Archives of Decolonization in the Middle East' 920–34.

[55] Hilde Henriksen Waage, 'Postscript to Oslo: The Mystery of Norway's Missing Files' (2008) 38(1) *Journal of Palestine Studies* 54–65.

[56] Jean Allman, 'Phantoms of the Archive: Kwame Nkrumah, a Nazi Pilot Named Hanna, and the Contingencies of Postcolonial History-Writing' (2013) 118(1) *American Historical Review* 104–29.

and non-elites.[57] This greatly expanded the scope of historical investigations, as new voices are discernable through such collections. UN Educational, Scientific and Cultural Organization (UNESCO) has a long history of working to preserve archives and to disseminate knowledge on good practices. Taking a cultural human rights approach to archival practices may strengthen these and other international efforts by emphasizing and exploring practical sides to realizing the rights of future people to their histories. While not specifically addressing problems of preservation of archives, *History* recommends that, following the safeguarding of privacy, states should secure access to archives and resources for research, facilitate digitalization and internet publishing, and put in place a system of scholarships for research into colonial archives.[58]

During the 2015 Copenhagen conference that produced this volume, the Special Rapporteur raised the question of whether the right to know one's cultural heritage in some cases includes, or should include, a right to control its historical relics. The case of indigenous communities was mentioned specifically. Who is entitled – legitimately and ethically – to manage and adjudicate existing collections? Does this include the right to move, restrict access to or even destroy testimonials, such as a collection of oral histories? A right to control historical relics is certainly problematic from a historian's point of view, but it also presents ethical issues as it gives people at one point in time the power to control which aspects of the past are available in the future.

Some historical persons and groups have left no written material. The *History* report criticizes the primacy of written over oral sources in historical research, especially in the case of post-colonial states where reliance on documents written by colonial administrators results in historical writing as carrier of a particular colonial perspective.[59] In taking this view, Shaheed seems to be inspired by an approach known as 'post-colonial critique'. The term stems from the work of a group of South Asian scholars who from the 1980s challenged conventional framings of the past by focusing instead on the lived experience and active roles of the subordinated masses. Due to their attempts to delocalize the centrality of Europe and of elites in South Asian history, their scholarship became known as 'subaltern studies'. Their approach

---

[57] Shepard, 'Of Sovereignty', 870–71.
[58] *History*, para. 47, pp. 13–14.
[59] Ibid., para. 33, p. 11.

gave rise to a critique of the modes of knowledge instituted by Europeans, including the academic discipline of history.[60] Their many contributions to historical theory and methods include strategies for how to read colonial archives to produce narratives that were neither colonial nor nationalist.[61]

The Special Rapporteur's criticism of historians for their disinterest or neglect of oral sources can come across as dated and simplistic: mainstream historical research acknowledged oral sources a long time ago. To take New Zealand as an example, a new generation of historians and anthropologists, including scholars with ethnic Maori backgrounds, became aware and vocal from the mid-1970s onwards that Maori historical narratives, carried largely by oral tradition, and European historical narratives, belonging to a written tradition, represent 'radically different ways of knowing the past and being in the world'.[62] They focused attention on the significance of perspective in terms of which questions were asked and which sources used. Bain Attwood has described how drawing on Maori oral history traditions, these scholars reconstructed narratives of the past that differed radically from the existing historical narratives of the same geographic space and its inhabitants. This fed into a larger, ongoing process at a time when historians were broadening their focus from political and official spheres to social and cultural ones, sensitizing historians to aspects of the past that had not been told or that called for reinterpretation. The result upended the conventional narrative and was nothing less than the rewriting of the history of New Zealand, including the rereading of written sources and use of previously unexplored materials.[63]

Adding new perspectives have also altered areas of study such as the history of pre-colonial and early modern America, Oceania and Africa. Here the descriptions of the first encounters between settlers and colonizers and the original populations, as well as the interior life of these populations following the encounters, are based on written and oral sources, material as well as archaeological and anthropological sources, methods and insights. Imaginative and skilful readings of elite and colonial writings have revealed insights into the lives and agency of

---

[60] Gyan Prakash, 'Postcolonial Criticism and History: Subaltern Studies' in Schneider and Wolff, *Historical Writing*, 74–92.

[61] Farina Mir, 'Introduction' in AHR Roundtable 'The Archives of Decolonization' (2015) *American Historical Review* 847.

[62] Bain Attwood, 'Settler Histories and Indigenous Pasts: New Zealand and Australia' in Schneider and Wolff, *Historical Writing*, 598–9.

[63] Ibid., 600–605.

illiterate or marginalized populations. This may include the internal lives of such communities and their interaction with other communities, extending far beyond their interactions with government agents and elites – and beyond contact with European authorities and settlers. Oral tradition, such as songs and stories, are assessed through methodologies in which the stability of the narratives of sources are corroborated by written evidence or through an assessment of the consistency of a particular narrative across geographic areas.[64]

The social and cultural turns in historical research made oral sources central evidence for many studies. More problematic than an outdated representation of historians' uses of oral sources, however, the critique voiced in the report may delegitimize sound history writing and methodological concerns. Such concerns include how individual recollections and oral tradition are excellent sources for mapping how individuals and communities remember the past, but may be less reliable for understanding those particular events and individuals. Oral tradition is biased in how it reflects power relations both at their point of origin and when these have been transmitted in time. Moreover, anyone studying contemporary history who has had the privilege of corroborating information from interviews with written sources will have experienced how individual recollection is prone to after-the-fact rationalizations and conflating actors and events, either consciously or subconsciously. Historians are trained to assess texts, oral testimonials and traditions critically, approaching them in light of other relevant materials and insights into the origins of the particular source, applying those norms for scrutiny of sources – an approach broadly known as the method of source criticism.

The Special Rapporteur rightly emphasizes that historical research, writing and teaching is always based on interpretations, and that narratives are 'viewpoints that, by definition, are partial'.[65] The cultural turn (also known as the 'linguistic turn') that has reshaped social sciences and humanities has also sensitized historians to the significant impact of our own experiences and perceptions on the questions we ask and how we work to answer them. Before historians start leafing through letters, diaries, diplomatic or business records, or collect oral testimonies, we have made choices about where to go and what to look for; and these

---

[64] For a theoretical intervention making the case for the use of oral tradition in historical reconstruction, see for example Jan Vansina, *Oral Tradition as History* (London: James Curry 1985). See also Toyin Falola and Jennings Christian (eds) *Sources and Methods in African History: Spoken Written Unearthed* (Rochester: University of Rochester Press 2003).

[65] *History*, para. 6, p. 5; para. 78, p. 20.

decisions are made on the basis of our own perspectives. We will never grasp the past as it was: we make 'a translation of the past into our time, an act of interpretation'.[66]

Emphasis on the subjectivity of historical research, however, should not be collapsed into a relativist position. Not all interpretations of the past have equal value: some are simply wrong, or invented. Academic norms dictate that historians consult and relate to the bodies of literature relevant to their topic of study. We must operate within this landscape of previously known facts, interpretations and theories, always trying to refine methods and challenge interpretations to gain new insights, both empirical and theoretical. Without losing sight of the subjective aspect of our profession, we have no choice but to continue insisting on the highest professional standards for how historians work to answer queries about the past and how those understandings should be narrated and published.[67]

This same insight seems to have guided several parts of the UN reports.[68] However, there is a tension between Shaheed's insistence on professional standards and truth-seeking and her repeated emphasis on the partiality of all historical narratives. The rapporteur would have done well to provide a more explicit rejection of relativist approaches to the past, in particular because emphasis on partiality may provide a smoke-screen for the very practices she seeks to end.

ON SILENCES AND THE RIGHT TO FORGET

The sense of injustice is one of the most compelling of emotions. Narratives of the past may lead not just to mourning, but to outrage and intense anger.[69] The overarching goals of *Memory* are to promote peace and recognize victims. The two are not always compatible and may be at odds with a third goal, voiced in both reports: to represent the past in a

---

[66] Bo Stråth, 'Methodological and Substantive Remarks on Myth, Memory and History in the Construction of a European Community' in special issue 'Confronting Memories – Reflecting History' (2005) 6(2) *German Law Journal* 256. For an earlier observation in a similar vein, see Edvard Hallett Carr, *What is History?* (New York: Vintage Books, 1961) 24–9.

[67] See for example David Lowenthal, 'History and Memory' (Spring 1997) 19(2) *The Public Historian* 32.

[68] *History*, para. 6, p. 5.

[69] See for example T.R. Tyler and H.J. Smith, 'Social Justice and Social Movements' in D. Gilbert, S.T. Fiske, and G. Lindzey (eds), *Handbook of Social Psychology* (4th edn McGraw-Hill, 1998).

documented, balanced and comprehensive way that conforms with 'best practice' for the discipline.

Public memorial culture has changed over time. Shaheed outlines how commemoration after war and mass atrocity from the 1980s onwards was expected to satisfy the needs of victims and at the same time forestall similar events in the future.[70] After the end of the Cold War, the will and commitment of groups and societies to confront particularly traumatic historical events and injustices has grown, in many instances.[71] International principles for state memorials were drawn up in 1997, building on the victims' right to know what took place, itself formulated as a collective right in order best to forestall the likelihood of such events in the future.[72]

There is much political capital to be harvested from memorial cultures, and Shaheed points out how public sites of remembrance have become an arena of competition in which adversaries vie to bolster and legitimize their 'moral, legal and ideological superiority'.[73] Contemporary memorialization predominantly recognizes victims but may evolve into 'memorial tyrannies' where a fast-growing number of public sites of memory ignore alternative stories of suffering or relations among the many groups involved.[74] Such remembrance may lead to victim cultures, cults of martyrdom and thirst for revenge.[75] Hierarchies of victimhood may emerge, resulting in what literary theorist Tzvetan Todorov terms 'an endless line of credit'.[76]

The presence or absence of specific memories in the public domain may result from promotion or suppression by governments, or from much more complex processes. One aspect of this is that individual and collective memory are intertwined with self-perception and so coloured by the need to retain a positive recollection of the past. Dealing with the darker sides of the past is inevitably problematic; this is particularly true when two or more collectives hold incompatible memories in the same

---

70 *Memorialization*, paras 9–10, p. 5.

71 See Chris Healey and Maria Tumerkin (eds), 'Special Issue: Social Memory and Historical Justice' (2011) 44(4) *Journal of Social History* 1007–18; Katherine E. McGregor, 'Time, Memory and Historical Justice: An Introduction' (2012) 21(1) *Time and Society* 5–20.

72 *Memorialization*, paras 25–32, pp. 8–9.

73 Ibid., para. 22, p. 7.

74 Ibid., paras 16 and 17, p. 6.

75 Ibid., para. 18, p. 7.

76 Ibid., para. 21, p. 7.

narrative space.[77] One example is the recent 'history wars' over Australia's settler past – specifically, the representation of the historical experiences of the aboriginal population.[78] Another example is how Palestinians and Israelis remember and frame the Palestinian exodus during the 1948 Arab-Israeli war.[79] Recognition of victimhood can carry material and political consequences. On Indonesia, Katharine E. McGregor points out how '[f]or indigenous peoples recognition of settler violence and harm validates their suffering' while the same historical revision for many settlers 'raises questions not only about their own identity as a group, but also about their ongoing rights'.[80]

The silencing of traumatic memories may come from efforts by particular memorial entrepreneurs (and even professional historians) to shape a narrative aimed at fostering reconciliation.[81] In this regard, a political perspective relevant to post-conflict societies is somewhat undercommunicated in *History*. In some national contexts, even those scholars committed to 'truth' are constrained by present-day exigencies and could leave some issues untouched for the sake of contemporary peace and stability. This can happen after war: the immediate post-war period may be cloaked with an 'instant amnesia' aimed at stabilizing the political order through collective solidarity among the survivors. This includes silence about collaboration, as Tony Judt argued in the case of European memories of the Second World War.[82] Another example is that historians of the Rwandan genocide are now presenting more complex stories than

---

77 Heisler, 'The Political Currency of the Past' 14.

78 For an overview over the controversies see Stuart Macintyre and Anna Clark, *The History Wars* (Carlton: Melbourne University Press, 2003); see also Anna Haebish, 'Forgetting Indigenous Histories: Cases from the History of Australia's Stolen Generations' (2011) 44(4) *Journal of Social History* 1033–46.

79 Many articles and books have dealt with issues of history and memory in the conflict between Israel and Palestinians. See notably Avi Shlaim, 'The Debate about 1948' (1995) 27(3) *International Journal of Middle East Studies* 287–304; and Robert Rothberg (ed.), *Israeli and Palestinian Narratives of Conflict: History's Double Helix* (Bloomington: Indiana University Press 2006), especially chapter by Mordechai Bar-On 142–74.

80 Katharine E McGregor, 'Time, Memory and Historical Justice: An Introduction' (2012) 21(1) *Time and Society* 17.

81 The process may be overt but also covert: see for example Vered Vinitzky-Seroussi and Chana Teeger 'Unpacking the Unspoken: Silence in Collective Memory and Forgetting' (2010) 88(3) *Social Forces* 1103–22.

82 Tony Judt, 'Myth and Memory in Post-war Europe' in Jan Werner Müller, *Memory and Power in Post-War Europe* (Cambridge, UK: Cambridge University Press, 2002) 157–83.

those appearing in the years directly after the conflict. This begs the question, raised by the Special Rapporteur in *Memory*, on whether the processes of memorialization may start too soon.[83]

It has become common for states and international organizations to intervene to address traumatic historical events, and we repeatedly hear the call for nations to come to terms with their past. Efforts in peace-making over the past couple of decades – ranging from truth and reconciliation commissions to legal procedures in courts – have been directed at 'transitional justice' with reconciliation as the declared goal. The *Memorialization* report shows how such commissions may be a buffer against states which might otherwise be 'tempted to destroy places of suffering' and thereby 'erase the memories attached to it'.[84] In such forums for dealing with traumas of the past, history and memory come face to face. The political affinities of these commissions may determine who is appointed to them, what materials they consult and how, and so skew the result. This has led some scholars to question whether such efforts in peace-making focus more on reconciliation than on truth and justice.[85] Can the past be negotiated? Truth and reconciliation processes purport to address two things simultaneously: the need to recognize the suffering of individual victims and survivors, and the need to establish facts about what happened and why.[86] The two are obviously of great significance to any post-conflict society, but is it possible to achieve them both at the same time? Or do we, at least in some instances, face a classic dilemma of competing rights? Which should be prioritized? Is it most important to reconcile – or does 'the truth' take precedence? Should we prioritize the latter even where this leads to strong controversies and potentially also to civil unrest? Shaheed mentions the two needs but does not explicitly weigh the conflicting concerns or advocate for either.[87]

---

[83] *Memorialization*, para. 57, p. 13. My thanks to Maja Gudim Burheim for pointing this out.

[84] *Memorialization*, para. 44, p. 11.

[85] <http://www.lrb.co.uk/v24/n21/david-blackbourn/more-reconciliation-than-truth>. See also C. Brants and K. Klep, 'Transitional Justice: History-Telling, Collective Memory, and the Victim-Witness' (2013) 7(1) *IJVC* 36–49; and Berber Bevernage, 'Writing the Past out of the Present: History and the Politics of Time in Transitional Justice' (2010) 69 *History Workshop Journal* 111–31.

[86] I wish to thank Maja Gudim Burheim for drawing this to my attention and the students of HIS2361/4361 at University of Oslo for their discussion of this issue.

[87] On lack of historical awareness in transnational justice mechanisms, see Paige Arthur, 'How "Transitions" Reshaped Human Rights: A Conceptual History of Transitional Justice' (2009) 31 *Human Rights Quarterly* 321–67.

With regard to more peaceful futures, Shaheed called for recognizing the collective or individual right to forget in a comment made during the Copenhagen conference in November 2015. *Memorialization* does not deal with this explicitly, but the report does warn that an active remembrance culture may harm societies rather than heal.[88] It also reminds us that '[a]ll post-conflict and divided societies confront the need to establish a delicate balance between forgetting and remembering'.[89] While forgetting may be perceived as necessary for social peace, censoring historical narratives could be a time bomb, by forcing upon a society an interpretation that conflicts with lived experiences.

Keeping the peace requires some level of consensus or mutual knowledge and recognition of the validity of other narratives. *History* describes how historians of different national origins have worked to establish a common understanding of a controversial past.[90] Collective works by Turkish and Armenian historians demonstrate that they can agree on important facts about the massacres and deportations of Armenians from Turkey in 1915, even though empirical and interpretative disagreements endure (the official Turkish government view diverges fundamentally from that of these historians).[91] Another example is the book by a group of Polish and Russian historians about historical relations between the two countries.[92] The impact of such efforts on public memory, however, is more limited than one might hope. In a different context, others have warned that politics-driven historical investigations aimed explicitly at reconciliation may represent a gulf between professional standards and the desire to achieve reconciliation.[93]

While it is crucial to acknowledge and rectify relatively recent wrongs, dealing with those in the very distant past holds particular problems. The

---

88 *Memorialization*, para. 17, p. 6. Whether this is at all possible is debated in Eric Stover and Harvey M. Weinstein (eds), *My Neighbor, My Enemy: Justice and Community in the Aftermath of Mass Atrocity* (Cambridge: Cambridge University Press, 2004).

89 *Memorialization*, para. 17, p. 6.

90 *History*, paras 81–85, pp. 21–22.

91 Ronald Gregory Suny, 'Truth in Telling: Reconciling Realities in the Genocide of the Ottoman Armenians' (2009) 114(4) *American Historical Review* 930–46.

92 For a similar effort on Polish-Jewish relations, see David Engel, 'On Reconciling the Histories of Two Chosen Peoples' (2009) *American Historical Review* 914–29.

93 For discussions of this tension with practical examples, see the AHR Forum edited by Elazar Barkan for the October 2009 issue of *American Historical Review*.

report mentions slavery and wrongs against indigenous populations. Can and should these be rectified? If so, how should the UN approach problems of what political scientist Martin O Heisler terms 'unwholesome actions or events' in the past that surface many years or even centuries later?[94] One aspect concerns the issue of time: Are we responsible for acts perpetrated by our ancestors? Who are the victims and who the perpetrators? In some cases, it is not possible to establish clear generational connections to either category of actors. A related problem is that what are clearly unlawful and hideous acts from a contemporary perspective took place in a very different normative historical context. Knowing about such events and debates is crucial, however. I agree with Heisler, who has pointed out that history textbooks are 'perhaps most encouraging in the long run … [as a] … medium for linking past and present'; these frame the past in its 'temporal and normative contexts' and can be updated to reflect new scholarship.[95] The rapporteur similarly emphasizes textbooks and, subsequently, global historical research with full protection of academic freedoms.

MULTI-VOICED INSTRUCTION IN HISTORY

Teaching history involves sound interpretations of past events based on a review of available sources; at the same time it often reflects attempts to shape a particular collective memory underpinning national identity. The reports reject this latter function, emphasizing that no indoctrination is acceptable,[96] and that instruction in history must never 'serve the purpose of strengthening patriotism, fortifying national identity or shaping the young in line with either the official ideology or the guidelines of the dominant religion'.[97] Multi-perspectivity constitutes a significant challenge to the status quo in most countries, as illustrated by the fierce debates in the 1990s among politicians and historians and in the media over the proposal to introduce a multicultural approach into the national curriculum of England and Wales.[98]

---

94 Heisler, 'The Political Currency of the Past' 20.

95 Ibid., p. 22. See also Ira Berlin, 'American Slavery in History and Memory' (2004) 90(4) *Journal of American History* 1251–68.

96 *History*, para. 87, p. 22.

97 Ibid., para. 88a, p. 23.

98 Robert Phillips, *History Teaching, Nationhood and the State: A Study in Educational Politics* (London: Cassel, 1998). For an exposition of the utility of adopting multi-perspectivity in history teaching, see Allan McCully, 'History

Lowenthal has observed that '[i]n most school texts, history remains one-dimensional even where controversy is rampant'.[99] Pointing out the diverging interpretations of the antiquity of Native American settlements in US history, he called for sensitizing students of history to the fact that there may be more than one accurate version of the same event. Similar observations are made in the UN report on the writing and teaching of history. The UN Special Rapporteur's main recommendation for a human rights-based approach to teaching history is multi-voiced/multi-perspective narratives; she does not however define these terms, which are used synonymously. The report associates the approach with the existence of peaceful relations within and across countries.

'Multi-perspectivity' is common in studies of fiction (literature, theatre). Marcus Hartner has pointed out that although the term has a variety of meanings, it should 'be restricted to cases where points of view interact in salient and significant ways and thus create multi-perspectivity by, for instance, repeatedly portraying the same event from various different angles'.[100] The term 'multi-voiced' is similarly found in works of literary theorists, while 'multiple narratives' describes a story-telling technique employed in books, films and theatre. Hartner differentiates between 'closed' and 'open' multi-perspective narratives, where the first category holds several incompatible points of view, and the second different views which are nevertheless included in one coherent narrative.[101]

In calling for multi-perspective/multi-voiced history education in schools, the rapporteur is in line with educational developments of the past 20 or more years. According to the historian Robert Stradling, the term 'multi-perspectivity' was rarely used in this context before the 1990s, despite first appearing in the 1970s. Educators in Europe focused increasingly on students' abilities to think historically and gain first-hand experience with interpreting sources, the moral being that a single event can be interpreted differently. They also recognized that the teaching of history had to become ever more inclusive and sensitive to the historical experiences of non-dominant linguistic, cultural and social groups, and

---

Teaching, Conflict, and the Legacy of the Past' (2012) 7(2) *Education, Citizenship and Social Justice* 145–59.

[99] David Lowenthal, 'History and Memory' (Spring 1997) 19(2) *The Public Historian* 37.

[100] Marcus Hartner, 'Multiperspectivity' in Peter Hühn et al (eds) *The Living Handbook of Narratology*. (Hamburg: Hamburg University) <http://www.lhn.uni-hamburg.de/> accessed 10 November 2015.

[101] Ibid.

had to accommodate the cultural heritages of recent immigration populations. Importantly, the interest in multi-perspective teaching grew as international institutions and organizations such as UNESCO and the Council of Europe sought to use history education as a tool for encouraging mutual understanding and reconciliation in Eastern and south-eastern Europe.[102] But what does the approach entail and how should it be implemented? As Stradling writes, 'multi-perspectivity is a term more often used than defined'.[103] This applies to the reports, in the context of which the conflation of terms is somewhat confounding. Should we stop aiming for synthesizing narratives? Or is the rapporteur merely calling for more nuances within such narratives? Does this entail a kind of kaleidoscopic pedagogy and, if so, would this enhance or inhibit an understanding of changes in time and space?[104]

Shaheed rejects any manipulation of historical narratives for nationalistic purposes.[105] Yet, she seems to consider state borders legitimate definers of culture and heritage. She points to UNESCO's recommendation about finding a balance between national and 'general history'.[106] At the same time, she decries an emphasis on political history (using a relatively archaic conception of what that is) and recommends that history be defined not just in terms of narratives that centre on military or political developments but also periods of peace and stability.[107] A better history, she argues, is a broader history that describes complex human relations and societies and the different kinds of causes for particular events.[108] She considers the general and regional history textbooks

---

[102] Robert Stradling, *Multiperspectivity in History Teaching: A Guide for Teachers* (Strasbourg: Council of Europe Publishing 2001) 9–12.

[103] Ibid., 13.

[104] See also ibid., 14–15, 25.

[105] See for example *Memorialization*, paras 54, 57, 60, pp. 12–13; para. 88a, p. 23.

[106] *History*, para. 60, p. 16. Another issue is that some smaller states may lack resources or the necessary competence to have local history researched and written: see ibid. para. 61, p. 16.

[107] *History*, para. 62, p. 16; para. 52, p. 14.

[108] Ibid., para. 63, p. 17; para. 71, p. 19. For an introduction to international textbook revision and research, see Henrik Åström Elmersjö, 'History Beyond Borders: Peace Education, History Textbook Revision, and the Internationalization of History Teaching in the Twentieth Century' (2014) 1(1) *Historical Encounters* 62–74 and Falk Pingel, 'Can the Truth be Negotiated? History Textbook Revisionism as a Means to Reconciliation' (May 2008) 617 *Annals AAPSS* 181–98. For a discussion of an unsuccessful history book project in Rwanda, see S. Warshauer Freedman, H.M. Weinstein, K.L. Murphy and

published by UNESCO to be 'one of the finest contributions to the dialogue between cultures and civilizations'.[109] Aiming for 'the greatest possible diversity', the editors of the books amicably took care to avoid giving priority to European turning-points over those of other regions.[110]

The Special Rapporteur expresses particular concern about segregated schools where children are taught different, mutually exclusive historical narratives and have limited opportunities to meet other children and see their worldviews challenged. In many places groups of people or communities relate to exclusive or conflicting understandings of their past or their present, in effect leading them to live – literally and not just metaphorically – in 'separate, hermetically sealed worlds.'[111] Even internationally mediated truces, such as the Dayton Agreement, can result in segregated communities.[112]

Shaheed makes several recommendations on how to safeguard multi-perspective historical instruction. One of these is the need for states to authorize more than a single textbook and to allow the use of supplementary teaching materials.[113] Instruction should aim at developing the abilities of the students to think critically, rather than activating emotions in a problematic way.[114] Teachers should be guaranteed independence in their professional work and they should receive an education that enables

---

T. Longman, 'Teaching History in Post-Genocide Rwanda' in Scott Strauss and Lars Waldorf (eds) *Remaking Rwanda: State Building and Human Rights after Mass Violence* (Wisconsin: University of Wisconsin Press 2011) 297–314.

[109] Ibid., para. 80, p. 20. Initiated in 1946, the book series focus on human scientific and cultural evolution. The second edition was prepared from 1980 and completed in 2009. Several volumes are available online at <http://www.unesco.org/new/en/social-and-human-sciences/themes/general-and-regional-histories/history-of-humanity/> accessed 1 September 2016.

[110] Charles Morazé, 'Foreword' in Peter Mathias and Nicolaï Todorow (eds), *History of Humanity – Scientific and Cultural Development: Volume V The Nineteenth Century* (Paris: UNESCO Publishing 2008), pp. x–xi. While UNESCO efforts advanced the historiographical field of world history, the books themselves have not been recognized as major academic contributions to the field. For a historical background to the UNESCO history-writing activities, see Poul Duedahl 'Selling Mankind: UNESCO and the Invention of Global History, 1945–1976' (2011) 22(1) *Journal of World History* 101–33.

[111] *History*, para. 56, p. 15.

[112] Pilvi Torsti 'How to Deal with a Difficult Past? History Textbooks Supporting Enemy Images in Post-war Bosnia and Herzegovina' (2007) 39(1) *Journal of Curriculum Studies* 77–96.

[113] *History*, paras 71–73, pp. 19–20.

[114] Ibid., para. 70(e), p. 18.

them to exercise this independence wisely.[115] Implementing multi-perspective teaching is a challenge even in relatively peaceful societies; in addition to the changes mentioned in *History*, such an approach presupposes more time allotted to teaching history in schools than is practiced in many places today.[116]

HISTORIANS AS GATEKEEPERS TO THE PAST

The reports stress repeatedly that states should avoid controlling the work of historians and that the community of historians should have free rein and act as the guarantors of a human rights-based approach to the past, one based on the norms of academic freedoms.

How do we make sure that the narratives of the past include the historical experiences of all relevant groups and stakeholders? Broadly speaking, the Special Rapporteur places her trust in historians as gatekeepers to the past. There is however a notable difference between the two reports in their emphasis on historians. In several places, *Memorialization* stresses the role of sites of memories as sites of knowledge[117] and argues that rigorous historical studies be 'respected and included' in debates over moral legitimacy in conflict situations.[118] How to achieve this could be better outlined, as could the role of history and historians in creating and using memorial sites or rituals. The report emphasizes the necessity of achieving multi-voiced memorial sites but focuses less on securing a balanced narrative that reflects historical research. Shaheed refers to the many advocates of establishing and using public sites of memory as 'memorial entrepreneurs'.[119] Non-state actors such as private organizations or groups are frequently memorial entrepreneurs, sometimes working with international organizations or foreign actors. The rapporteur cites artists and curators as particularly important in this respect[120] but makes only passing reference to the role of historians as critical actors and to history as a crucial academic discipline for public sites of memory.[121] Historians are not mentioned among the relevant actors in the conclusions and recommendations, although they do

---

115 Ibid., paras 74–78, p. 20.

116 Stradling, *Multiperspectivity in History Teaching*, 13, 60.

117 *Memorialization*, para. 65, p. 15.

118 *History*, para. 6, p. 5.

119 *Memorialization*, para. 14, p. 6; para. 92, p. 19; para. 101, p. 21.

120 Ibid., paras 66–73, pp. 15–16.

121 Ibid., para. 70, p. 16; paras 76 and 79, p. 17; para. 102, p. 21.

obliquely take centre stage when Shaheed writes that 'memorial practices [...] must be informed by rigorous historical research and study'[122] and that artists should work with historians and other academics.[123]

In contrast, *History* unequivocally places historians as the guarantors of a human rights-based approach to the past. Shaheed advocates securing multi-voiced narratives by letting independent, professional organizations of historians define the history curriculums for primary and secondary schools[124] and by limiting interference from politicians, religious thinkers and other intellectuals.[125] Does it matter who the historians are? History departments in universities across the world are often populated by (predominantly male) historians with ethnic, racial, religious and socioeconomic backgrounds that do not reflect the diversity of the general population. Historians are trained to work to achieve multiperspectivity in their research; nevertheless it is a fact that point of view is shaped by background and may colour the choice of research topic and perspectives.[126]

Related to this point, the issue of who should be allowed to narrate the past of a particular group is a highly contested one. In both New Zealand and Australia, indigenous activists and academics have argued since the 1980s that writing about the past be reserved for individuals of the same ethnic origin.[127] However, if protests by particular interested parties result in a revised history textbook that does not reflect well-founded research or the initiation of independent research, this is deeply problematic and can lead to propaganda or myth-making. These are fine lines to tread. It is very important to safeguard avenues for debating the preconceptions of historians – including blind spots when it comes to minorities. Historians should not – and cannot – operate untouched by the events, ideas and concerns of their time, and we categorically should not wish for a historical profession insulated from the societies in which they live or

---

122 Ibid., para. 102, p. 21.

123 Ibid., para. 70, p. 16.

124 *History*, para. 51, p. 14; para. 88(b) and (g), p. 23.

125 Ibid., para. 88, p. 23.

126 For a similar remark see comment by Patrick Manning, 'Diversity: Among Historical Practitioners, in Research, and in Teaching' May 2016 <https://www.historians.org/publications-and-directories/perspectives-on-history/may-2016/diversity-among-historical-practitioners-in-research-and-in-teaching> accessed 1 June 2016.

127 Attwood, 'Settler Histories and Indigenous Pasts', 609.

about whose history they write. However, this must not lead to myth-making or the creation of separate academic standards or closed communities of research on particular topics. The key here, it seems, is transparency and non-discrimination in employment practices at universities, as *History* emphasizes.[128] But equally important, we need an ongoing public and professional debate on how we should research, teach and remember the past; Shaheed's two reports are significant contributions to this end.

FUTURE CHALLENGES FOR THE CURRENT SPECIAL RAPPORTEUR

What is the future of the past in a globalizing world that is at once coming together and moving apart? Collective memories are by definition shared by a group of people, and in the context of the two reports we are primarily interested in collectives of some scale – ethnic groups, diasporas, even nations. Have the conditions for or the dynamics of collective memorialization changed significantly from only a few years ago? If so, what are the implications for the recommendations in these reports?

The report on memorialization processes mentions virtual sites of memory. I would like to extend this line of reasoning about the significance of new information technologies a bit further. We have over the past few years seen revolutionary changes in the relations between the virtual and physical worlds. With the advent of the internet and the emergence and global reach of social media, the speed and scale of information dissemination globally has changed dramatically, as have the forms and geography of interactions among people responding to events both local and in faraway places.[129] Lately, software curates much of the information most readily accessible to us online, not merely ads. This reflects our past online behaviour – we are presented with more of what we have demonstrated an interest in. Combined with the diminished

---

128 *History*, para. 89 (a), pp. 23–24.

129 See for example Peter Joseph Gloviczki, *Journalism and Memorialization in the Age of the Social Media* (Palgrave Macmillan 2015). Much public debate has centered on memorialization at the level of the individual: see Geoffrey A. Fowler, 'Who Controls a Digital Legacy?' (*Wall Street Journal*, 5 January 2013) <http://www.wsj.com/articles/SB10001424127887324677204578188220364231346> accessed 11 September 2016.

significance of print newspapers, real-time radio or television, or linear broadcasts on non-commercial, public channels for shaping our knowledge of what happens in the world and why, we are experiencing 'disconnected realities'[130] on a much larger scale than in the recent past. Information technologies facilitate the creation of virtual memorial collectives of groups large and small. These bolster each other's interpretations of the past, in ways that are in principle detached from collective memories shared by people of any one particular state or (majority) population of a territory. The potential of such virtual communities to mobilize is demonstrated in the flocking of foreign fighters to Syria. While foreigners fighting wars that do not directly involve their own state, on a voluntary basis and for ideological reasons, is not a new phenomenon, what *is* new is the way virtual worlds dilute the potency of geography for collective memorialization and mobilizing the past for political or social action.

This new technological landscape also has implications for the teaching of history. *History* emphasizes how narratives of the past are communicated though textbooks and instruction in schools. These books are usually produced in a national context, but the controversies over the narratives they relate may be international or even global. Increasingly, children will seek information about the past in an ever more global and virtual world. The printed book is under duress. For many children, computer games are now the dominant vector of representations of the past. History textbooks for primary and secondary education are already obsolete in many places, replaced by digital learning platforms and resources available online. The digital revolution of the classroom adds qualitatively and quantitatively new kinds of supplementary teaching materials, including oral, iconographic and textual primary sources. Without a doubt, this revolution will be countered by censorship in many states. And it will not reach all children everywhere, due to resource constraints and lack of infrastructure. Nevertheless, it represents opportunities and challenges on many levels and will manifest differently in various contexts. The Special Rapporteur is well placed to explore and make recommendations as to how states, international organizations, scholars, teachers and other agents of memory in various contexts should deploy digital technologies in the future teaching of history.

---

130 *Memorialization*, para. 28, pp. 9–10.

9. The impact of commercial advertising and marketing practices on the enjoyment of cultural rights – Report 2014 (A/69/286)

Dalindyebo Shabalala

I. HOW DOES THE MANDATE ENCOMPASS THIS ISSUE?

When reading the report of the Special Rapporteur (SR), one of the striking frames she uses is the idea that cultural rights are exercised within a community. While she notes that these are exercised both individually and in community[1] with others, similar to other expressive rights such as the right to free expression, I believe that this report and others by her, rightly emphasize the peculiar communitarian nature of cultural rights. Culture does not and cannot exist outside the commune, is created by and with the commune, and has value only because it is shared with the commune. Thus we are concerned about the nature and the health of that commune. I argue that this is what is at the core of the SR's justification: that those actors with undue power use the force of advertising to impose a specific narrative and set of cultural preferences on the citizens of the commune.[2] It is this that justifies, she argues addressing the issue in the cultural rights context and in the context of paragraph 9(b) of the original mandate.[3] In particular she points to the threat this poses to: cultural diversity; cultural freedom; and freedom of thought and opinion. How these threats are manifested is one of the things that the SR struggles with and I think may not have been

[1] United Nations General Assembly Doc A/69/286.

[2] Paras 3 and 5, SR Report.

[3] 'To identify possible obstacles to the promotion and protection of cultural rights, and to submit proposals and/or recommendations to the Council on possible actions in that regard.'

altogether successful in delineating, and I address the issue of definition of harms later. Nevertheless, it is the threat to equal participation in generating and defining the common culture that seems to be the driver for addressing the issue, and one of the tensions in the report is between the driver for the report, and the analytical framework that the SR adopts, that limits the extent to which the broader concern can really be addressed.

II. FRAMEWORK TENSIONS IN THE REPORT

II.1 Cultural Commoditization and Culturalization of Commodity

The twentieth century did not create the privatization of cultural production and distribution, but it turned it from an activity performed by the few for the wealthy to one where the masses became the target. As much as the industrial revolution revolutionized production and distribution of goods, it did the same for the cultural goods and culture embedded in those products. The twentieth century is the era of literacy and mass book culture; mass music culture; mass radio, television and film culture. Success and cultural significance became defined by ubiquity and quality, reducing the role of cultural gatekeepers and reifying individual consumer choice as an expression of the self. This is what we call the commoditization of culture: mass production of cultural products for the mass of consumers.[4] This chapter does not intend to engage in the debate about high culture versus low culture and the class and wealth signifiers that supposedly separate one from the other. For the purposes of this analysis what matters is the understanding that culture *qua* culture became a major commodity and the right to access and consume culture became central to our understanding of what it means to meaningfully participate in the polity. This process of commoditization has been accompanied by the instrumentalization of cultural products as well: the use of art, music and literature to sell other products. This had two pathways of growth: the growth and primacy of industrial and graphic design as art, as a vector for conveying artistic and other ideas while embedded in utilitarian products such as furniture, clothing, cars, kitchen appliances, electronics; and the growth in advertising. The SR's report

---

[4] Many of these developments were captured in the broad field of study of Consumer Culture Theory, nicely described in Eric J. Arnould and Craig J. Thompson, 'Consumer Culture Theory: Twenty Years of Research' (2005) 31 *Journal of Consumer Research* 868.

concerns itself with the second path and the harms that come from using cultural products to sell other goods and services and the way that distorts the content of the cultural products that come to dominate the cultural sphere. In essence, by harnessing cultural products in service of selling other goods, only those products with a proven ability to draw people in and make them feel good about a product are being made and distributed and those that are more purely creative and have less commercial utility are side-lined. A pure advertising in this sense is the logical end point of cultural commoditization that emphasizes popularity, ubiquity and sales volume over other values that culture provides. Both of these trends resulted in the blurring, perhaps even obliteration, of the line between culture and commerce.[5]

Any approach to try and address and rebalance the harms caused by cultural commoditization at its most pernicious (i.e. advertising) needs to answer this question: if artistic and cultural products can be advertised and art used to persuade and influence, argue and ask people to pay and support artists and their commercial intermediaries, why should industrial and manufactured products and producers not take advantage of that, given that they have greater utility for people?

This is crucial, when we understand that advertising is central to the business model of the creation and dissemination of some art forms and cultural products e.g. television, but also magazines and magazine writing. We can also point to the key role of industrial design and graphic design as art forms in and of themselves whose advertising and mass communication aspects are crucial to their existence. This is a form of culture that is central to expressions in the mass industrial age and converses and engages with that modern construct in ways that other art forms do not. The essence of these products is that they are bought, that the design communicates and advertises the product and that it is part and parcel of it. There is no separation between the advertising, the design and the product. How do we view and value this in the context of concerns about the harms of advertising on cultural rights? I argue that

---

[5] As argued by consumer culture theory. See Arnould and Thompson, ibid., p. 871. They point out that consumer culture is constituted by combinations of the ways in which consumption relates to identity; define the boundaries and meaning of specific markets in products and services; the mechanisms, symbols and processes by which market cultures are sustained; and the role of commercial media in all three. In this sense, consumer culture theory is a useful theoretical framework for understanding how advertising operates and is fundamental to the nature of modern cultural consumption and it informs the cultural ecology metaphor I use later in this chapter.

consistent distinctions between commercial cultural activity and non-commercial cultural activity are impossible,[6] and may even be undesirable given that we do not want to stifle the explosion in creativity and distribution mechanisms that bypass traditional gatekeepers. These are large and difficult questions of theory which the SRs report does not explicitly address but which underlie much of the analysis and recommendation. This chapter aims to tease out some of the underlying framework and discuss what they imply for which of her recommendations may work best to address the harms she identifies.[7]

II.2 Metaphors of Progress and Competition and Metaphors of Cultural Ecology

There is clearly a struggle between metaphors and analytical frameworks in the SR's Report. These tensions are not always clearly resolved and they lend themselves to different solutions of different scope some that address key concerns of the SR and some that do not.

In the SR's Report, the competition metaphor takes over in the analysis in contrast to the broad way in which she outlines the harms. Cultural production and distribution is a marketplace, a marketplace of ideas,

---

[6] Where expression is properly understood to go beyond politics but to the generation and distribution of culture (as embodied in goods and services), there can be no coherent dividing line between personal, self-regarding expression which receives less protection and other regarding expression which receives greater protection because of its political import. This narrow view of expression fails in the cultural rights context where we understand participation in the culture to simultaneously be both personal and communal, and artistic expressions to function both in the realm of ideas and in the realm of the market. As the SR notes, advertising sells an image of the self, an image of society and the role of the product or service in that individual and communal identity – the essence of culture.

[7] This is less a critique than an observation that the encounter between human rights and the field of study that relates to advertising is not successfully negotiated by the SR report. In part because the description and understanding of advertising's roles in the generation and distribution of cultural products and in the ways that such products are embedded in advertising as well as part of mass consumer culture, the description of harms suffers, as does the description of the ways in which the harms occurs suffers. That this is true of most special procedures when they first begin to tackle controversial areas at the intersection with other fields does not negate the need for developing a much stronger analysis and understanding of the fields which study advertising as part of culture.

driven by choice and the consent of rational actors.[8] She adopts some of the language from Article 6 of the UNESCO Universal Declaration on Cultural Diversity which places the ability of individuals to choose cultural expressions as the guarantor of cultural diversity. Thus she places damages to choice or limitations on choice at the heart of her analytical framework. Choice therefore implies the individual works within a marketplace of ideas, the value of which is not intrinsic or objectively determined but whose value is determined primarily by the sum of individual choices. In this context, the autonomy of the citizen is the paramount justification both for the generation and expression as well as for participation.[9]

Thus, interference in this market is aimed at maintaining healthy competition – cultural diversity is a product of individuals seeking to have more choices and these being provided by the providers who become aware of this need out of the system and are free to express themselves in ways that others can see, view and exchange expressions with them. In some sense, the only equality the system is concerned with is equality of opportunity to express and choose, but not with equality of outcomes in the sense of selecting one set of cultural expressions over another. In this we look to the primacy of choice then as the means and the mechanism to enable and support.[10] Advertising then plays a key role in the reduction of search costs for individuals and we regulate it to ensure accuracy and truthfulness but not much else.

---

[8] In this she situates herself within the broad consumer culture tradition that views consumer culture as the web of interrelations and meaning derived from sets of individual choices in the market as to which cultural goods to engage with and when. See Arnould and Thompson, note 4, p. 869.

[9] As well articulated by Victor Brudney, 'The First Amendment and Commercial Speech' (2012) 53 *Boston College Law Review* 1153, p. 1163. Brudney notes that the American First Amendment is underpinned by two axes – the autonomy axis and the democratic participation axis. While there are some parallels between the cultural ecology approach I discuss below and the democratic participation axis he outlines, I envision a much larger public goods approach that moves beyond enabling individual participation in democratic process and places the health of the cultural commune at the center. And of course, I address something far larger than just political participation which is his primary concern is discussing the traditional justifications for US First Amendment jurisprudence.

[10] Para. 4, SR Report. Consumer culture theory also provides a framework for understanding that while traditional theories of consumer choice and competition can be useful, the actuality of consumer choice on the ground is not driven by rationality but by sociocultural and historic elements. See Arnould and Thompson, note 4, pp. 875–7.

By contrast, a cultural ecology approach[11] does not privilege individual choice in the market but looks at the health of the ecology, and seeks to limit unhealthy growth and encourage healthy growth, maintaining sufficient diversity to support sustainable growth, but limiting growth where it is not appropriate, by limiting the vectors of transmission such as advertising. This is in tension with individual rights where these are conceived and pursued counter to the health of the whole, where these perform the role of a cancerous or other sickly growth. One can see the unease that such a metaphor raises because it justifies larger intrusions into the rights to receive and impart culture and expression that might be greater than that allowed by a traditional individual human rights approach to freedom of expression. Nevertheless, it may be the one that allows us to address the big concern of displacement of cultural space by concentrated global firms through advertising that seems to drive the SR's report. Thus, to some extent, the SR leaves a significant amount of work to be done regarding the extent to which intrusions into the advertising space can extend, and part of the problem is really the issue of harms and the nature of harms.

III. SPECIFIC TRIUMPHS AND CHALLENGES WITHIN THE REPORT

III.1 Definitions

The report struggles with and I think does not necessarily succeed at defining two core concepts: what is advertising and what constitutes commercial speech?[12] This is especially important given the role of advertising in the dissemination of cultural products themselves and in

---

[11] As a metaphor that draws from both consumer culture theory as well as actual study of cultural ecology. Cultural ecology emphasizes the interaction between culture and environment how one affects and creates change in the other and either results in sustained and sustainable communities or degraded and dysfunctional ones. The environmental metaphor is useful in the context of discussions around cultural diversity as well. See Arnould and Thompson, ibid.; Charles O. Frake, 'Cultural Ecology and Ethnography' (1962) 64(1) *American Anthropologist* 53.

[12] Here I adopt some traditional American nomenclature but which is particularly apt for the core concern that the SR struggles with: the division between commercial and non-commercial advertising. Here the SR parallels the historic discussion in the US as to whether there is a principled distinction to be made between commercial and non-commercial speech and the extent to which

communicating about the value and need for such cultural products. Consider a simple market: books. We live in a blockbuster age, perhaps we have always done so, but such blockbusters are created things and the success of a book in the cultural marketplace[13] lives by the extent to which it was made known through advertising. The SR notes that advertising and marketing practices are meant to encompass 'a diversity of tools and methods to sell and promote services or products'. I believe however that she means to say something more than this; that the definition she would truly like to use involves a value judgement in some manner. Not that we wish to make a distinction between 'good' and 'bad' advertising but that there is something about the nature of advertising that is structurally inclined to specific kinds of harms. With that in mind I think we can point to several key characteristics of advertising that she is concerned about:

- it is communication to the public or specific publics by persons who, by definition, are driven by pure self-interest in engaging in that communication;
- it is, by nature not just informational, but aimed to persuade and influence that public to purchase and or adopt the products and services being sold;
- the seller has no inherent duties to the public that constrain the incentives they have to advertise as often as possible, to as many of the relevant people as possible, as untruthfully as they can get away with regarding harms and weakness, strengths and benefits of the product or services;
- the seller has no inherent duty to refrain from the use of persuasive methods that deceive the public into believing that they have all the necessary information or that they are not actually being advertised to.

In this sense then advertising is different from state propaganda where the state or the government *does* have duties to the public and these are clearly violated when the state acts for its own interests or that of the governing party in communicating to the public.

This allows us to consider that we are primarily not concerned about advertising that is in the public interest, or that is constrained by public

---

the first amendments for protection of speech should be less protective of commercial speech.

[13] And here I realize I fall into the language trap myself.

duties of truthfulness. We are really talking about 'commercial propaganda' rather than advertising as a whole. This also allows us to elide the commercial v non-commercial distinction that the SR also struggles with.[14] This also means that, to the extent that we are concerned about the harms above, perhaps it is not the commercial nature of the speaker but the way and method used by that actor that is harmful. Thus it is not just advertising, but even political and religious speech that may involve such harms. Simply because an actor is a non-profit or a religious organization does not remove the incentives that we note above. Where the actor has those incentives and has the cash to support itself in such action the harms from non-profits are no different from those of commercial actors. It is perhaps only in the scale that one may be concerned but, one has only to look at the scale of influence the Mormon Church in America is able to exert in political realms through advertising,[15] the Catholic Church in its campaigns against contraception, or the Wahhabi sect of Islam in its modesty and the role of women campaigns. Thus, I argue that the aim should not be to counterbalance the corporate sector as the SR notes,[16] but to target the methodology and the set of incentives by imposing duties on all advertising actors. This means not focusing so much on the nature of the actor doing the speaking but on the methods and the incentives underlying the advertising in which the speaker is engaging. The danger is the persuasiveness and the uses of persuasiveness to shift rationality and incentives to achieve other ends than expression of one's own creative, political, religious and cultural beliefs and ideas. Once you seek to persuade others to adopt a viewpoint, or provide you with support, via money, or other resources, then you have the same set of incentives to engage in harmful advertising that seem indistinguishable from those that relate to 'commercial' advertising. The harms of advertising, as outlined by the SR make it very difficult to make a principled distinction between commercial and non-commercial advertising. Where the harms are cultural or diversity harms and concerns about the ideology propagated by commercial advertising, the SR makes it clear that, if political or ideological advertising is protected, then 'commercial' advertising that has such political or ideological content or viewpoints should also be protected from regulation to a similar extent.

---

[14] This is a struggle shared by legal scholarship and courts across the world. In the US, there is a long-standing, but fundamentally incoherent, line of cases that has struggled to make such a distinction. See Brudney, note 3.

[15] Jesse Mckinley and Kirk Johnson "Mormons Tipped Scale in Ban on Gay Marriage" *New York Times*, Nov. 14, 2008.

[16] Para. 38 SR Report.

Only by focusing on the methods used rather than the nature of the actor doing the advertising can the SR rescue the project as outlined in the report. Where my own argument may fall apart here is with respect to the instrumentality of much advertising. Where the advertising truly is purely functional i.e. communicating specific information about the nature and characteristics of a product or service, requiring that the information be accurate and transparent seems obvious. However, traditionally, we do not extend such a requirement to non-commercial speakers doing the very same thing. There is no duty or regulation placed on a person expressing a political opinion and referencing a factual matter e.g. the number of refugees flowing across the Mediterranean, to be truthful and accurate as to that factual matter. There is a traditional margin of appreciation provided to such actors regarding such statements, including intentional falsehoods, that is not extended to commercial actors regarding products.[17] Thus even if the information is factual, the margin differs depending on the speaker and the purpose for which the speaker uses the information. There are many rationales for why such a distinction is made, but one pertinent one, is that the best corrective for political speech is likely to be more political speech which can challenge and contradict such statements, whereas commercial speech, absent a counter-narrative from another commercial actor/competitor, is not likely to be corrected before the harm takes place i.e. the consumer makes the purchase.[18] However, as Brudney notes, this privileges the autonomy of the speaker over those of the listener or advertised to. As Strauss notes, emphasizing the autonomy of the listener allows for restrictions on false or misleading expression in order to enable the exercise of rational decision-making.[19] This issue of where to draw the line between commercial and non-commercial expression infects the attempt by the SR to draw a line between commercial and non-commercial advertising. I argue that focusing on the nature of the actor doing the advertising is not coherent or useful in the context of addressing the harms she identifies because these are generalized harms; they either are autonomy harms which are not limited to commercial advertising but to *any* lack of truthfulness or deception, or they are harms to the body politic or the culture at large, which are also not limited to commercial advertising and which we are much more reluctant to regulate because they impinge on the autonomy of speakers and require us to make, at a communal level,

---

[17] See e.g. Brudney, note 3, pp. 1166–7.

[18] This is the approach in the US for example. See ibid.

[19] See David A. Strauss, 'Persuasion, Autonomy, and Freedom of Expression' (1991) 91 *Columbia Law Review* 334, p. 357.

judgements about the desirability of the content of expressions.[20] This issue of harms is significantly under-examined in the SR report and weakens the basis for her recommendations but it remains very difficult to see how the contradictions in making reasoned distinctions between commercial and non-commercial advertising can be solved within the framework of the mandate, when so much relies on the freedom of expression framework already elucidated by the SR on Freedom of Expression.

This suggests that the evaluation of whether the advertising is inappropriate cannot be left to the persons doing the advertising no matter what category they fall into but must be assessed by independent authorities attuned to the harms enunciated and the related remedies. The government cannot be the determiner because the methods and harms so easily overlap with those related to political, religious and other advertising, and self-regulation is inappropriate precisely because the incentives of the actors are so distorted. The independence of the bodies is crucial to the set of proposed remedies made by the SR. However, as I discuss in the section below, even this may not allow us to deal with one of the broader harms that the SR is concerned with: the sheer volume and ubiquity of advertising as a mode of communication.

III.2 What is the Nature of the Harms Identified by the SR?

III.2.1 The imposition and manipulation of choice and options of those not yet capable or literate enough to make informed choices; or temporarily incapable of doing so

This is a market place structure the remedy for which is primarily ensuring minimal exposure of these people (e.g. children, those permanently or temporarily unable to make balanced rational decisions for themselves) to advertising where they make decisions for themselves or influence decisions and choices that they make in the near term. The classic case is children and tobacco advertising, but extends as the SR

---

[20] A separate argument can be made however that some forms of political speech (negative political advertising) result in harms to the body politic and discourage voter participation and turnout, thus justifying action to restrict the content of such speech where it is false or misleading. In this sense it much more parallels the justification for restricting commercial speech. See e.g. Clay Calvert, 'When First Amendment Principles Collide: Negative Political Advertising and the Demobilization of Democratic Self-Governance' (1997) 30 *Loy. L.A. L. Rev.* 1497.

notes to unhealthy food,[21] sugary beverages, risky sports and age-inappropriate behaviors such as sex, etc. This presents the strongest case for the SR that extends across all the available analytical frameworks, that children should be protected from advertising as a whole and that even informational advertising is inappropriate because of their lack of capacity to properly assess the utility and relevance of the information being provided. Thus, in looking to business obligations, the clearest ones she finds relate to children and children's rights.[22] However, neither she nor the Committee on the Rights of the Child (in General Comment 16) go so far as to argue that children should never be advertised to, but that care should be taken not to allow harmful advertising. In part, this is driven by concerns that children have rights to freedom of expression, to receive and impart information and culture.[23] How to determine what information is age appropriate to be transmitted and advertised to children is left to the state but the SR's frame here does not allow us to address the core issue of assessment and analysis: do we know what kind of information allows children to engage in choices (rational or otherwise) that benefit the advertiser and themselves. Does this entail regulating the methods by which such advertising is made to children as well as the substantive content? Should we limit the type of advertising that we understand is more likely to limit or inhibit children's rational decision-making because it emphasizes excitement and novelty, for example? I argue that where it is considered necessary to actually impart healthy and useful information to children, beyond specific substantive restrictions such as tobacco and obesity, there is no principled way provided by the SR's report to allow banning advertising to children more generally based on their capacity, even though that is the exact implication of her analysis.[24]

---

[21] See Samantha Graff, Dale Kunkel and Seth E. Mermin 'Government can Regulate Food Advertising to Children Because Cognitive Research shows that it is Inherently Misleading' (2012) 31 *Health Affairs* 392.

[22] Paras 15–17, section II.B SR Report. See also Johanna von Bahr, 'Regulating the Impacts of Advertising and Marketing on Children's Rights – A Multicountry Comparison' Working Paper prepared for the Global Child Forum 2015, ActionLab: Responsible marketing to children, Royal Palace in Stockholm, Sweden.

[23] See Committee on the Rights of the Child General Comment No.16, para. 59.

[24] von Bahr notes several EU states where the general rules that disallow television broadcast content 'which are likely to harm the physical, mental or moral development of children' and focus on methods by which such harm can take place e.g. encourage children to purchase products or services by exploiting

By implication, although she does not emphasize this as such, the SRs analysis of the harm extends to advertising of addictive products which by definition make the persons and users incapable of engaging in rational choice-making regarding the actual risks of the product, even where these are communicated. Within this framework falls tobacco, for example, as well as alcohol. Additionally, we can argue that restrictions on advertising of medical products are premised on the assessment that laypersons are never in a position to rationally assess the risk of medical products and services and thus should not be advertised to directly. This is especially true of people who are ill, who are not in a position to refuse treatment but cannot and do not have sufficient information and knowledge to make rationale choices about their treatment options as presented by a self-interested advertiser. Only a disinterested medical professional is seen as capable of presenting options in a manner sufficiently complete and independent to allow patients to be capable of making such decisions.

III.2.2 The deception and hidden manipulation of choice options of those capable of making informed choices

A key concern of the SR is the distorted influence that advertising can have on people by bypassing the rational choice mechanisms that they have. These can be evaded by using false information, but also, as the SR argues, by manipulation that reaches to subconscious biases, and behaviors.[25] As noted above, this is another autonomy harm.

Here it is where the advertising is hidden or manipulated in a way so as to hide key characteristics of the product, or key characteristics of the means by which the advertising is done so as to lower barriers to accepting the information provided at face value. Thus the construct is that the advertiser is always self-interested and has an incentive to distort

---

their inexperience or credulity; encourage children to convince their parents or any other person to purchase products or services; exploit children's special trust in parents, teachers or any other persons; unjustifiably show children in dangerous situations. This approach does go some way to targeting specific vulnerabilities of children in terms of methods of advertising. Other countries such as Sweden opt for a simple ban on advertising to children below the age of 12, which comports more generally with the rationale the SR provides. See von Bahr, note 22, pp. 13–14.

[25] Paras 5, 28, 31, SR Report. See also Jon Alexander, Tom Crompton and Guy Shrubsole *Think of me as Evil? Opening the Ethical Debates in Advertising* Public Interest Research Centre (PIRC) WWF-UK (October 2011); John Alan Cohan 'Towards a New Paradigm in the Ethics of Women's Advertising' (2001) 33 *Journal of Business Ethics* 323, p. 324.

or lie about the service or product or the means by which they are letting you know about the service or product. In either case accuracy is paramount – thus we ensure two things: a strong system for distinguishing between different advertisers and communicators – trademarks, trade dress, design protection etc, so that we can then enforce a clear obligation of truthfulness and accuracy on them – when they are speaking of themselves – and when they are speaking of others – comparative advertising. Additionally, a strong system for ensuring that advertisers state as clearly as possible when they are engaging in advertising, so that there is sufficient distinction between advertising and other content.

In this framework, the evidence of harms is crucial: what then does the psychological and scientific data say about the nature and the ways in which people are manipulated, and are unaware that this is the case? The Nudge cases, where choices are presented differently especially given options between opting-out or opting-in are one such example and thus limits could be placed on specific uses, or require disclosure of the method being used.[26] The evidence for subliminal advertising[27] is thin at best and thus makes this harm difficult to use as a basis for regulation. Suggestibility through use of existing predilections and biases, as for example through the use of visual sexual cues has clearly been shown to be an effective means of advertising, but is also seen to have harms relating to equality of women and respect for autonomy of women. This harm occurs by using and emphasizing cultural cues to perhaps make viewers more susceptible to messages associated with sexual imagery, but it remains difficult to argue that this 'bypasses' rational thinking in a way that impinges on the autonomy of individuals to make decisions.

'Neuromarketing' also plays a significant area of concern for the SR but it may be that there is a gap between the claims of the advertisers to be able to exert certain kinds of influence and the reality of what they can actually do. Where the aim is to test the actual effectiveness of an advertising campaign, and the methods that are most effective at advertising, the generation and use of such data do not raise specific harms. It is where the claim is made that such data can pinpoint methods for changing or determining responses to specific advertising messages and bypassing rational decision making that problems may arise. Again however, the data for the reality of that second claim is inconclusive at best and thus cannot form a basis for seeking to regulate.

---

[26] R. Thaler and C. Sunstein *Nudge* (New York: Penguin 2008).

[27] There may be more evidence for something more broadly defined as creating suggestibility. See Cohan, note 25, p. 326.

This is in line with other methods such as viral marketing where firms claim to be able to influence product adoption by sending actors and models into key market environments such as clubs and having these actors and models, as part of their conversations and socialization with patrons, promote and praise products. The data on these methods is proprietary and spotty but suggests that they are not as successful as claimed by marketers. Nevertheless, the broader concern and harm that can be pointed to, is not the actuality of the influence, but the methodology by which such influence is claimed to be done. These are essentially unsanctioned human psychology experiments, with the potential to shift human behavior, as the SR herself points out in paragraph 32 of the Report. This is similar to Facebook secretly altering the proportion of negative or positive elements of people's timelines to see how this affects their moods.[28] It may be here that the real concern is that individuals should be in a position to consent to such experimentation in an informed manner as for any human subjects experiment that would be carried out by academic or other researchers. In the absence of such consent, a system for approval of non-consensual research could be set up, much like Institutional Review Boards in universities. Rules on transparency, truthfulness and on comparative advertising go a long way to addressing the other concerns, so the harms here appear not so great, at least if one takes the approach of the harms above.

III.2.3 Harms to the health of the system

Other harms that the SR is concerned with are more nebulous and difficult to show but may justify stronger action. These go beyond autonomy harms and even beyond harms to participation in the body politic. Some of these harms can come under the rubric of diversity harms. Advertising here then is a vector in the ecology for the growth and acceptance of ideas about products and services, which are good, which are bad, which are valuable and which are worthless. An ecology approach argues that the determinant of which are good and which are bad, is not something that is a product of market competition purely, but a product of an ecology, of which competition is only one element. This suggests that there are cultural niches that fit into the cultural ecology and that each niche has value and should be enabled to flourish and those niches should not be displaced by mono-cultural growths that displace or

---

[28] See 'Facebook tinkers with users emotions in news feed experiment, stirring outcry' Available at http://www.nytimes.com/2014/06/30/technology/facebook-tinkers-with-users-emotions-in-news-feed-experiment-stirring-outcry.html?_r=0Facebook experiment.

overgrow all. It suggests a sustainable growth that is not static, but that has an objective reality in the network of relationships between the occupiers of the niches. The niches may change, albeit slowly, the persons and institutions occupying those niches may shift under the pressure of competition, which can happen rapidly and is a necessary part of the evolution of the ecology, new ideas and seeds may enter and shift the ecology, but the premise is that there is an objective good in sustaining, slowly growing and changing slowly at the macro level while allowing rapid change at the individual and institutional level. Thus to the extent that advertising or specific tools for advertising, or the scale and volume of advertising interfere with that, or encourage overgrowth at the macro level, or the displacement or disappearance of niches, such advertising could then be restricted. This does not rely on a choice model and requires, rather than a multitude of individual assessments as to 'the good', implies a collective assessment of what 'the good' is. It argues for a managed ecology rather than a wild ecology, in which products and services are freely available but the means for creating, distributing and sharing them such as advertising are limited based on the community's assessment of that which should be allowed to grow quickly and that which should be allowed to grow slowly. We can think of wild ecology in the sense of Dawkin's idea of memes and their transmission in culture and the ways that successful memes can lodge in the culture due to specific ways in which they attach to historical behaviors and prejudices.[29] More precisely it is in this frame that the SR's concerns about the ways that advertising and its effect on cultural diversity and the ways that it can usurp or displace other means of transmitting and valuing culture by harnessing it to the sale of service and goods can best be understood.[30] The SR is clearly concerned that advertising, as a business and as a methodology has an inherent value system i.e. that everything is a commodity and that all can be used in the service of persuading people to buy or sell to meet their aspirations. She also points out that advertising can impose specific kinds of aspirations such as extreme wealth, youth culture that involves excess drinking and drug-taking, selection of specific gender roles and hyper-sexualization of women.[31] Within a

---

[29] Richard Dawkins *The Selfish Gene* (Oxford University Press: London, 1976).

[30] Paras 44–47, SR report; Keynote Address by Farida Shaheed, United Nations Special Rapporteur in the field of cultural rights 'United Cities and Local Governments Culture Summit: Culture and Sustainable Cities', Bilbao – 18–20 March 2015.

[31] See also Cohan, note 25.

market place of ideas where choice is paramount, there are no bad or detrimental ideas as such, although it selects for those that most easily plug into existing biases, prejudices and historical cultural behaviors.[32] Under the traditional framework, there is no mechanism for determining which ideas are bad or detrimental.[33] The SR seems content to rely on existing democratic processes for determining when to restrict certain kinds of advertising or to whom, but as she points out, even those states have largely operated by requiring transparency, and information for adults, and only resorted to bans for advertising to children.[34] Even in arguing for stronger safeguards, the SR acknowledges that simply providing information and transparency is insufficient if that information is not as equally salient and available as the advertising itself. This however remains within the choice framework and within the marketplace of ideas metaphor.

As such, she seems to want to push back against the 'mentality of the souk' that advertising encourages and appears to be spreading to all arenas. Again, only outside the marketplace of ideas framework can one really consider such regulation as the cry of the souk is inescapable in the market, and is essential to its functioning. In an ecology, there are natural channels and flows (word of mouth, performance, independent third-party assessments) rather than artificial ones created by commercial exchanges and advertising, and the burden is thus flipped – advertising is only allowed where a need for it exists, where there is lack of growth that advertising can help feed.[35] The limits of this approach then lie in the extent to which the right to freedom of expression imposes limits on the state regarding communication to the public.

---

[32] Ibid., p. 324.

[33] See Strauss, note 19, noting that a traditional free speech approach that focuses on autonomy in the marketplace of ideas cannot restrict expressions simply because they are too effective at communicating to others. In this principle, expressions may only be limited if it bypasses the rational process of being persuaded by, contrasted to those that seek to influence the unconscious or subconscious, or through deceit.

[34] Paras 48–50 SR Report.

[35] It is hard to escape the sense that the SR objects to the sheer commercialization of cultural products and services that underpins modern cultural activity. Absent a return to some Cartesian paradise, commerce and cultural exchange have always been inextricable and what modernity has changed is the ubiquity, scale and centralized control over distribution channels of culture. I share this discomfort but may be more sanguine that commerciality is not the core problem but the erosion and elision of consensual and cooperative forms of creation, expression and sharing.

In addition, it is primarily within this framework that the other substrata of the SR's concerns is also best understood: concerns about *who* is doing the advertising.[36] To the extent that advertising is done primarily by large concentrated global enterprises, both as the creators of advertising and the clients of advertisers, the SR considers this problematic because of three key issues:

- the lack of any real public duties of such enterprises;
- the scale and disproportionate power they wield over points of access and points of distribution to allow and advertise only certain kinds of cultural products; and
- the sheer amount of advertising that such conglomerates with singular visions, missions and values can engage in.

In the absence of a cultural ecology approach, the justification for interfering with such legal persons lies in the hope for a reasoned distinction between commercial and non-commercial advertising that allows you to impose significant restrictions on commercial advertising. I argue that the SR does not provide this and this makes the target of her action thus harder to hit as noted above in the discussion on definitions.

As discussed above, the SR report implies a communitarian approach to culture that would favour such a model, with an appropriate rights substrate, but the language used and the solutions suggested all seem to lie in the competition, choice and marketplace frameworks.

IV. RADICAL CONSENT AND CHOICE

In the end a cultural ecology approach encounters far too many obstacles, including its compatibility with a rights approach. What may be the best approach here is not so much to seek a right that restricts the communicator but one that seeks to expand the ability of the advertised to, the listener, to consent. This is something the SR points to in Paragraph 33 of the report but does not elaborate on.[37] A radical approach would require that advertisers obtain real, true, prior informed consent before presenting advertising to a person. That this would be an extension of the right to choose which products, services to buy, which cultural products to consume seems inarguable. How radical you would wish to be would then be constrained by both technical limits and transaction costs. You

---

36 Section III.B SR Report.

37 Also suggested in Alexander, Crompton and Shrubsole, note 25, pp. 51–2.

can imagine a system whereby advertisers were obligated to provide, in the market, the means for consumers to turn the advertising off or refuse to listen or consume it as part of their participation. While this seems easy for consumption in private spaces, it is advertising in the public spaces, especially visual advertising that would need to be managed. Size, colour and other elements of billboards and other public space would be controlled to allow for individuals to choose not to look as the SR suggests and recommends but for which the analytical justification is not as strongly based in a right and is more located in a cultural ecology mode than a radical choice and consent mode. Audio would only be allowed if a person made an affirmative choice to do so by pointing an audio device or walking up to a speaker. This would require volume controls and standards. The SR does not operate within this framework either, although it is the one that best explains the recommendations she makes, but I believe that the implications of that choice are much stronger, that they are based in some form of radical consent and choice which implies a far stronger set of recommendations here. Just as someone should be free to seek to speak or express themselves, an individual has the right to refuse to hear or listen. It is this negative right that I think presents the strongest argument for the SR and has the best link to the freedom of expression framework. It is also the strongest argument for addressing how the public space needs to be managed. The SR rightly points out that public space is an arena of competition for the attention of individuals and where private spaces are used to intrude speech into those public spaces, as individuals and firms have a right to do, how are we to address the ability of the individual to make choices in that environment? It cannot just be an ability to choose between the cacophony of expressions in the public space but the ability to choose not to listen to any of those except those that are necessary for the act of navigating. In this sense public spaces are thus not simply physical but extend to social spaces on the internet such as Twitter and Facebook which although managed by private firms, are located within the public infrastructure of the internet and thus take on some of the role of public providers in that context. Where participation in those spaces cannot be avoided, there can be no real consent to terms that impose a requirement to be exposed to advertising and thus a radical consent approach would require the ability to opt out of advertising, but perhaps then a requirement to pay a subscription fee instead, one that would not be prohibitive, but aimed to cover the cost of access and use. In physical spaces, visual clutter can use zoning to limit the number and size of billboards. Again, her prescription falls within this radical consent framework even though it is not articulated as such. Finally, this approach also encompasses limits on advertising to children who can never be considered to have given consent except in a very limited set of circumstances.

It is also clear that this negative aspect of the right to seek and impart information as discussed by the Human Rights Committee in General Comments and reports of the SR is much less well-developed and discussed as the concern has been driven largely by ensuring access and the right to speak. But the development of the negative aspect of the right may be the best defense against the HRC's assertion that commercial advertising is included within the broader subject matter of freedom of expression.[38] Without the development of this radical right to consent to listen or right to refuse to listen, the framework for protecting expression places significant limits on what can be done and is not able to address the core concern of the SR – the dominance and cultural displacement that advertising can have, when wielded by concentrated global enterprises. This is not to say that we should not accept the margin of freedom that the SR points out is made available under the SR reports on freedom expression and by courts such as the ECHR.[39]

It is also important to note that some aspects of this radical choice and consent approach could be developed within the right to participate in cultural life, premised on the understanding that advertising is a major conduit for the transmission of cultural values and products and aspirations. The extent to which the right also implies a right *not* to participate in certain forms of cultural activity, there is little guidance from the CESCR General Comment 21.[40] Paragraph 7 does suggest that part of the right is the right to choose whether or not to participate:

> The decision by a person *whether or not to exercise the right* to take part in cultural life individually, or in association with others, is a cultural choice and, as such, should be recognized, respected and protected on the basis of equality' (my emphasis)

However, this is not further developed in the section on participation and thus may need to be addressed in order for a radical choice framework to be effective. There might however be further guidance in the standards that the Rapporteur points to in those instruments related to rights of minorities, protection of indigenous peoples, and the rights of women.

---

38 Para. 7, SR Report.

39 Para. 9, 10 SR Report.

40 General Comment 21 Available at: http://www2.ohchr.org/english/bodies/cescr/docs/gc/E-C-12-GC-21.doc.

CESCR General Comment 21 recognizes that Minorities[41] and indigenous peoples[42] may have an interest in preserving and conserving their culture which therefore implies refusal to take on or participate in the consumption or adoption of non-minority or non-indigenous cultural products and services. Further elaboration of these rights to refuse or to exclude may also be useful in justifying choice at the communal level and not just at the individual level.

This radical consent approach however, is a fundamentally anti-communitarian approach that looks at culture merely as the sum of the individual choices and consents rather than a collectively chosen and managed construct.

V. ENFORCEMENT

I believe the most successful finding by the SR is the extent to which regulation in this area is ad hoc, disaggregated, and a mix of self-regulatory and regulatory mechanisms. I argue as I did above that one of the prerequisites that the SR should focus on is that the regulator must be independent. Additionally, the regulation must target *conduct* not necessarily categories of persons. The basis and justification for that regulation may have to be left up to the individual states but the SR should perhaps think about providing some basis for the analytical approaches and outline the limits that human rights frameworks impose on them and the limits on the kinds of problems each approach can address.

Importantly, the SR emphasizes in her report the lack of enforcement and access to enforcement against violators of the rules. One of the solutions to consider, premised on a consent model is pre-approval processes for advertising rather than reactive mechanisms. This extends the SR's own recommendations and suggests that it encompass all forms of advertising and not just the limited print and billboard type that it now largely applies to. This would thus form both a bottleneck for managing the volume and the nature and placement of advertising. An Advertising Standards Authority, whose decisions would be appealable as any other independent administrative regulatory body should engage in pre-surveillance rather than post-violation corrective measures.

41 Ibid., para. 31.
42 Ibid., paras 36–37.

10. Copyright policy and the right to science and culture – Report 2015 (A/HRC/28/57)

Fiona Macmillan

INTRODUCTION: THE REPORT

From the outset, one thing should be clear: The *Report* of the Special Rapporteur in the field of cultural rights on Copyright Policy and the Right to Science and Culture[1] is fundamentally critical of the current international copyright system. By this I mean that it would take a particularly original approach to construing textual meaning to read the report as a lament against a system of property rights that has, perhaps, gone a little overboard from time to time and consequently requires some tinkering around the edges. Rather the depth of its critical stance makes it a novelty in the international law discourse around copyright,[2] which generally tiptoes around difficult issues in its anxiety not to offend. And the influence of those likely to be offended should not be underestimated bearing in mind that they include a powerful lobby of corporate interests and an intimidating constellation of the leading states of the neo-liberal era, which have collectively advanced the interests of the corporate sector through the extension of copyright at the international level.

The *Report* commences in a straightforward fashion, noting that despite the fact that they cover the same subject matter (science and culture) 'two influential paradigms of international law – intellectual property and human rights – have evolved largely separately' (para. 2). As private rights over intellectual property become ever stronger, the *Report* notes, the tension between these two regimes has increased (para.

[1] Report of the Special Rapporteur in the field of cultural rights, Farida Shaheed, *Copyright Policy and the Right to Science and Culture*, UNGA Doc. A/HRC/28/57, 24 December 2014.

[2] Perhaps the *Report's* festive timing helped it slip under the radar.

3). According to the *Report*, some of the consequences and/or risks of this separate evolution are: the privatization of human knowledge; the restriction of artistic and creative freedom; the squeezing of the public domain with the consequent reduction in the capacity of everyone to take part in cultural life; restrictions on the general right to freedom of expression, including the right to receive information; and a failure to recognise the 'unique concerns of indigenous peoples' (para. 56). Generally, the *Report* tends to proceed with careful diplomatic phrasing on these points, often warning against adverse consequences rather than proclaiming their existence. It states, for example, that 'human knowledge' is 'a global public good and … States should guard against promoting the privatization of knowledge to an extent that deprives individuals of opportunities to take part in cultural life' (para. 14). Cautious language is also used with respect to the impact of copyright on artistic freedom. On this point the *Report* notes that the width of the exclusive rights afforded to copyright holders enables them 'to monetize a wide variety of uses and to prevent adaptations they find objectionable. Consequently, the creative freedom of other artists to build upon and adapt existing cultural works may become dependent upon their ability to pay a licensing fee' (para. 22). Similarly, on the question of the contracting of public domain or cultural commons, the *Report* draws attention to the way in which the long duration of the copyright interest may interfere with the protection of 'a vibrant public domain of shared cultural heritage, from which all creators are free to draw' (para. 50).

If, however, the *Report* is diplomatic on the copyright/human rights nexus, it is considerably less equivocal on the legal and institutional environment of international copyright law making. One punch that it packs, especially bearing in mind that it was presented in the Human Rights Council of the United Nations General Assembly, is its rejection of the claim that the copyright system is an expression of, or might be justified by, Article 15(1)(c) of the International Covenant on Economic, Social and Cultural Rights,[3] requiring the protection of authors' moral and material rights. As the *Report* observes, nothing in that provision requires the protection of these rights through the proprietary apparatus of copyright (paras 26–29). It draws welcome attention to the fact that there are a range of other legal instruments that are relevant to protecting the rights of authors:

---

[3] The progenitor of which is contained in the Universal Declaration of Human Rights, art. 27(2).

> Artistic livelihoods may be supported by, for example, minimum wage protections, collective bargaining power, social security guarantees, budgetary support for the arts, artistic education, library purchasing, immigration and visa policies and measures to promote cultural tourism. Copyright laws should be understood as part of a larger set of policies to promote the cultural sector and the right to science and culture. (para. 49)

The obsession with copyright seems often to obscure these other instruments.

However, the *Report's* punchiest sections are directed at issues arising from the presence and activities of the media and entertainment corporations in the copyright context. The *Report* goes behind the figure of the copyright owner, drawing the critical distinction between the owner of the copyright interest, often a corporation, and the author of the copyright work. It is important to understand that the interests of these two figures may be not only different but 'opposing' (para. 38), says the *Report*, and that the contractual relations between them regarding commercialization and distribution of works 'are often marked by an imbalance of power between the parties' (para. 43). Applying its critical human rights eye, it notes that the economic interests of corporate rights holders 'do not enjoy the status of human rights' (para. 41). Accordingly, '[f]rom the human rights perspective, copyright policy and industry practices must be judged by how well they serve the interests of human authors, as well as the public's interest in cultural participation' (para. 41).

The *Report* criticizes the overwhelming influence of the corporate sector in the political economy of international copyright law making, which it describes as a 'democratic deficit in international policymaking on copyright' (para. 19):

> Of particular concern is the tendency for trade negotiations to be conducted amid great secrecy, with substantial corporate participation but without an equivalent participation of elected officials and other public interest voices. For example, the recent negotiations around the Anti-Counterfeiting Trade Agreement and the Trans-Pacific Partnership have involved a few countries negotiating substantial commitments on copyright policy, without the benefit of public participation and debate. (para 19)

SO FAR, SO GOOD

In drawing critical attention to a wide range of issues impacting on the operation of copyright law and, especially, the international copyright regime, the *Report* has courageously gone where few other institutions of public international governance have dared to go. This territory is, however, not uncharted. A considerable number of academic and activist commentators have already set up camp there. The challenge now is to build upon the *Report* by bringing to light further matters of substantial importance in understanding the relationship between copyright and the realization of cultural rights. In this chapter I offer comments on a range of issues raised or touched on in the *Report*, but which I consider deserve further consideration. Of course, there is a yardstick according to which these issues have been selected and this yardstick is a set of principles and observations that I suggest are fundamental to finding our way to a system that recognizes and promotes creativity and cultural rights.

The first of these is the proposition that cultural production and the use of cultural goods/services and other intangible resources are a part of the same process. This means that every moment of cultural production implies the use in some form of cultural products or resources that already exist. So, in this sense, cultural production is always a collective undertaking. However, acknowledging that cultural production is a collective process does not mean that authors should be required to abandon their rights with respect to specific instances of that process for which they are responsible. So the second notch on my yardstick is that authors/creators should have the right to be recognised and remunerated for their work. Thirdly, an accommodation must be found between the importance of securing this outcome and the recognition that, by its nature, cultural creativity in the arts is a common good. What is needed, therefore, is a balance between community rights and individual (private) rights. Finally, I proceed on the (admittedly optimistic) basis that law has the capacity to be liberatory and thus to offer solution to problems, even where – as in this case – those problems have been created by the law itself. The idea of copyright as a model to encourage production and diffusion of intangible cultural resources has come under significant pressure in recent years. The essential reason for this is that what the copyright model has produced is a system of the commodification of creativity and the privatization of culture.[4] The winners in this system are the big production houses and other private commercial interests.[5]

[4] This is an argument that I have made at length in other places: see, eg, F. Macmillan, 'The Cruel ©: Copyright and Film' (2002) *European Intellectual Property Review* 483–92; F. Macmillan, 'Commodification and Cultural Ownership' in J Griffiths and U Suthersanen, *Copyright and Free Speech: Comparative and International Analyses* (Oxford: OUP, 2005) 35–65.

[5] See, eg, R. Bettig, *Copyrighting Culture: The Political Economy of Intellectual Property* (Boulder: Westview Press, 1996); F. Macmillan, 'Public Interest and the Public Domain in an Era of Corporate Dominance' in

However, the fact that copyright law has produced, at this point in history, a problematic system of private property protection over cultural goods does not necessarily mean that it is incapable of having a part in securing the balance, mentioned above, between community rights and individual (private) rights.

Measuring itself according to this yardstick, this chapter examines six critical issues raised by the *Report*: private property over cultural output; the problem of corporate ownership of copyright; the uses of human rights discourse; the particular position of Indigenous Peoples; the challenges posed by digital technologies; and the problem of the apparently ever-decreasing (or, maybe, ever-increasing) cultural commons.

PRIVATE PROPERTIZATION

We have become so used to the idea that copyright, and other intellectual property rights, grant private property rights over intangibles that perhaps we have stopped seeing the strangeness of this idea and its possible pernicious consequences. The *Report* acknowledges some of the consequences of the fact that what copyright creates is private property rights over cultural output. In particular, it focuses on the way in which this plays out in relation to the author/owner distinction. As already mentioned, it notes, for example, that as a consequence of this distinction granting copyright is not the same thing as ensuring that creators of such works are able to enjoy material and moral rights in relation to them. Its concern about the way in which rights granted to human authors end up in corporate hands, often as a consequence of contractual negotiations that are affected by a power imbalance, also flows from the author/owner distinction.

What the *Report* does not say, however, is that the creation of private property rights over cultural products is part of a system designed to make those products into liquid investments and that the purpose of making culture – or any other asset – liquid is to facilitate investment. In other words, the design of the system favours the accumulation of capital by those best able to harvest profits off that accumulation. Those best able to harvest profits off the liquid assets represented by copyright are the corporations engaged in the production and distribution of cultural products. When the copyright system is seen in this light, one might

---

B. Andersen (ed.), *Intellectual Property Rights: Innovation, Governance and the Institutional Environment* (Cheltenham UK and Northampton, MA: Edward Elgar, 2006), 46–69.

reasonably query the nature of the 'the social and human values *inherent* in copyright law' (para. 60, my emphasis), to which the *Report* makes reference or 'the social function and human dimension of intellectual property' (para. 90). It is, of course, true that the system of authors' rights derives its fundamental justification from the notion that an author's personality is embedded in the work,[6] but this theory has very little purchase in the now internationally dominant Anglo-American concept of copyright.[7] That concept has traditionally justified the allocation of monopoly rights to creators and distributors of creative works on the basis that they will incentivize such creation and distribution. Nevertheless, the operation of the international copyright system appears to prioritize accumulation of investment capital over 'social values' or 'social functions'.

From the point of view of the *Report*, which measures the intellectual property system against that of human rights, one might think that – worthy as it is – it is not really enough to identify disjunctions between the copyright system and the human rights system that can be remedied by adjustments here and there. Rather, it needs to be acknowledged that the systems are aiming at fundamentally different things. This is not to say that reconciling their aims is impossible, but more that achieving this is of the same order of magnitude as imposing human rights limits on other systems of capital accumulation, such as the various forms of the stock and futures market.

When the *Report* claims that 'copyright laws should be understood as part of a larger set of policies to promote the cultural sector and the right to science and culture' (para. 49) it is not clear whether it is talking about the copyright system as it is or some idealised version of the system yet to come. Only the second meaning is credible. As long as copyright is primarily an instrument of investment it remains a potent instrument for – and, in fact, an ideal example of – the replication of the labour/capital division, where the labour of the author is separated from the capital in the property. Trying my best, it seems to me to be difficult to question this claim. Whether or not it is a good or bad thing is, of course, another question over which much fierce debate can be, and has, raged. However,

---

6 See, eg, J. Hughes, 'The Philosophy of Intellectual Property' (1988) 77 *Georgetown Law Journal* 287–366; J. Waldron, 'From Authors to Copiers: Individual Rights and Social Values in Intellectual Property' (1993) 69 *Chicago-Kent Law Review* 841–87.

7 Cf. J. Ginsburg, 'A Tale of Two Copyrights: Literary Property in Revolutionary France and America' (1990) 64 *Tulane Law Review* 991–1031.

from the human rights perspective of the *Report*, the merits of copyright law as a system of investment might be reasonably regarded as questionable.

CORPORATE OWNERS

The *Report* speaks about the role of corporate actors in the operation of the copyright system, including their role in shaping copyright laws transnationally, as though they enter into consideration only as the recipients of transfers (either by assignment or licence) of copyright interests from human authors, possibly negotiated in circumstances of unequal bargaining power. There are, however, two evident problems with this characterisation.

One of these is, as I have already noted above, that it fundamentally underrates the centrality of corporate systems of distribution in the accumulation of capital in copyrights as liquid assets. The other is that, precisely for this reason, the media and entertainment corporations that are involved in both production and distribution of cultural products, are granted copyright interests in some forms of cultural products *as if they were authors*. That is, not because they have taken some form of assignment or licence from a human being in circumstances of uneven bargaining power (or not), but because they have been granted copyright by operation of law from the outset as if they were authors. Music production companies, not the musicians, own *from the outset*, the exclusive rights over the sound recording that will become the commercially distributed product; in many jurisdictions, film production companies own, or own jointly with the director, *from the outset* copyright in the film; broadcasting corporations own copyright in their broadcasts *from the outset*; publishers own the copyright in the appearance of the pages of works they publish (whether printed or electronic) *from the outset*. All these rights – none of which are mentioned in the *Report* – are owned by the corporations before we even start talking about other rights they may acquire by contractual transfer from human authors under circumstances affected by unequal bargaining power. Besides anything else, this means that the problems with the owner/author distinction are in fact much more profound than the *Report* acknowledges. The problem is not just that copyright law embraces a distinction between authors and owners, which tends to militate against the interests of authors. In fact, it is characterized by a confusion between these two concepts that means that the interests of so-called 'authors' cannot easily be identified or generalised.

The *Report* is, of course, absolutely right to say that the role of corporations in forming international copyright law should be limited. When it says that '[c]orporate right holders must not be presumed to speak for the interests of authors' (para. 99), the context makes it relatively clear that it is referring to human authors. But this statement also makes it clear that the *Report* underrates how much these corporations are insiders in the copyright system – exactly because they are not just rights holders.

HUMAN RIGHTS DISCOURSE

One of the most pernicious, intellectually unjustified and dangerous discourses in intellectual property scholarship and commentary is that which claims that the Article 15(1)(c) of the UN Charter on Economic Social and Cultural Rights gives a human rights justification for the grant of intellectual property protection.[8] This is particularly so when it is accompanied by a discourse that claims a human right to property. The baselessness of the former claim is acknowledged in the *Report* (paras 26–29). However, the latter claim seems to be accepted by the *Report* (paras 52–54), which cites Article 17(2) of the Charter of Fundamental Rights of the European Union as the source of this claim. Bearing in mind that the claim in Article 17(2) seems to be based on Article 15(1)(c) of the United Nations Charter on Economic Social and Cultural Rights – already rejected by the Report as a basis for private property protection of cultural and scientific works – this seems a little strange.

But more than this, if we are constrained to accept that this so-called fundamental right to property is a human right then, frankly, it brings the whole discourse of human rights – already under pressure for its Euro-centrism, if not neo-colonialism – into disrepute. In a world where international human rights law has done so little to protect so many from fundamental abuses of the most basic human rights – the right to life, for example – does it really do any credit to human rights discourse to claim the right to a form of property which is central to not just capitalist processes of accumulation, but the perfection of such processes in the neo-liberal period, as being of somehow an equivalent order or type?

And then perhaps there are also shortcomings in relying on the human rights system as a yardstick against which to measure the achievements of the intellectual property system in its 'social function and human

[8] To be clear, that is intellectual property protection in the form of an alienable private property right.

dimension' (para. 90). Here we might cite the extremely vexed question of the gradual disappearance of labour rights from the central concerns of human rights law. The *Report* says that copyright should be only one part of a legal structure to protect its concept of authors, which it envisages as human workers in creative and cultural production, and it mentions the importance in this context of 'minimum wage protections' and 'collective bargaining power' (para. 49). However, it perhaps overlooks the extent to which these rights have been marginalized in human rights law and discourse.[9] Another major shortcoming in relying on the human rights system as a yardstick arises from the legitimate concern that the rights of us all to our cultural heritage, and the particular rights of Indigenous Peoples to protect rights in their heritage, are not adequately recognised in mainstream human rights law.

INDIGENOUS PEOPLES

So far as the relationship between intellectual property rights and cultural heritage is concerned, the particular position of Indigenous Peoples is recognised in the United Nations Declaration on the Rights of Indigenous Peoples (DRIPs).[10] Article 31(1) of the DRIPs seeks to assure to Indigenous Peoples 'the right to maintain, control, protect and develop their intellectual property over their cultural heritage, traditional knowledge and traditional cultural expressions'. For reasons that are surely located in the historic and continuing injustice meted out to Indigenous Peoples – including the forced dispossession and misappropriation of their lands and culture, and their political marginalisation and disempowerment – the *Report* endorses the approach of Article 31(1). And it urges the observance of the values and principles embodied in the 1995 United Nations Guidelines for the Protection of the Heritage of Indigenous Peoples,[11] especially that:

> indigenous peoples' ownership and custody of their heritage must continue to be collective, permanent and inalienable; that the free and informed consent of the traditional owners be a precondition of any agreements for the recording, study, use or display of indigenous peoples' heritage: and that

---

[9] See, eg, V. Mantouvalou, 'Are Labour Rights Human Rights?' (2012) 3 *European Labour Law Journal* 151–72.

[10] GA Res. 61/295 (UN Doc. A/61/L.67 and Add.1), adopted on 13 September 2007.

[11] E/CN.4/Sub.2/1995/26.

concerned peoples be the primary beneficiaries of commercial application of their heritage (para. 58).

While in no way questioning the validity of the concern about the treatment of Indigenous Peoples that provides the context of this endorsement of both the 1995 Guidelines for the Protection of the Heritage of Indigenous Peoples and the 2007 DRIPs, one might wonder if the endorsement of Article 31(1) of DRIPs is consistent with the general position of the *Report* rejecting the proposition that Article 15(1)(c) of the Charter on Economic Social and Cultural Rights (and/or Article 27(2) of the Universal Declaration of Human Rights) mandates protection in the form of private property rights. Similarly, doubts might be raised (and will be in what follows) about whether Article 31(1)(c) is consistent with the idea of the protection of cultural heritage as a community right. And, on this basis, even whether it is consistent with the 1995 United Nations Guidelines for the Protection of the Heritage of Indigenous Peoples, cited in the *Report*. It is not only that a form of private property protection is an inherently problematic way to protect what is said to be a community or collective right.[12] It is also that protecting the cultural heritage of Indigenous Peoples through a private property device developed according to an understanding of creativity propounded by the ideals of the European enlightenment may have consequences for the development of that heritage that are deleterious to its protection. This is because one result of such a process is that the cultural heritage in question has to be corralled into the shape of Western intellectual property law.[13] If the item of cultural heritage is a story, music, or artwork then it has to be fitted into copyright law; designs and symbols must fit into the netherworld of the relationship between copyright, designs and trademarks; knowledge about local flora and fauna must be fitted somewhere into patent law, plants breeder's rights, geographical indications. This will mean that different levels of protection will apply to different types of Indigenous cultural heritage. In short, the end result is that occidental intellectual property law comes to constitute Indigenous (and other non-Western)

---

[12] I do not discount here the possibility that certain cultural property might be privately owned by individuals comprising part of an Indigenous community, but this is not the situation to which I make reference here.

[13] M. Blakeney, 'The Protection of Traditional Knowledge Under Intellectual Property Law' (2000) 22 *European Intellectual Property Law Review* 251–61.

cultural heritage.[14] In so doing, it may change the shape of that heritage in ways that are not necessarily the consequence of the reflexive cultural practice that constitutes it. Overall, it seems to me to be questionable that intellectual property rights can ever – or could ever be expected to – do the things that the 1995 UN Principles and Guidelines for the Protection of the Heritage of Indigenous Peoples envisaged.[15]

Paragraph 56 of the *Report* states (taking no hostages) that '[i]ntellectual property regimes have historically failed to take into account the unique concerns of indigenous peoples'. In this, I suggest, that intellectual property law is not alone. The same observation is arguably true of almost all international law in the post-colonial period. This is because the 'unique concerns of indigenous peoples' are, by definition, that they constitute a political formation that is not recognised as a state in international law. As a result they lack self-determination domestically and have been excluded from the process of international lawmaking, including international lawmaking with respect to intellectual property and with respect to culture and cultural heritage. Under these circumstances it is appropriate and just for the international political and lawmaking community to take seriously their well-founded claims to both political and cultural self-determination. The fact that we are prepared to concede them the latter (which is part and parcel of the former), but not the former is hardly an adequate response.

And then, looking again at the words of the 1995 United Nations Guidelines, should it not be a concern of all of us that our heritage is not 'collective, permanent and inalienable', that we are not afforded the opportunity to consent to the 'recording, study, use or display' of our heritage? As has already been argued, we should take account of the particular historical position of Indigenous Peoples, but this should not blind us to the fact that it is not only Indigenous Peoples that have, or should have a right, to the enjoyment of their heritage.[16] One of the particularly strange results of the saturating effect of the intellectual

---

[14] P. Fitzpatrick and R. Joyce, 'Copying Right: Cultural Property and the Limits of (Occidental) Law' in F. Macmillan (ed.), *New Directions in Copyright Law: Volume 4* (Cheltenham, UK and Northampton, MA: Edward Elgar, 2007), 169–90.

[15] See F. Macmillan, 'The Problematic Relationship between Traditional Knowledge and the Commons' in S. Pinton and L. Zagato, *Cultural Heritage: Scenarios 2016* (University Ca Foscari Press, 2016) (in press).

[16] See further, F. Macmillan, 'Cultural Property and Community Rights to Cultural Heritage' in T. Xu and J. Allain (eds), *Property and Human Rights in a Global Context* (Oxford: Hart, 2015), 41–62.

property system is our acceptance, as Slaughter argues, of a state of affairs in which we in the global north have intellectual property and the rest of the world has cultural property.[17] While Slaughter argues that the rest of the world suffers from the burdensomeness and lack of prestige arising from this state of affairs, it is worth also noting what a culturally impoverishing idea this is for the global north. And, assuming that we do have some cultural heritage/property, are we really supposed to be happy with the idea that when elements of our own heritage are privatised by large media and entertainment corporations we have to pay to enjoy, use or re-use it, with the result that that a large corporation is the 'primar[y] beneficiar[y] of the commercial application' of our heritage (see para. 58, *op cit*)? Do we think this is all right because we in the global north are all one big (although not happy) community? The implicit idea that the law regards me as being in community with Disney, so that when Disney privatises collective cultural heritage for its private profit that is not a problem, seems to me to be a bit of a problem.

DIGITAL TECHNOLOGY

The *Report* is, in my view, quite correct to question the excessive and sometimes almost hysterical reaction among certain copyright owners to the advent of the Internet, digitization, social media and the like. It is true that the ease of copying works available in digital form allied with the difficulty in identifying and proceeding against unauthorised copiers has demonstrated some of the inherent limits of the intellectual property construct in the current world juridical order. However, this does not justify the introduction of excessive and oppressive rules and sanctions. As the *Report* says, controlling (so-called) digital 'piracy' through things like 'website blocking, content filtering and other limits on access to content … as well as the liability imposed on intermediaries for infringing content disseminated by users … could result in restrictions that are not compatible with the right to freedom of expression and the right to science and culture' (para. 51).

In particular, criminal sanctions are inappropriate in cases of 'non-commercial infringement' the *Report* says (para. 51). But we might

[17] J. R. Slaughter, 'Form & Informality: An Unliterary Look at World Literature' in R. Warhol (ed.), *The Work of Genre: Selected Essays from the English Institute* (English Institute in Collaboration with the American Council of Learned Societies, 2011), http://quod.lib.umich.edu/cgi/t/text/text-idx?c=acls;idno=heb90055, 177–240.

wonder whether they are more generally inappropriate in relation to copyright infringement. It is true, of course, that the criminal law has been, traditionally, extensively used to protect private rights in tangible property. Advocates of strong intellectual property rights like to draw comparisons between the theft of physical property and that of intellectual property, sometimes employing emotive metaphors that have somehow abandoned their metaphorical nature and acquired a life of their own within the lexicon of intellectual property.[18] However, to accept uncritically that what applies with respect to the protection of private property rights in tangibles is appropriate with respect to the same rights in intangible property is also to accept that there are no important differences between these forms of property or in the political, cultural and social consequences stemming from their protection. There are good reasons why this is not an intellectually convincing elision.

Unlike tangibles, intangibles are both non-rivalrous and non-wastable. They are non-rivalrous in the sense that there are no limits on the number of people that can use a piece of intangible property at the same time; and they are non-wastable because they are not degraded by use. The non-rivalrous and non-wastable nature of intangible property means that its 'theft' is of an entirely different order than that of tangible property. Like taking someone's physical property, taking someone's intellectual property may be ethically questionable, but this is not because taking it deprives the owner or anyone else of its further use. Justifications for creating private property rights over intangibles cannot, therefore, depend on the need to prevent the 'infringer' wrongfully depriving the 'owner' of the right to use the intangible. Nor can they depend on some sort of benevolent response to the famous 'tragedy of the commons',[19] according to which resources held commonly are plundered, degraded and eventually exhausted.[20] Rather, justifications must depend on one (or both) of two frequently posited claims. One of these claims is that there is some sort of natural or fundamental right of the author/creator over the thing produced. The other is that, in the absence of a restriction or reward or incentive in the nature of a property right, rather than creating new things

---

[18] The classic example of this is the use of the word 'piracy', uncritically used in the *Report*, for systematic copyright infringements, despite the absence of unconstrained physical violence that is the hallmark of high-seas piracy.

[19] See G. Hardin, 'The Tragedy of the Commons' (1968) 162 *Science* 1243, 1244.

[20] See further, eg, Hardin, ibid.; and E. Ostrom, *Governing the Commons: The Evolution of Institutions or Collective Action* (Cambridge and New York, Cambridge University Press, 1990), esp Ch. 1.

everyone would just copy what already exists with dire consequences for human productivity and creativity.[21] Perhaps arguments from natural rights or based on incentive or reward theories might justify the creation of private property rights over intangible things. But none of these arguments suggests in any particularly compelling fashion that we should attach the same legal, political, social or cultural consequences to the infringements of those rights as we do to the infringement of property rights over tangibles.

In the context of the digital revolution focusing only on the question of enforcement and tightening sanctions means following the agenda of the big copyright owners, the media and entertainment corporations. This is a pity when there are also other ways, not mentioned in the *Report*, in which the logic of new wine in old bottles is worth questioning in the context of digital technology. Changes in practices of cultural production as a result of this technology challenge many of the assumptions of copyright law and may have important implications for its application. In particular, there are four distinctions at the heart of copyright that these new modes of cultural production bring into stark relief. These distinctions, which are examined below, are: the distinction between authorship and collaboration; the distinction between product and process; the distinction between author and user; and the distinction between capital and labour.

The Distinction Between Authorship and Collaboration

The copyright paradigm has long been criticised for its focus on the author or individual genius, because of the way that this focus ignores the relationship between authorship and the use of what already exists. Digitisation has increased both the conscious and the sub-conscious use of collaborative practices, without this being well recognised in the copyright paradigm. A number of different consequences might flow from this. One of these is that the tendency of copyright to become a 'winner take all' right is enhanced because the strongest economic players, who are always best able to defend legal rights, claim to own the rights in works to which a range of authors have contributed. This is not different in principle to what can take place in the non-digital environment, but differences in practice in the digital environment may exponentially increase the gap between the reality of 'authorship' and the ownership of the copyright interest. Another way of looking at the same

---

[21] See, eg, Waldron, n. 6 *supra*.

problem is to say that copyright law does not facilitate collective works. In particular, it lacks a clear concept of the public domain or cultural commons in which collective work, untrammelled by private property rights, is facilitated. As part and parcel of this, it lacks any concept of a community of creators working freely within the community, but protecting their work from use outside the community by the use of property rights.[22]

The Distinction Between Product and Process

Copyright always focuses on the final product, the protected 'work'. In the kingdom of copyright law production and consumption of the work are always distinct moments. In the digital environment what we often see instead is a continual process of revision and innovation, in which production of the work and its consumption are not differentiated. Consequently, it may be difficult, if not impossible, to identify the final 'work'. Some argue that this is exactly how things should be because the focus on a final work negates the reality of the creative process.[23] Others say that focusing on process at the expense of product, especially the idea of a final product, undervalues cognitive work.[24]

The Distinction Between Author and User

The idea, strictly connected with working practices in some parts of the so-called digital economy, that it is all about the process, not the final product, carries with it the suggestion that everyone can be a creator. The idea of universal and undifferentiated authorship tends to suggest that creativity is banal.[25] In other words, if it is true that everyone is a creator then there is nothing exceptional about creativity. This means that the lack of differentiation between production and consumption also goes to the heart of one of copyright's most beloved distinctions, that between author and user. The idea of the author or the individual genius is

---

[22] See, eg, Macmillan, n. 15 *supra*.

[23] C. DiBona, S. Ockman and M. Stone (eds), *Open Sources: Voices from the Open Source Revolution* (Sebastopol: O'Reilly, 1999).

[24] Eg, T. Terranova, 'Free Labour: Producing Culture for the Digital Economy' in P. K. Nayar (ed.), *The New Media and Cybercultures Anthology* (Oxford: Wiley-Blackwell, 2010), 335–56.

[25] Ibid.

embedded in the heart of copyright.[26] It is the very power of this idea that is at the base of the maximalist protection claims by, among others, the media and entertainment corporations. Perhaps it is premature to do away with the distinctions between product and process, and between author and user, but some recalibration of these concepts in the light of the digitally based creative practices may restore a semblance of reality.

The Distinction Between Capital and Labour

Like the three distinctions already considered, the way in which copyright law understands the distinction between capital and labour is a consequence of the central position of the author in copyright's theoretical worldview. The irony of this is that, as has already been mentioned in this chapter, in practical legal terms the author counts for little, but this is probably a minor quibble for those who understand copyright to be founded on the strict relation between investment of labour on the part of the author and property rights.[27] However, the phenomena described above, including the difficulty (or unreality) of identifying an author or a work, interrupts this connection and eliminates the author as the incarnation of capital. The effect is to produce a net separation between labour and capital. The distinction between author and owner in copyright law has long been part of the Marxist critique of copyright's commodification of creativity.[28] However, the combination of the severing of capital and labour, on the one hand, and the reality of creative practices in the digital environment, on the other, has produced the phenomena of work without payment, the fruits of which are subsequently propertised – using copyright – by a corporate interest. This is an issue that has recently attracted particular attention on the part of theorists of technology.[29] Aside from the obvious problem of working without payment, it appears that these practices are having a negative effect on salaries and job-security in some industries concerned with cultural production. Another way of describing this phenomenon is that thanks to the strange coalition between new ways of working and old ways of appropriating the fruits of

---

26 M. Woodmansee, *The Author, Art, and the Market: Rereading the History of Aesthetics* (New York: Columbia University Press, 1994).

27 See further, Hughes, n. 6 *supra*.

28 Macmillan, 'Copyright and Corporate Power', n. 5 *supra*.

29 N. Dyer-Witheford, *Cyber-Proletariat: Global Labour in the Digital Vortex* (Chicago: University of Chicago Press, 2015); O. Fraysse and M. O'Neil (eds), *Digital Labour and Prosumer Capitalism: The US Matrix* (New York: Palgrave Macmillan, 2015).

labour (through copyright) we have a situation in which we can all be a part of the new 'creative and cultural economy'. We can all be a part of the market, and we can all be exploited in it.

THE CULTURAL COMMONS

It has been frequently suggested, that one way of dealing with the problems that copyright poses to the enjoyment of human rights, of cultural heritage, of labour rights and so on, is to develop a better concept of something which variously goes by names like the public domain, public goods or the cultural commons.

Whatever we call it, the idea is that we should secure an area of cultural production, exchange, use, enjoyment that is free from copyright restrictions. In a partial – but inadequate[30] – sense copyright already does a bit of this work through its exceptions and limitations. Part IV of the *Report* identifies the importance of extending and strengthening these exceptions and limitations. It observes that the way that the exceptions and limitations are framed is crucial to ensuring the types of access, use and re-use that are critical to realising cultural rights. This is especially so with respect to: ensuring artists' livelihoods (para. 62); facilitating creativity, particularly in certain artistic forms, such as parody, appropriation art, documentary making (para. 63); expanding educational opportunity (para. 64); facilitating cultural access for people with disabilities (para. 67); facilitating cultural access for people who speak languages other than English, French or Spanish; and promoting development (para. 70). The *Report* recommends international harmonisation of the exceptions and limitations in international copyright law (paras 74–76). (This is arguably without having given due attention to the fact that international intellectual property lawmaking is, as the *Report* says (para. 19) dominated by corporate copyright maximalists representing private interests, which means that it might be more effective to embed these exceptions in non-intellectual property instruments.)

The *Report* also makes positive reference to the role of licensing, especially of the sort going under the banner of 'Creative Commons' in creating and preserving the cultural commons (para. 78). The concept of Creative Commons is a perfectly reasonable one. However, seeing it as a solution to the problem of copyright's foreclosure of the cultural commons is, I think, misguided. Creative Commons licences effectively

[30] F. Macmillan, 'Many Analogies, Some Metaphors, Little Imagination: The Public Domain in Intellectual Space' (2010) 2 *Pòlemos* 25–44.

accept the copyright system as it is and constitute a good hortatory, but always voluntary, use of its licensing function. The Creative Commons movement, unfortunately, can do nothing about the vast quantity of culturally valuable material that is in the hands of private parties – particularly, but not only, the media and entertainment corporations – whose only concern about the cultural commons is to limit it as far as possible.

So, in the end, this is another and, perhaps, the most important place in which the *Report* does not go far enough. I have a suggestion of how the *Report* could have gone further and have dealt effectively with the anxieties it identifies around the maintenance and extension of the exceptions and limitations. This is a simple suggestion that turns the current copyright regime on its head.[31] Instead of copyright being a right, subject to appropriate limitations, and use, re-use and enjoyment of its protected works through the exceptions and limitations being privileges (literally exceptions), we should recalibrate the law so that monopoly ownership of proprietary rights over cultural products is a privilege while use and re-use of those works, subject to appropriate limitations, is a right. This way copyright will be the exception and use, re-use and enjoyment of cultural heritage, and our human rights in relation to that heritage, will be the rule.

[31] See also C. Geiger and E. Izyumenko, 'Copyright on the Human Rights' Trial: Redefining the Boundaries of Exclusivity Through. Freedom of Expression' (2014) 45 IIC – *International Review of Intellectual Property and Competition Law* 316–42, 325 http://link.springer.com/10.1007/s40319-014-0181-3.

11. Patent policy and the right to science and culture – Report 2015 (A/70/279)

Comment on Report of the Special Rapporteur in the field of cultural rights, Farida Shaheed 4 August 2015

Jannice Käll

INTRODUCTION TO THE REPORT

The debates about the effects of intellectual property on human culture and science under the current forms of capitalism have been discussed for a long while. Not least, such debates have been pursued through social movements that may be categorized under the umbrella term, Access to Knowledge.[1] The report on patent policy and cultural rights presented by the Special Rapporteur, Farida Shaheed should, in a similar manner to these movements be understood as raising crucial aspects of the intellectual property rights construct (for example, para. 2). As she notes, the tension between intellectual property rights and human rights is common to all fields of essential technologies, beyond the areas of health, food or the environment (para. 3).

The report on the relation between patent rights and human rights to science and culture is the second of two consecutive studies by the Special Rapporteur in the field of cultural rights and the right to science and culture. The first report (A/HRC/28/57 and Add.1 and 2) focused on how copyright policy interfaces, on the one hand, with the protection of authors' moral and material interests and, on the other, with the right of everyone to benefit from scientific and cultural creativity. As the two reports are very much connected, the comment on copyright policy by

1 See e.g., Kapczynski, 2010.

Fiona Macmillan[2] may fruitfully be read in connection with this comment on the patent construct.

As already hinted at, the Report can in general be understood as being skeptical about the current formulation and exercise of patent rights, and critical of the manner in which they conflict with interests related to human rights to science and culture. This is signalled in the way that the Special Rapporteur stresses that the right to science and culture does not establish a human right to patent protection (para. 5). She goes on to state that she does not recognize a direct link between the realization of rights to science and culture and the existence or exercise of intellectual property rights such as patent rights. A similar point was also made in the report on copyright.[3]

The point that patents are not human rights is also reiterated in relation to the suggestion that patent rights may be conceived as being capable of defending the moral and material interests of inventors. In this regard, it is specifically noted that Article 15 of the International Covenant on Economic, Social and Cultural rights does not recognize a human right to protection of intellectual property as it defined in the international intellectual property treaties (para. 32). As is specifically argued by the Special Rapporteur:

> Whereas the human right to benefit from the protection of the moral and material interests resulting from one's scientific, literary and artistic productions safeguards the personal link between authors and their creations and between peoples, communities or other groups and their collective cultural heritage, as well as their basic material interests, which are necessary to enable authors to enjoy an adequate standard of living, intellectual property regimes primarily protect business and corporate interests and investments. In addition, contrary to intellectual property rights, human rights are inalienable (para. 32)

The Special Rapporteur further emphasizes that even in cases where patents have been conceptualized as property, it should be noted that a right to property as a human right is not an unlimited right. Specifically, as she puts it 'the right to property is subject to very far-reaching government power to regulate its use in line with its social function' (para. 33). This is further exemplified by the fact that a rejection of a patent application or the granting of a compulsory license on the public health ground could be understood as an interference with the right to property. However, the Special Rapporteur argues that it is difficult to see how either of these

2 Macmillan, 2017.
3 See the comment on the report on copyright: Macmillan, ibid.

cases could be viewed as a violation of the human right to property if not done in 'an arbitrary or capricious way' (para. 33). Subsequently, the report is generally skeptical in regarding property rights to human rights. I will here further such understanding by advancing a critical perspective on the patent construct and its functioning as a property right.

In order to organize my comments under a somewhat coherent theoretical framework, I will here make use of the idea that we currently live under 'advanced capitalism' as suggested by a stream of theorists falling within the *new materialist* grouping.[4] In this comment, I will argue that the conflicts between patents and human rights make very specific sense in relation to an understanding of capitalism through such theory, and subsequently how the conceptual battle between patents and human rights could be fought.

I will address a number of areas where the Special Rapporteur has identified the control exercised through patents to be problematic in relation to human rights to science and culture. Following this, I will focus on those things identified as being potential practices that may rebalance the excessive power that patents appear to have gained over access to science and culture. I will further, from a theoretical point of view, focus on rupturing the dominant idea of *the human* as a person that produces and has control over culture and science through the property device.

As a starting point in highlighting the nature of the patent regime in its current alignment with capitalism, I will first turn to the problems with the patent construct as outlined in the Report in relation to the TRIPs and TRIPs plus agreements (for example, paras 21, 60, 61, 64, 67). I will then focus on the attention placed in the Report on the social or communal aspect of patent rights. This is a theme that runs through the entire Report. However, it is also specifically mentioned in several places (for example, in paras 11, 61, 62). The theme is most strongly emphasized in relation to the human rights of indigenous peoples and local communities (paras 35–45). Based on my analysis of this theme, I will argue that the Report exposes the danger that, if patents are treated as unconditional individual property rights, what is at stake is not only the diminished potential of such communities, but also of communal values in general.

The chapter will then address the general emphasis in the Report on the means of supporting the creation of free and non-political forms of science (para. 13) within the context of the *International Covenant on Economic, Social and Cultural Rights*, Article 15(3). As outlined in the Report, it is a

---

[4] Dolphijn and van der Tuin, 2011; Coole and Frost, 2010, p. 5; Braidotti, 2013, p. 57.

matter of some current concern that patent control has become a means of governing science, even in cases where it is publicly funded (para. 58). Thus, the politicization of science through its marketization may be understood as a specific threat to the realization of its fundamental tenets. I will expand on this perspective through further emphasizing the role of neoliberalism in turning the university into something more akin to a corporate entity than a place for the advancement of truly free science. Apart from the problems flowing from the patenting (whether university-lead or researcher-lead) of research results, I also address further issues arising from the neo-liberalisation of the university.

THE PRODUCTION OF SCIENCE AND CULTURE UNDER ADVANCED CAPITALISM: LIFE AS SURPLUS AND MONOCULTURES OF THE MIND

Through the advancement of critical theoretical accounts in the (digital) humanities and social sciences in general, including in particular those coming from new materialist theorists, the critique of advanced capitalism is becoming increasingly pervasive. Theorists such as Rosi Braidotti, Karen Barad and Melinda Cooper have all made significant contributions in connecting the use of intellectual property control as a power regime under conditions of advanced capitalism with negative effects on the production of science and culture. Their accounts, like the Report, address the control pursued through intellectual property constructs such as patents in relation to, for example, general concerns of indigenous peoples, global scale access to medicine in the Global South, as well as research production in the Global North (see for example paras 38, 2, 58 in the Report).[5] As mentioned above, I will therefore utilize their theoretical contributions to open up an even more pervasive critique of intellectual property rights systems in general, and patents in particular, in the light of the effects that current forms of capitalism have on human, as well as in-human, and possibly post-human[6], cultures and sciences.

One central starting point for the conceptualization of advanced capitalism is the notion that in advanced capitalism, as argued by Melinda Cooper, 'Life itself', is the main capital. This capitalization of life itself implies the production of a new economy. As Cooper argues, globalization in this manner suggests that the Earth as a whole is being

[5] Braidotti, ibid., passim; Barad, 2007, p. 383; and Cooper, 2008, p. 3.
[6] See e.g. Braidotti, ibid.

capitalized through inter-connected operations.[7] An example of such a phenomenon discussed in the Report is the advancement of the TRIPs Agreement. It has furthermore been suggested that the modality of advanced capitalism is to engage in a multitude of discursive and material political techniques of population control, which transcend Foucault's idea of bio-political governance.[8] More specifically, this implies that a techno-scientific culture as a dominant culture is constructed on the convergence between biotechnology and information technology.[9] This is arguably visible in the current emergence of the scientific field of *bioinformatics*.[10] As furthermore noted by, Vandana Shiva, the capitalist culture of biology is tightly linked to other post-colonial practices. These practices take form, for example, in the construction of what Shiva refers to as *monocultures of the mind.* Thus, the practises of controlling biology through capitalism is in several instances (foresting, seed control) identified as a culture of reducing biological difference in order to achieve market benefits.[11]

Such a radical critique of intellectual property and property in general is, in spite of the generally critical outlook of the Special Rapporteur's Report, limited by a generally positive approach to patents. As an example of this, the Report, as a starting point, stresses the need to note that the connection between human rights and intellectual property is 'important and complex' (para. 2). Subsequently, it argues that the central challenge is to recognize and reward human creativity and innovation while simultaneously providing public access to the outcomes of such creations (para. 4). In this manner, the Report, while making very welcome contributions to a more radical approach towards the control

---

7 Cooper, 2008, p. 3.

8 Braidotti, 2013, p. 61.

9 See e.g. Braidotti The Human/Inhuman Synposium: https://www.youtube.com/watch?v=gNJPR78DptA&feature=youtu.be.

10 See e.g. the description for the Masters program in Bioinformatics at Uppsala University:

> The Master Programme in Bioinformatics is designed for those of you who wish to focus on the exciting interdisciplinary field of bioinformatics, which combines computer sciences, mathematics and biology. Uppsala University possesses exceptional competence in bioinformatics and computer sciences. The tools and knowledge you will acquire as a student in this programme are central elements in many areas of research, such as studying the function of human hereditary characteristics or developing new types of pharmaceuticals.

http://www.uu.se/en/admissions/master/selma/program/?pKod=TBK2M.

11 Shiva, 1993.

over central aspects of science through intellectual property, still appears to embrace the possibility that property rights such as patents may be fruitful for human science and culture in some abstract sense. It is worth noting in this context the Special Rapporteur's comments to the effect that:

> [w]ell-designed patent laws and policies play a vital role in encouraging private investment in scientific research and development, making an important contribution to scientific progress and well-being (para. 4).

In her comment on the Report, 'Intellectual Property and Access to Science and Culture: Convergence or Conflict?'[12] Cooper Dreyfuss has welcomed the fact that this is (at least) not an entirely radical perspective on property rights.[13] However, such an abstract understanding of intellectual property rights as a necessary means to realize scientific research and development disconnects intellectual property rights, such as patents, from their very materialist underpinnings. More specifically, it detaches patents from the role that they currently play in the development of advanced capitalism. Such a disconnection may be understood as problematic considering the other very radical suggestions made in the Report with respect to how patents have tended to make possible market control over essential life technologies, both in medicine generally and specifically in relation to the life of indigenous peoples and local communities.

A GLOBAL, NON-NEGOTIABLE AND SECRETLY AGREED INTELLECTUAL PROPERTY REGIME?

Through the TRIPs system, as discussed in the Report, the patent construct has become a tool for global capitalism as a result of the harmonization of patent rights that aims to achieve a position of power that reaches beyond the regulatory capacity of nation states (paras 16–20). As further noted, and as is well known by now, this development means not just an extension in the geographic scope of patent protection, it also sustains a property-oriented discourse according to which the ability to impose limits on the patent monopoly is substantially undermined. An even stronger assertion of the illimitability of property controls over patented inventions has furthermore, as the Report discusses, been suggested through so-called TRIPs-Plus provisions. As

[12] Geiger, 2016.
[13] Cooper Dreyfuss, 2016, p. 61.

noted in the Report, such provisions could increasingly 'limit opposition to patent applications; prohibit national regulatory authorities from approving generic patent applications; maintain data exclusivity, thereby delaying the approval of biogenetic drugs; and require new forms of protection, such as anti-counterfeiting measures.' (para. 21) As noted by the Special Rapporteur, this can also be understood as part of a general trend where the ultimate goal of 'developed countries' is the universal harmonization of intellectual property laws according to their own intellectual property standards and measures (para. 22).

TRIPs as well as TRIPs-Plus also allows commodification of resources that previously were not considered commodifiable and restricts the exceptions to the grant and exercise of intellectual property rights. Naturally occurring elements, including the human body, are examples of resources once considered to be outside the purview of the patent system and its process of commodification. The commodification of these types of 'resources' clearly falls within the thesis of capitalist expansion advanced by, for example, Braidotti and Cooper.[14] The seriousness of this development, which moves power from states to market agreements that are difficult to opt out of, cannot be stressed enough. It is therefore very much to be welcomed that the Special Rapporteur makes this point, even if it may not seem to be a particularly new idea among intellectual property theorists. The mentions of the serious impacts, in this respect, of the Trans-Pacific Partnership Agreement (TTIP), as well as the general tendency to negotiate and settle large trade agreements in secret (para 73–75), should also be noted as important discussions in the Report.

ADVANCED CAPITALISM AND POST-COLONIAL CONTROL: ACCESS TO INNOVATIONS ESSENTIAL FOR A LIFE WITH DIGNITY

Probably the best-known example of advanced capitalism as a form of capitalism that is intrinsically linked with intellectual property culture and post-colonialism is the problem caused by patent control and access to medicines. As the Special Rapporteur points out, there is currently a significant tension between the manner in which patents are being used and the affordability of medicines. This in turn can be understood as a conflict between patent rights and the human right to health (para. 2). It should therefore be noted that the Special Rapporteur also highlights the

[14] Braidotti, 2013, passim and Cooper, 2008, p. 3.

well-recognized problem with access to what she refers to as *essential* technologies. Examples given of such 'technologies' are medicines, seeds, and information and communication technologies that are essential to lives and/or cultures (paras 48–55).

As noted in paragraph 56, the Special Rapporteur argues that: '[p]atent policies and practices may divert research priorities away from matters of greatest public concern'. Such an insight is furthermore exemplified by the fact that intellectual property may only function as an efficient tool for everyone to gain access to new medicines when the interests of people in rich and poor countries overlap. When they differ, the fact that patents are constructed as tools for gaining control over market output will value the interests of those that can pay higher prices for medicines (para. 56).

In relation to such concerns, the Special Rapporteur argues that 'innovations essential for a life with dignity' should be accessible to everyone. She also specifically indicates the areas of energy, information and communication technologies, nanotechnology and synthetic biology as fields that are likely to have such an impact in the future (para. 4). In order to pursue proper access to innovations essential for human life, the Special Rapporteur suggests an enforced use of the exceptions to the exercise of patent rights. One example of such an exception, suggested as achieving a balance between patents and human rights, is the exception that allows so-called *compulsory licensing* (para. 68). The Special Rapporteur also highlights the potential of the limit on the grant of patents for surgical methods in improving access to medicine (para. 65).

Another aspect of improving access to medicines relates to the use of 'inventive step' as a criterion for the grant of a patent (para. 64). It is well known that the distinction between what is to be considered an invention as opposed to a discovery (which falls below the barrier of the inventive step) has not been well observed in the patenting of biotechnologies. The potential to patent what certainly as easily could have been considered part of nature but is now considered to be biotechnology will likely affect access to medicine even more in the future when biomedicine has become even more developed. The Special Rapporteur however draws attention to the *Myriad Genetics* case, in which some of the patent claims over genes were invalidated, as demonstrating good practice (para. 78). The Human Genome Project, and its aim of making the human genome public in order to hinder patenting is also highlighted as good practice (para. 81).

In spite of this quite balanced understanding of which exemptions in patent law could improve the protection of human rights, there is still a risk that even these fairly basic suggestions of 'balancing' patent law through means that are already present within the legal construction of patents will be understood as too radical. The reason for this is, again, that the general assumption in society today is that market actors, through the utilization of property rights that are as unconditional as possible, are best equipped to control the production of innovations essential for a life with dignity.[15]

As an example, it is worth noting the comments of Cooper Dreyfuss on the Report's approach to the question of the limitations on the patent monopoly that are built into the patent construct. As she puts it, the Report may be understood to be on 'dubious ground when it suggests that a commitment to human rights must be read as barring more developed nations, including emerging economies ... from enacting stronger protection'.[16] The reason for this, she argues, is that '[n]ew fields may present unique challenges that require new law. In emerging economies, more robust protection might better attract foreign investment, create jobs and opportunities for training technological workers, and improve the ability of these countries to invent for themselves – and ultimately, for the global marketplace'.[17] For this reason, she argues, compulsory licensing can be 'particularly questionable'.[18]

Such a comment must not be understood as exceptional in relation to the construction of patent rights. Rather it acts as just one example of how the patent construct, while conceptually leaving open the possibility of functioning in diverse ways as a result of the exemptions that are already included in most patent laws, still cannot be considered to be outside the forces of advanced capitalism. Cooper Dreyfuss may indeed be right that compulsory licensing would likely produce effects that hinder the global marketplace from expanding. This in turn could be specifically harmful to those economies that at this stage have not been able to reap the benefits of (intellectual) property systems through capitalism to the same extent as most industry-heavy countries in the Global North. However, no matter whether this is understood as the 'economically' most efficient decision to make or not, the question still remains: is it acceptable that we assume that advanced capitalism is the only, and non-negotiable, world order and that this order is the one that best supports cultural and scientific production?

---

15 See e.g., Kapczynski, 2010, p. 26.
16 Cooper Dreyfuss, 2016, p. 60.
17 Ibid.
18 Ibid.

Assuming that the aim of property, intellectual property, and patents in particular, is to support the progressive improvement of human lives,[19] questions must be raised about their current operation. The fact that one may, as for example Cooper Dreyfuss does, put forward the argument that inventors may be cautious about investing in inventions that require a large financial input that cannot be recuperated if their property rights in the invention are unduly limited,[20] arguably only highlights the seriousness of the situation we now find ourselves in. If we sincerely believe in the human rights to science and culture, it is arguably questionable to assert that market actors know how to best pursue such goals, especially bearing in mind that such goals are not profit generating.

ADVANCED CAPITALISM AND POST-COLONIAL CONTROL: RIGHTS OF INDIGENOUS PEOPLES AND LOCAL COMMUNITIES

More focused discussion about protecting people from what may be understood as post-colonial forces of advanced capitalism[21] has generally centered on the possibility of granting specific rights of protection to so-called indigenous peoples and local communities. The Report is no exception to this. As it points out, it has been established in the United Nations Declaration on the Rights of Indigenous Peoples (DRIPS) that indigenous peoples have the right to maintain, control, protect and develop their intellectual property (art. 31, para. 1). As noted in the Report (para. 36) this construction differs from the Universal Declaration of Human Rights and the International Covenant on Economic, Social and Cultural Rights in that it specifically enunciates a right to intellectual property, rather than to the protection of moral and material interests (para. 36). The discussion around what may be protected has, as noted in the Report, been framed around traditional cultural expressions, traditional knowledge and genetic resources (para. 36). As furthermore noted by the Special Rapporteur, several motivations underlie this right, including the right of indigenous peoples to self-determination, their right to maintain and develop their culture and their struggle for cultural survival (para. 36).

---

19 See e.g., Chon, 1993.
20 Cooper Dreyfuss, 2016, p. 60.
21 Shiva, 1993, e.g., pp. 9–122.

The Special Rapporteur starts by noting that there is a 'defensive' as well as a 'positive' approach to using intellectual property to protect the bio-cultural heritage of indigenous peoples and local communities (para. 35). This defensive approach aims at patenting important resources before someone else does. The offensive approach aims at patenting resources in order to leverage them in a manner that provides incomes to the respective indigenous peoples and/or local communities (para. 38). This is specifically exemplified by the interest in maintaining control over non-commercial, communally created and historically rooted cultural assets, which 'tend to fall through the cracks of intellectual property regimes' (para. 38). The standard example of this, which is also reiterated in the Report, is the type of traditional knowledge that has been made available to the public and is thus regarded as being in the public domain. According to the intellectual property regime, this implies that it is free for *anyone* to use (para. 38).

In whatever way (offensive or defensive) intellectual property rights are to be utilized to protect such interests, however, it appears as if they only make sense if we assume both a threat against, as well as a potential for, the pursuit of the moral and material interests of the persons engaging in such cultures/cultural expressions. Thus, they only make sense if we assume that intellectual property rights may either threaten or create avenues for income. If other means, such as exemplified in the Report (para. 10), could hinder/respectively provide for such an end, there seems to be no rationale for an unconditional trust in intellectual property rights in this context.

However, this question is of course complex as indigenous peoples and local communities, due to the damage inflicted on their cultures by advanced capitalism, already have little protection from further exploitation of their culture and knowledge. The potential to protect whatever may be protected through the seemingly unconditional right to intellectual property granted through DRIPS should therefore certainly not be the first intellectual property construct to be addressed for revision under the idea of human rights to culture and science.[22]

The observation that the cultures of indigenous peoples and local communities may not necessarily be protected by current intellectual property rights systems could *however* be utilized as an inspiration for a wider insight into intellectual property rights. This is the insight that suggests that intellectual property rights in general might have a negative effect on all kinds of communal values. Such an approach is both

---

22 Macmillan, 2017.

communicated as well as partly refuted in the Report, which highlights the social function of intellectual property rights (para. 11) while at the same time suggesting that there is something very specific about the cultures of indigenous peoples and local communities that does not lend itself to the use of Western concepts of property as a means of control (para. 38). In relation to such a terminology of exception, it should be noted that Macmillan, for example, has pointed out that there seems to be an assumption that only some peoples (indigenous, and local communities) have intangible cultural heritage, whereas the rest have intellectual property.[23] The underlying reasoning behind such claims appears to be that cultures that are not indigenous or local are in fact appropriately sustained through intellectual property.

Considering the development of advanced capitalism, one may arguably wonder if property as it functions under the conceptual regime of liberalism and the material force of advanced capitalism actually provides protection for *any* kind of community culture that is not market-based. Thus, as has been consistently argued here, it is difficult to understand the current form of capitalism and the constant expansion of property rights, patents included, as anything other than a phenomena which makes a lot of cultural elements 'fall through the cracks' of the (intellectual) property regime.

For this reason I suggest that a more fruitful way forward in relation to the human rights to science and culture could be to treat the insights from communal cultures, such as indigenous cultures and local communities, as a rule rather than as an exception. Thus, the problems that advanced capitalism causes for such cultures may be understood as examples of how intellectual property functions in *any* culture which does not aim at commodifying cultural elements in order to capitalize upon them.[24] This leads to the subjection of all cultures that do not lend themselves to such commodification and capitalization, which in turn decreases cultural and scientific diversity. As Vandana Shiva argues: 'Dominant knowledge [also] destroys the very *conditions* for alternatives to exist, very much like the introduction of monocultures destroying the very conditions for diverse species to exist.'[25] As will be discussed next, and as is also discussed in the Report, the issue of a displacement of non-market based communal culture is now also forcing changes to the university, which is

---

23 Ibid., p. 10.
24 Ibid.
25 Shiva, 1993, p. 12.

consequently losing its character as a public institution for the production of free scientific inquiry.

THE UNIVERSITY AS A MARKET ACTOR AND PATENT HOLDER

As already indicated, a well-known problem with current forms of patent regimes is that patent rights appear to create and uphold so-called problems of *access* to knowledge in relation to medical inventions for peoples in the Global South. Furthermore, attention has also been given to the way in which Western concepts of culture in general, as well as aggressive intellectual property strategies, potentially hurt indigenous peoples. However, what is less discussed in intellectual property rights theory and by movements advocating increased *access to knowledge* is how intellectual property and advanced capitalism also destroy certain scientific practices in countries of the Global North. Such questions have, however, increasingly been addressed in the context of the neoliberalisation of education processes. As an example, Wendy Brown highlights the way in which the neoliberal world order creates a situation in which knowledge is no longer understood as something that may be good in general, but as a means to become an employable person, or 'human capital', in a market. This in turn implies that universities are no longer (as) free to function as hubs for free scientific production as previously.[26] Rather, they, as noted by Brown, are also supposed to function as market actors.[27] As noted by Cooper, the turning of the university into a market actor is not only visible in the manner described by Brown, but also through the increasing capitalization of science through, for example, patents.[28] This market orientation of the university function through patenting is also noted and criticized by the Special Rapporteur (para. 58).

The emphasis on the destruction of scientific potential through patenting in university settings should therefore be understood as a valuable contribution of the Report. As Shaheed puts it, the result of such processes is that research that has been funded by public money ends up in the hands of market actors, under terms of exclusive ownership. The fact that patents incentivize research in a manner that is directly related to an idea of its value in a market economy is also problematized in the

---

26 Brown, 2015, e.g., p. 176.
27 Ibid., p. 186.
28 Cooper, 2008, p. 27.

Report. As Shaheed further points out, this trend is worsened by the turn of public research towards activities that target commercial applications rather than general 'public good and human advancement' (para. 58). As noted by, for example, Cooper, in the US this has been facilitated through the so-called Bayh-Dole Act,[29] which grants the right to US universities to patent the research that its employed researchers have carried out.[30] Similar legislation is now in place in most of the world.[31]

The need for universities to be able to patent research is generally justified by the fact that it is argued that research, and specifically life sciences, involve high costs.[32] For this reason, it is welcome that the Special Rapporteur stresses the need for more transparency with regard to the actual costs of patenting (para. 76).

No matter the reasons for patenting, it should however also be added that turning the university into a market actor through the imposition of a market logic necessarily benefits those knowledge fields that have the capacity to package their resources in a manner that allows them to become the material of market transactions. As stressed by Cooper, the development of life science as a research field can clearly be understood in relation the drive to create revenues for universities.[33] This implies that, for example, scientific disciplines where research outputs may lead to innovations that may be controlled through intellectual property rights and traded in high-priced markets will gain more revenues in the form of university and other public funding than those disciplines that do not have the capacity to convert their output into value of this sort.

The risk is thus, apart from the commodification of research in general, that the disciplines of the humanities may suffer while science disciplines will thrive. Such a development should be understood as a serious problem as scientific innovations become increasingly organic and/or intelligent in the manner in which they push our understanding of what

---

[29] The Bayh–Dole Act or Patent and Trademark Law Amendments Act (Pub. L. 96-517, December 12, 1980).

[30] Cooper, 2008, p. 27.

[31] A notable exception to this standard may be found in Sweden where researchers in general still have the right to decide over their research results, and thus to decide whether they should be pursued through patents or not. As noted by e.g., Ulf Petrusson however, due to the financing of research by business actors, in effect, this still leads to researchers signing over their results of the research (in advance or after research has been carried out) to industrial companies to large degree. Petrusson, 2007.

[32] See e.g. Cooper Dreyfuss, 2016, p. 58 and the Report para. 76. Cf. Correa, 2016, p. 48.

[33] Cooper, 2008.

'the human' is and may become. As argued by Rosi Braidotti, a combined and critical understanding of science and humanities will likely soon be needed in order to manage 'strictly' scientific outputs as they will pose ethical dilemmas for humanity. If market rationalities do not support such inquiries, this may arguably pose a serious challenge for human culture, as well as science, in the future.[34]

OPENINGS FOR A MORE RADICAL APPROACH TO THE PATENT CONSTRUCTION FROM A HUMAN RIGHTS PERSPECTIVE

As mentioned at the beginning of this chapter, the connection between patent rights and their effects on the potential for differentiated cultural expressions have been much debated during the last decades in connection with the question of access to knowledge. In spite of this, it is still rare that the relationship between patents, intellectual property, and property is characterized as being in direct conflict with the possibility of realizing the full potential of human culture.

A significant reason for this may be that property rights (no matter if one considers intellectual property different from other property rights or not)[35] are believed to confer rights that enhance the lives of humans. Behind such reasoning lies the liberal idea that property and the potential to hold property is intrinsic to human personhood/subjectivity. This divide between persons and things in liberal ideology is also, as argued by Davies and Naffine, bundled up with a central notion of *free* individuals.[36] Claiming property in oneself thus works as 'an assertion of self-possession and self-control, of a fundamental right to exclude others from one's very being.'[37] Furthermore, such an understanding enables, as well as is coupled with, ideas according to which property is believed to function as a crucial tool for the establishment of free markets. Implicit in this is also the claim that free markets optimize human flourishing. As argued by Amy Kapczynski in relation to such narratives of intellectual property:

---

[34] Braidotti, 2013, e.g., pp. 164–5.

[35] I here follow Davies and Naffine in their theorization of intellectual property rights as anomalous yet included in the general conceptualization of personhood under the liberal property concept. See: Davies and Naffine, 2001, p. 135.

[36] Ibid., p. 1.

[37] Ibid., p. 6.

> The legitimation narrative of intellectual property today is not a coherent theory, but a thaumatrope – two different images on a card or disk, recto and verso, that when spun on an axis give the appearance of a single, unified image. One image is derived from the field of information economics, but omits the skepticism about intellectual property present in that field. The other screen is derived from the theories of the Chicago School of economics about the superiority of private-property rights in material resources, but suppresses the many significant differences between the economics of land and the economics of information.[38]

Markets, and the creation of market efficiency on a global level as an important, not to say primary, role of societies, may then furthermore be understood as a part of a neoliberal regime of governance.[39] In light of the assertion that property is directly linked to the production of an improved human condition, it is not difficult to understand how property (and this *certainly* includes intellectual property) has increasingly been understood as something akin to a *human* right. For this reason, it is also understandable that it has rarely been questioned whether property *in fact* fulfils the promises of increased human subjectivity, a freer personhood, and generally increased welfare that prevail in liberal as well as neo-liberal discourse.

The fact that the Special Rapporteur makes clearly visible a conflict between property, in the form of patent rights, and human cultures in the form of a number of scientific cultural interests should therefore be understood as both radical and very much welcomed. The reason for this is that such questioning has the potential to rupture a liberal doxa where personhood is directly linked to ownership over property. The Report furthermore identifies several tensions between, specifically, intellectual property and the right to science and culture.

With this said, the Report seems to remain connected to the reasoning that technology may only be created if (fully globalized) capitalism exists. Such an understanding is certainly not unique today. One might rather say that there is an almost all-prevailing assumption that humanity should live in this kind of society. For this reason, it is also easy to dismiss any type of effort to limit intellectual property rights, especially in relation to 'costly' innovations, on the basis that 'market actors' would place their investments otherwise (para. 76).

Furthermore, it appears almost consensual that constant innovation in technology always results in improvements in society. As an example of this, Cooper Dreyfuss argues that we need to have patent rights in order

38 Kapczynski, 2010, p. 26.
39 Brown, 2015, pp. 122–31.

to promote technological development, especially in these times, as we face challenges such as 'new and ever more terrifying diseases, drastic climate changes, increasing pollution, growing populations, and threats of terrorism'.[40] This assumption that technological development will hinder and not contribute further to such problems seems, in relation to the functions of capitalism today, slightly problematic. As noted by Braidotti, technologies function today *both* as means to promote immortality as well as in producing a 'forensic turn' of humanity. An example of such technologies are those that aim at optimizing warfare.[41] As Braidotti argues, these processes may also be directly linked to advanced capitalism.[42] The belief that a capitalist rationality, such as an enforced (or even sustained) intellectual property regime, will hinder rather than increase these problems therefore seems a bit too vague.

In relation to this it needs to be clearly understood, and reiterated, that as Verzola for example has argued: 'The business firm is programmed to maximize its return on investment – no more, no less.'[43] If there still is a potential for improvement of the human condition through property rights such as patents, as suggested by Shaheed (para. 4), it does not seem entirely likely that it will come to fruition on its own under the current market system.

A good starting point in finding a way out of our current subjection to the patent construct, which is also propounded in the Report, could therefore rather be to visualize a regime of intellectual property that takes into account the 'social dimension' of intellectual property (para. 11).[44] Such a social, or relational, dimension necessarily needs to reach beyond advanced capitalism in order to produce sustainable cultural and scientific expressions. If it is not capable of doing this, it risks, as new materialist theorists argue, continuously erasing differences that are not valuable in a market. The observation of the Special Rapporteur that such differences include a range of communal interests should be understood as an important step in making such an alternative vision of human rights to science and culture possible.

---

40 Cooper Dreyfuss, 2016, p. 65.
41 Braidotti, 2013, p. 125.
42 Ibid., p. 112.
43 Verzola, 2010, p. 270.
44 See also Shaheed, 2016, pp. 19–20.

REFERENCES

Literature

Barad, K., 'The ontology of knowing, the intra-activity of becoming, and the ethics of mattering' in K. Barad (ed), *Meeting the Universe Halfway* (Duke University Press, USA, 2007).

Braidotti, R. *The Posthuman* (Polity Press, USA, 2013).

Brown, W., *Undoing the Demos* (Zone Books, USA, 2015).

Chon, M., 'Postmodern progress: reconsidering the copyright and patent power' (1993) 43 *DePaul L. Rev.* 97 available at: http://via.library.depaul.edu/law-review/vol43/iss1/3.

Coole, D. and S. Frost, 'Introducing the new materialisms', in D. Coole and S. Frost (eds) *New Materialisms, Ontology, Agency, and Politics* (Duke University Press, USA, 2010).

Cooper, M. *Life as Surplus, Biotechnology and Capitalism in the Neoliberal Era* (University of Washington Press, USA, 2008).

Cooper Dreyfuss, R., 'Patents and human rights: the paradox re-examined' in C. Geiger (ed.) *Intellectual Property and Access to Science and Culture: Convergence or Conflict?* (2016) CEIPI/ICTSD, US.

Correa, C.M., 'Intellectual property and access to science' in C. Geiger (ed.) *Intellectual Property and Access to Science and Culture: Convergence or Conflict?* (2016) CEIPI/ICTSD, US.

Davies, M. and N. Naffine, A*re Persons Property?: Legal Debates about Property and Personality* (Ashgate Dartmouth UK, 2001).

Dolphijn, R, and I. van der Tuin, 'Pushing dualism to an extreme: On the philosophical impetus of a new materialism' (2011) 44 *Cont Philos Rev* 383–400.

Geiger, C. (ed.) 'Intellectual Property and Access to Science and Culture: Convergence or Conflict?' CEIPI/ICTSD, USA (2016).

Kapczynski, A., 'Access to Knowledge: A Conceptual Genealogy' in A. Kapczynski and G. Krikorian, *Access to Knowledge in the Age of Intellectual Property* (Zone Books, USA, 2010).

Macmillan, F. *Copyright policy and the right to science and culture* – Report 2015 (A/HRC/28/57) (2017).

Petrusson, U. *Universitetet i kunskapsekonomin* (Vinnova, Sweden, 2007).

Shaheed, F. *Introductory Remarks by the Special Rapporteur* in ed. *Intellectual Property and Access to Science and Culture: Convergence or Conflict?* (2016) CEIPI/ICTSD, US.

Shiva, V. *Monocultures of the Mind* (Zed Books Ltd. UK/USA, 1993).

Verzola, R., 'Undermining abundance: counterproductive uses of technology and law in nature, agriculture, and the information sector' in A. Kapczynski and G. Krikorian, *Access to Knowledge in the Age of Intellectual Property* (Zone Books, USA, 2010).

Acts and Conventions

The Bayh–Dole Act or Patent and Trademark Law Amendments Act (Pub. L. 96-517, December 12, 1980).

International Covenant on Economic, Social and Cultural Rights, Adopted and opened for signature, ratification and accession by General Assembly resolution 2200A (XXI) of 16 December 1966, entry into force 3 January 1976, in accordance with article 27.

The United Nations Declaration on the Rights of Indigenous Peoples (UNDRIP). Adopted by the General Assembly on Thursday, 13 September 2007.

Index